The attractions, fascinations there are in sea and shore! How one dwells on their simplicity, even vacuity! What is it in us, arous'd by those indirections and directions? That spread of waves and gray-white beach, salt, monotonous, senseless—such an entire absence of art, books, talk, elegance—so indescribably comforting, even this winter day —grim, yet so delicate-looking, so spiritual—striking emotional, impalpable depths, subtler than all the poems, paintings, music, I have ever read, seen, heard. (Yet let me be fair, perhaps it is because I have read those poems and heard that music.)

—WALT WHITMAN
Specimen Days (1882)

Bob & Wilma Knox

National Park Service

U.S. Department of Agriculture

Rapho Guillumette

U.S. Forest Service

AMERICA

OUTDOORS

Edited by

Edwin A. Roberts, Jr.

NEWSBOOK

The National Observer
Silver Spring, Md.

NEWSBOOK®
(A Trademark of Dow Jones & Company, Inc.)

Published by The National Observer
11501 Columbia Pike, Silver Spring, Md.

Library of Congress Catalog Number: 66-14738

Printed in the United States of America
By Danner Press of Canton, Inc., Canton, Ohio

Contents

America Outdoors is the eighth in the Newsbook series of special reports on important topics in the news. Recent titles include *The Stock Market, Vietnam: The War,* and *Education—A New Era.*

America Outdoors was prepared for publication in the news room of The National Observer. Heidi Fiske assisted in the research and general preparation of the book. The cover design, illustrations, and page layouts are by Kathryn Henkel. This Newsbook report was written by the staff writers and special correspondents of The National Observer.

The front-cover photo of Odell Lake in the Oregon Cascades is by the Southern Pacific Company. The back-cover photo of Mirror Lake in Yosemite National Park is by American Airlines. All other photos are credited where they appear.

Cape Cod National Seashore. Photo by National Park Service.

Rapho Guillumette

With Time Enough and Money, Americans Are Pausing to Look Beyond Their Artifacts to Ask—

Where Now Is the Countryside?

THE United States, like a woman of 30, is young, but not quite so young. Time has accelerated of late and the beginnings of maturity have impressed themselves almost everywhere. Youthful beauty is still apparent but it is no longer as certain as the sunrise. Nor as promising. What there is compares unfavorably to what there was, but that is only in the order of things. While extracting payment in years, maturity offers the gift of good sense—the sense to know that beauty is increasingly vulnerable. More than admired, it must be scrupulously maintained.

Happily, most Americans seem to agree that this is so. Never in history has the natural beauty of the United States been so much a topic of discussion and a cause for action. This is true partly because many influential people in Washington are committed to the physical and aesthetic values of the outdoors. But another reason is that, in these affluent times, millions of Americans are getting about the coun-

try to see at firsthand what a diverse park their country is. And they want the best of it preserved for their children's children.

The use of the outdoors was only intermittently an issue during the century of American expansion. Generally and understandably, Americans took the view that they possessed more of the outdoors than they needed. More important then were plowing the plains, unrolling railroad track, and building cities and factories near rivers and roads. The sportsman could find fish and game enough in the ponds and fields at the edge of town. The Sunday picnicker did not look far for an accommodating glade. Wilderness was first of all something to contend with; it seemed well equipped to conserve itself.

It is all the more remarkable, therefore, that as long ago as 1872, a small group of prescient men decided to keep in its natural state the forested mountains in the northwest corner of Wyoming. The decision is especially re-

Rapho Guillumette

Coney Island, New York: Some sunbathers and the sea around them.

markable because it was made to stick during the administration of President Grant, a man not remembered for his interest in conservation. Thus, the area that was to become the first national park in the world—Yellowstone—was preserved intact, even when the West was barely the white man's dominion.

Almost 100 years later, America is realizing that what was desirable in 1872 is essential now. Nor is the issue so simple as setting aside wilderness areas for recreation (national parks) or for various controlled uses (national forests). The Johnson Administration, with no little help from the First Lady, is out to beautify the country, even those parts of the country long ago claimed by civilization. Thus, late in 1965, the President signed into law a measure restricting billboards along highways, and providing for the removal or masking of junkyards near Federally financed roads.

The dominant outdoor themes, then, are conservation and beautification, at least as far as the nation's leaders are concerned. For the individual citizen, the goal is a less elevated one. With spending money to spare, many Americans are thinking of the outdoors in terms of their own personal requirements.

It should be no mystery why more and more Americans are pursuing outdoor activities. We live in the age of the sedentary man, whether the desk he confronts each morning is cigaret-scarred oak or hand-carved teak. Our civilization demands that for much of our waking day we sit—on trains, on buses, in autos, in offices, at the dinner table, in the easy chair. Americans are the sitting champions of the world.

But inside every sitter there burns a little aspiration. One day, he promises himself, he will get off his chair and take to the outdoors, there to swagger along a mountain trail, bathe in an icy stream, build a friendly fire of sticks he has broken over his knee, and cook to perfection the rainbow trout he caught in the pool beneath the waterfall. Some day, some day.

For many Americans, some day has arrived. Aided considerably by the Federal Interstate Highway System which has made long-distance motor travel easier than ever, that little aspiration is being acted upon. In station wagons, tent-trailers, camper trucks, and luxurious land cruisers, Americans are getting out in the outdoors, to experience the serenity of the wilderness and, perhaps, to find a few answers.

After the boom years immediately following World War II, it became evident that the country would soon run short of land and water for recreation if no attempt were made to conserve them. Finally, in 1958, Congress established the Outdoor Recreation Resources Review Commission (ORRRC) to make a wide-ranging study of America outdoors.

Congress gave ORRRC three jobs: To estimate current participation in outdoor recreation and the projected participation for 1976 and the year 2000; to estimate the supply of recreation land and facilities for the same years; and to draw conclusions and make recommendations on the basis of the data collected. In 1962, ORRRC reported to Congress that recreation needs were not matched by available areas and facilities, and that the problem would quickly get worse. For a variety of reasons, said ORRRC, while the population can be expected to double by the year 2000, participation in outdoor recreation will triple.

Unfortunately, while most of the U.S. population is in the East, most land available for recreation is in the West and Alaska. This is particularly true of Federal lands. Alaska accounts for 31 per cent of the national-park land, 65 per cent of wildlife-refuge lands, 11 per cent of the national forests, and 64 per cent of Federally owned land listed in the broad category of "public domain." But Alaska, aside from being inconveniently located for most Americans, accounts for less than 1 per cent of the population.

Within individual states, this imbalance is duplicated. Recreation areas and the people who would use them are often widely separated.

Too, much recreation land is in large tracts, with few roads and facilities in the interior, so only the perimeter can be used. Tracts of 100,-000 acres or more account for 88 per cent of the recreation land available. Conversely, more than two-thirds of the number of recreation areas are under 40 acres, but they amount to

less than 0.1 per cent of the total acreage suitable for recreation. Thus, statistics dealing with the total U.S. land area available for recreational purposes can be misleading.

ORRRC concluded that more recreational facilities should be provided near the great cities, and that imagination as well as money should be employed.

Some ORRRC recommendations: Multiple use should be made of facilities primarily designed for a purpose other than recreation (such as reservoirs). Bicycle and pedestrian paths should be included in highway-building plans. Scenic vistas should be preserved. Housing developers should lay out their homes in clusters, leaving large patches of nature between clusters, rather than building all houses equidistant and set in dreary, lookalike grids.

Interestingly, natural beauty can pay off, the ORRRC study shows. In some cases where a city has established a park, the value of abutting land has risen so much that the tax revenues have exceeded what they would have been if the value of nearby real estate remained unchanged and the park area was used for taxable purposes.

A direct result of the ORRRC report was the forming of the Bureau of Outdoor Recreation in the Interior Department. The new agency: Provides technical assistance to states, local gov-

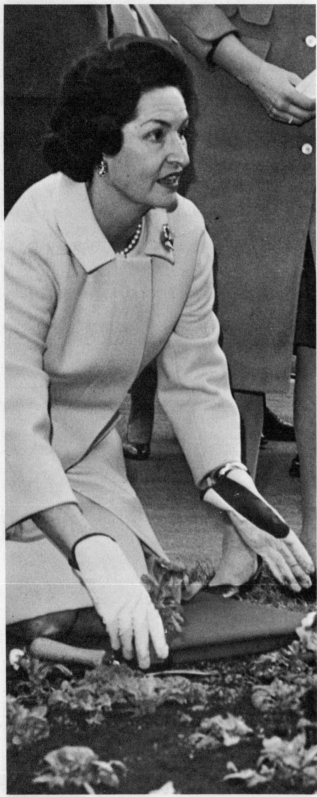

The First Lady: It's always planting time.

ernments, and individuals; encourages state and regional co-operation in solving recreation problems; acts as a clearinghouse for research, information, and public education on outdoor recreation; co-ordinates the work of the more than 30 Federal agencies whose responsibilities bear upon the outdoors; administers grants-in-aid to states according to a formula approved by Congress; and "accepts and uses donations" for the cause of recreation.

The Bureau of Outdoor Recreation has a certain amount of muscle. Its policies are decided by the Recreation Advisory Council, whose membership consists of the Secretaries of Interior, Agriculture, Defense, Health-Education-Welfare, and Commerce, plus the administrator of the Housing and Home Finance Agency.

But one of the foremost champions of recreation and natural beauty has been Mrs. Lyndon B. Johnson who, while she holds no Cabinet post, is not entirely without influence in Washington. Lady Bird Johnson has made natural beauty her pet cause. She has delivered several very good speeches railing against billboards and junkyards that spoil scenic highways and, when she's not making speeches, she can usually be found planting flowers here or a little tree there.

Declared the First Lady: "Ugliness creates bitterness. Ugliness is an eroding force on the people of our land. . . . It seems to me that one of the most pressing challenges for the individual is the depression and the tension resulting from existence in a world which is increasingly less pleasant to the eye."

Mrs. Johnson, as women will, had her way, and when Congress late in 1965 passed the law to restrict billboards and junkyards along Federally financed highways, the First Lady was given much of the credit.

Natural beauty, conservation, recreation—all these things are very much in the air in Washington, partly because they are laudable in themselves and partly because popular feeling is running in their favor as it never did before.

There is a 33-mile, barrier-reef island off the coasts of Maryland and Virginia, separated from the mainland by Sinepuxent and Chincoteague Bays. The northern three-quarters of the island lies in Maryland, with the Virginia quarter comprising the Chincoteague National Wildlife Refuge, where visitors can watch 200 varie-

Larry Stevens

Roadside vista.

Washington Post Photo

Even children require hills.

ties of birds as well as the famous Chincoteague wild ponies.

The whole of Assateague Island was first proposed as a national seashore in 1935, but it was not until September 21, 1965, that the proposal became a reality. Some measures must wait a long time for the right climate.

America Outdoors focuses upon the nation's most pressing problems in the area of recreational resources. Often, as in the case of water, the discussion must be broadened to include other social ramifications. Contaminated rivers, for instance, are bad news for swimmers and fishermen, but they might well be catastrophic news for water-short cities. Therefore, this book's area of inquiry is occasionally widened to take up the problem of industrial and municipal wastes, new desalination techniques, and the political problems that develop when two or more states seek to tap the same water sources.

Millions of Americans each year visit, at small expense, the national parks and forests. These areas offer a particular kind of vacation experience, far from the boardwalk amusements of the seashore, far from the planned activities and conspicuous luxuries of mountain resorts. National parks are very different from national forests, and these differences are explained in the succeeding pages. Too, there are close looks at several of the most popular national parks, with many hints about how to enjoy them.

Included also is a concise guide to the Alaskan outdoors, plus an unusual account of a hiking adventure in Hawaii. Readers will also find out what it's like to climb Mount Rainier, fish for dolphin in the Florida Straits, join a remarkable sailing club on Long Island Sound, discover a particularly abundant lake in Maine, explore a ghost town in the Southwest, hike the hills of Yosemite, inspect old sailing hulks at Cape Hatteras, feel the beauty and isolation of Zion Canyon, trudge through the Everglades, canoe upwind in the Minnesota wilderness, spend the night at an Indian reservation, admire the trash cans in Taos, New Mexico, and do many other things vicariously that few of us are able to fit into one lifetime.

In all these places and activities, there is one natural resource that in at least a basic way is uniformly essential. And it's a resource that's giving the nation serious trouble. How ironic that something as durable as water should damage so easily. ♦

A Rocky Mountain stream.

DPI

Water

BECAUSE the land around it is so much a desert, Lake Mead appears illusive, especially when it comes suddenly into view from the steep, winding highway that descends from Boulder City, Nevada. When the breeze is still, the huge lake looks like a mirage, a plain of pale blue set a-twinkle by the sunlight. It is an unlikely spectacle among the parched brown hills and, while not quite pretty as scenery, it is beautiful because it is so very welcome.

There is little humidity in the southeast corner of Nevada and it almost never rains. Humans broil in the 115-degree heat of summer, but they don't perspire noticeably because where the humidity is only 6 per cent, perspiration evaporates instantly. The land is very fertile but only desert plants are hardy enough to survive on six inches of rainfall a year. Because the climate is so dry, the people who live in the American Southwest regard water with a respect akin to reverence. "Water." They pronounce it as solemnly as a medieval schoolman might have pronounced "life."

There was a time when such an attitude toward so common a substance would never have occurred to inhabitants of the American Northeast and elsewhere outside the desert. The country, after all, abounds in lakes and streams, in broad rivers and bays, in the sea water that washes the Atlantic and Pacific shores. Thirty inches of rainfall is the nation's annual average and, although evaporation and transpiration return three-quarters of the total to the atmos-

phere, the remaining water amounts to 1.3 trillion gallons daily.

But pumps and pipelines can recover only about half of this volume for human use. Today, the United States requires 355 billion gallons daily for all the many ways water is used in a highly industrialized civilization. By the year 2000, however, the nation is expected to require a trillion gallons daily, or 350 billion gallons more than the most engineers can recover by digging wells, tapping lakes, and building reservoirs.

Nor need we look into the future to find water-shortage problems. The Northeast—and especially New York City—has been experiencing a shortage of water so severe that the President in 1965 declared part of that section a disaster area.

And beyond the obvious primary uses of water—in homes, factories, and on farms—there is also the need for abundant clean water for recreation, a use that is also listed as "primary" by many Government experts.

The National Recreation Survey, sponsored by the Outdoor Recreation Resources Review Commission, shows that 44 per cent of the population prefers recreational activities directly involving water. The Commission has also calculated that by the year 2000, swimming will be the number one summer recreation in popularity (that position is now held by pleasure driving). Too, the presence of water greatly enhances many other outdoor activities. There's

to Live With

Lake Mead, Nevada.

U.S. Bureau of Reclamation

Camping begins with clean water.

no denying the importance of mountain-gully water to clean a camper's dishes, the value of a waterfall as a scenic delight, or the usefulness of a breeze from off a crystal lake.

Water, then, is closely connected to many outdoor pursuits. But it must be *clean* water. When lakes and streams are polluted, there is no swimming, no fishing, poor hunting (animals get thirsty, too), difficult camping (men cannot live on beans alone), and various other hindrances to enjoying the outdoor life.

The water problems now facing the nation are largely man-made, because when nature provisioned the United States with resources, it was especially generous with water.

Fresh waters within the 48 contiguous states cover a vast area. Almost 1,000,000 miles of streams and rivers, more than 100,000 natural lakes and 10,000,000 acres of reservoirs and other impoundments make up the 95,000-square-mile total.

But not all this water is accessible to the public. Many lakes, for instance, are completely surrounded by privately owned land, and industry long ago staked out thousands of miles of river frontage. Public rights-of-way to such waters, which are legally open to the public, are comparatively few. Thus, states and local governments have the difficult and delicate job of balancing private-property rights with the democratic notion of the greatest good for the greatest number. Tax prods, the concept of eminent domain, access laws, and easements are some of the devices for getting the public to the water.

A bright spot: Reservoirs can be constructed (within certain limits) near population centers; where they can be used for recreation. Reservoirs administered by the Army Corps of Engineers, the Tennessee Valley Authority, and the U.S. Bureau of Reclamation attract far more visitors each year than all the national parks and forests combined.

But whether water is confronted in a reservoir or a bathtub, it is never "free"—although most Americans have always considered it so. And not only Americans.

When Russian troops advanced into Germany near the end of World War II, some of the boys from upcountry Siberia goggled at a remarkable example of Teutonic ingenuity: Through odd little metal things, water came out of the walls. Comical though this ignorance seems, it is basically an ignorance widely shared.

It took an emergency, for instance, to instruct New Yorkers that, however lavish their bathroom fixtures, their supply of water is finite. The water that "comes out of the walls" actually comes out of reservoirs, and a four-year drought had dangerously reduced their contents. New Yorkers, surrounded by filthy rivers, are as dependent on rain as the most primitive Indians. City folk may even be worse off—they probably don't know the right dances.

Nevertheless, the city folk do have science on their side. But a scientist finds water as awesome as does any rain dancer. The only substance that occurs simultaneously in nature as liquid, solid, and gas, water is one of the few that occupies more space when "dry" than when wet, as those who leave milk out in freezing weather soon learn. The molecular structure of liquid water is unknown; as steam, its molecules move about independently without form; as ice, water takes the shape of six-sided crystals.

"All its chemical characteristics considered together, water ought to be a gas at room temperature—but the inescapable fact is that it's a liquid," says a Government researcher.

Water is an almost universal solvent, which is to say that most substances dissolve in it—more than in any other known liquid. While reducing the dissolved substance (solute) to invisible ions, water itself remains unchanged, and can therefore be saved for reuse. More than 60 of the elements found in nature can be detected in nearly all ocean water.

Aside from impurities it may contain, water taken from any random fresh-water source, such as a lake, may contain up to 32 water-like substances besides the

Magnum

Confluence of Hudson River (foreground) and East River at tip of Manhattan: An open sewer for the millions.

U.S. Bureau of Reclamation

Spraying a reservoir with a compound that retards evaporation.

well known H2O. These include D2O, better known as "heavy water," which is used to aid fission in nuclear reactors. Heavy water looks like ordinary water, but it boils at a slightly higher temperature. Seeds watered with it won't sprout; rats given only heavy water to drink die of thirst.

A major problem in retaining water in reservoirs is evaporation (some reservoirs in the West lose as much as two feet of water in this manner during the month of August).

To combat this "leak," scientists are experimenting with a compound that would coat the surface of the water and keep it from evaporating. The compound, which possesses a peculiar molecular structure (16 carbon chains plus a bond of oxygen and hydrogen), is poured over the water. The oxygen and hydrogen are attracted to the H2O, and so they cling next to the surface, leaving the carbon chains "standing up just like little soldiers," in the words of Jack Hilf of the Office of Water Resources Research in the Interior Department.

This chemical battalion inhibits evaporation effectively—in the laboratory. But when the wind blows across a reservoir, the covering compound is swept into a corner and does not respread itself.

A second major kind of water loss—plant transpiration (or sweating)—seems insoluble. But since it has been suspected that plants do not need to transpire to survive, scientists are trying out covering plants, too, in a thin film. Putting every bush and begonia in a raincoat seems like a formidable undertaking, but the Office of Water Resources Research believes the basic idea—coating plants with a spray—is worth testing.

Human beings waste a relatively small but, in crowded cities, vital amount of water. If a faucet drips only one drop a second it will waste four gallons a day, and a toilet-bowl leak which is noticeable only as a hum in the pipes can waste 13,000 gallons a year and more. New faucets have been developed which, if closed only partially by a careless householder, will turn themselves all the way off. Most faucets, however, still require a certain amount of human resolution.

The most intriguing hope for increasing

Public Health Service

This irritated bird was grounded after a dip in an oil-polluted river. Below: A trickling filter is one method used to remove bacteria in treatment of sewage.

the usable water supply, especially near the coastlines, is desalination. Many fancy methods have been tried. In a process under study for nine years called "reverse osmosis," salt water is forced against a plastic membrane. Only fresh water goes through the membrane, leaving the salt behind. Although it's still too slow for mass commercial use, it works beautifully on a small scale. "But we don't know why it works," comments a researcher. "It's not a filtration process because the salt and water particles are so nearly the same size. If we just knew how the membrane separates the fresh water from the salt, we might very well be able to find or make far more efficient membranes."

A desalting method called "electrodialysis" runs a current of electricity through salt water. The current forces salt particles, which acquire electrical charges when dissolved in water, out of the solution through membranes and so leaves pure water behind.

More everyday methods have been tried, too. There is freezing; when brine is frozen, the ice crystals are pure water. Salt clinging to the ice is washed off with fresh water and then the ice is melted into pure liquid water.

Related to freezing is the "hydration" process in which water under specialized conditions

Public Health Service

forms ice-like crystals at more than 60 degrees Fahrenheit around natural gas molecules.

The commonest and, so far, the cheapest method of desalting water is the simplest of all: Boil the water, recondense the salt-free vapor, and the result is fresh water.

But this cheapest method is not very cheap at all. Water can absorb so much heat without vaporizing that it is used as a measure of the heat-absorbing capacity of other substances. No method has yet been found that will heat large tanks of water to make the process economical. The coal or atomic energy required to do the job makes the method too expensive for general use, although various desalination plants are operating in arid parts of the world and, on an experimental basis, in some water-short sections of the United States.

One source of heat is plentiful and "free." But if sunshine itself is free, the various ways of putting the sunshine to work are very expensive. Nevertheless, scientists at the Universities of Sonora (Mexico) and Arizona have worked out a new solar process called "the low thermal technique."

Salt water is placed in black-bottomed trenches (400 feet long, 4 feet wide, 2 inches deep) covered with two layers of plastic. One layer lies right on the water to prevent vaporization; a second layer forms a convex reflector to catch the sun. When the sun has raised the temperature inside the trench to between 150 and 160 degrees, the water is pumped through an evaporator, where 5 per cent becomes salt-free vapor and the other heavily brackish 95 per cent flows out to sea. The vapor then enters a condenser, where it is cooled again to become water—fresh water now.

The process used to cool the vapor heats even more sea water: A column of sea water is pumped upwards through the center of the condenser. Entering from the sea at about 80 degrees, by the top of the tube the brine has absorbed so much heat from the condensing vapor

Waste from a Buffalo steel plant pours into Lake Erie.

Public Health Service

that it has reached about 130 degrees. It then flows into the plastic-covered trenches and the process begins all over again.

Residents of the Mexican town where this experiment is in operation had been paying $6.50 for 1,000 gallons of water. Now they pay one-third that amount, which is still expensive —too expensive for use in irrigation, for instance. (Most cities spend between 17 cents and 35 cents to provide 1,000 gallons of sweet water.)

Since the cost of fuel makes the boiling process expensive, a solution is to reduce the atmospheric pressure around the water, thereby lowering the temperature at which the liquid will boil, and the amount of fuel needed to boil it. When water is placed in a near-vacuum, the temperature at which it boils is so low that the amount of heat lost in the vaporizing process freezes the remaining water. The vapor is recondensed and the ice melted to get liquid—

A steel retaining wall corroded by acids.

Public Health Service

"It's simply teeming! Now we won't have to drink Lake Erie!"
Drawing by Alan Dunn; © 1965 The New Yorker Magazine, Inc.

The sea is the beginning and the end of the water cycle. More and more it is being tapped by man's desalination devices, even as it is being eternally tapped by the atmosphere. But the sea is also the final sewer. Declares Interior Secretary Udall: "The oceans . . . are beginning to back up and belch over the mounting load of effluvient which they are required to digest."

from a process that boils and freezes water simultaneously.

Unfortunately the cost of creating a near-vacuum is greater than the cost of fuel to boil water at normal pressures.

The best-known U.S. desalination plant was built originally at San Diego, then hurriedly dismantled and transferred early in 1964 to the U.S. Naval Base at Guantanamo Bay in Cuba when Premier Castro threatened to shut off the base's fresh-water supply. This plant now is producing about 2,250,000 gallons of fresh water daily, enough for the whole base. Another plant is scheduled to be built at San Diego.

In mid-August 1965, President Johnson signed into law a measure extending the Federal desalting effort, begun in 1952, through mid-1972. Vastly expanded spending totaling $240,000,000 beginning in fiscal year 1966 has been tentatively approved by Congress. The $55,000,000 made available through mid-1967 is more than double the spending rate in most previous years.

Holding out more hope for solving the na-

tion's water-supply problems than desalination, however, is the cleaning of available water that man has sullied.

Thirsty New York City, for instance, needs 1.25 billion gallons a day, and in the same period the Hudson River pours almost 10 times that amount past the city. Yet the river is so filthy from its share of the sewage (equivalent to 500,000,000 gallons of raw wastes daily) which New York pours into the Hudson and East Rivers, that the Hudson cannot be tapped to meet the city's needs.

Many users damage water, and industry is the leader among them. Interestingly, most water used by industry (94 per cent) goes for cooling. If returned hot to the source, this water may raise the temperature of the stream to the point where fish and other aquatic life cannot survive. In addition, heat reduces the amount of oxygen which water can dissolve, draining the water of its main, natural purifier.

Industry also uses water to clean, to carry away wastes, to transport products (logs, for instance), and in the manufacture of such things as cosmetics, drinks, soups, and paints.

Sewage is a major cause of pollution, and another is land runoff, which carries into the nearest stream sediments, insecticides, and such urban material as rubber left on streets by millions of automobile tires.

One might think that river water would be purged of these wastes in a modern manner, perhaps by raking the water with laser beams or dumping in frothing beakers of wondrous chemicals. One might think that, but if one did one would be wrong.

Methods for ridding water of wastes are peculiarly primitive. The simplest is to place the water in large vats and allow suspended solids to settle to the bottom. This physical process, called primary treatment, settles out a sludge which goes through about seven processes to become a dry, harmless substance known as sludge cake and used as mulch. The market in sludge cake does not boom. In fact, the treatment plant is lucky if it can give the stuff away. None of the seven processes kill viruses, so where they may be present, the sludge cake must be burned.

After the suspended solids are removed, the water may undergo secondary treatment, a biological process designed to get rid of dissolved organic matter and colloids. Bacteria which consume the material are introduced either by aeration or by passing the wastes over beds of stones where the bacteria are housed.

Either way, this process creates two problems. The first—more bacteria—is not serious. The bacteria multiply so that after 15 minutes the mix may contain twice as many organisms as it started with. In order to get rid of the bacteria which got rid of the dissolved organic material (like chewing gum, the problem transfers itself instead of disappearing), the water is resettled in a third tank, and the bacteria are either killed or returned to the secondary tank for another go.

The second bacteria problem is very serious, however. By breaking down nutrients from the soil, the tiny organisms release nitrogen which combines with oxygen to form nitrates. These and the phosphates which come into the sewage plant from detergents, among other things, are the stuff of which fertilizer is made, and they fertilize the stream into which they are injected after the treatment process.

In small quantities the algae thus nurtured in the stream are desirable, as they pro-

Public Health Service

Suds that last and last: The water in this stream has already passed through a sewage treatment plant. Detergent from thousands of homes was unaffected by the treatment and is now on its way to a river—there to upset myriad aquatic life balances.

27

Waste oil and other industrial leftovers are plainly visible in the water at the Chicago wharves. But boys have to swim some place.

Public Health Service

vide food for fish. In large numbers, however, they make water murky and block out sunlight. The plants on the bottom die and the ducks which feed on them are forced to desert the premises.

When the sun is shining, algae exude oxygen into the water, but they take it out when the sun goes down. Thus, after a few cloudy days over an algae-filled stream, the plants begin to suffocate. Their decaying saps even more of the stream's oxygen and soon the surface of the water is dotted with dead fish. Oxygen is no longer available as a natural purifier and the stream is quickly reduced to an odious mess.

Detergents are a main source of the phosphates which, together with nitrates, feed the algae. Developed because they work well in hard water, form no soap film, and are far cheaper to produce than soap, detergents have enjoyed amazing popularity. Housewives now use 2,400,000 tons of detergent a year.

Another detergent component which, like the phosphates, resists every attempt of standard sewage treatment to decompose it, is alkyl benzyne sulfonate (ABS), which causes foaming. On heavy washdays water taps have been known to froth at the mouth and, in the 1950s, "detergent blizzards" covered many waterways.

The detergent industry has recently come up with a substitute for ABS known as linear alkylate sulphonate (LAS), but this compound ups the phosphate load. You can't win—cer-

Public Health Service

This third-time-through might involve chemical, physical, or biological processes. The tertiary treatment preferred by those in the sewage-disposal line is to inject the effluent from secondary treatment not into a river but onto the ground, allowing nature to filter the waste as it seeps through the soil on its return trip to the nearest water system. Water from treated sewage in the increasingly crowded Lake Tahoe area, on the California-Nevada border, is returned to the lake by this indirect method.

As rising populations demand more clean water while they make surrounding water dirtier, tertiary treatment will become vital, for cities must reuse water through which sewage has passed.

As unattractive as this idea may be, it is eminently practical because waste waters are available in the largest quantity where water supply is the worst problem—in the crowded cities.

In the far future, a few thousand gallons of water may be delivered to each house by truck. Once the water has been used, a self-contained sewage treatment package, now in experimental use in the United States and Canada, would treat it so it could be used again and again. No water mains, no sewer pipes to the outside, no domestic pollution of nearby lakes and streams. And, unless the American population expands to cover every inch of the continent including the Grand Canyon and Pike's Peak, no water shortage.

Will people be squeamish about reusing sewage water? A recent experiment suggests not. In the town of Santee, near San Diego, California, waste waters are really put through their paces. Given primary, secondary, and tertiary treatment, the water then trickles down 400-foot gravel beds, dropping out viruses en route. (To test for virus elimination, polio viruses were injected into the water. They had disappeared 200 feet from the point of injection).

Clean and sparkling after leaving the gravel beds, the water passes into four recreation lakes. A swimming area at one displays a sign announcing that the lake is composed entirely of treated sewage. Nevertheless, children line up for a two-hour wait to get a one-hour swim.

But more fundamental to curing pollution than the technology are the economic and human factors.

"People talk so much about pollution in

tainly the outdoorsman loses.

The end product of water treatment, primary or secondary, is mixed with chemicals such as chlorine and fluoride to kill as many bacteria as possible before returning the effluent (that is, the treated water) to the stream.

Primary sewage treatment serves 32,700,000 people in the United States, primary plus secondary treatment serves another 61,200,000. The sewage of the rest of the population—more than half the people in the nation—goes into the ground or water entirely untreated.

"The coming thing in water pollution control," says Roland Renne, director of the Office of Water Resources Research, "is tertiary treatment of wastes."

the water," grumbled a Geological Survey engineer as he passed acquaintances in an Interior Department corridor. "If they'd just get the politics and the confusion out of it they'd be in much better shape."

Co-operation is essential, for water has no respect for political boundaries. The 15,000,000 gallons of raw sewage spewed forth each day into the Mohawk River by the city of Utica, New York, flow downstream to befoul the Hudson at Troy and Albany, from whence the sewage is borne south to Kingston and Poughkeepsie

and finally through New York harbor.

As the filth passes from community to community, so does the buck. Everyone wants clean water but nobody wants to pay for it. Cities are not interested in building sewage treatment plants to benefit other municipalities downriver. Thus, the financing role passes to the state. Estimating that it will cost $1 billion over the next five years to clean up just the Hudson and the Mohawk, New York Governor Nelson Rockefeller has pushed ahead with a $1.7 billion antipollution program for the state.

U.S. Forest Service

Sliding Rock on Lookingglass Creek at Pisqah National Forest, North Carolina: Clean water is a versatile resource. Below: Close-up of creek bed covered with algae.

Public Health Service

The complexity of such a situation is well illustrated by New York City's experience. Vital to that city is the supply of water in the upper Delaware River Valley. Downstream, the Delaware River estuary provides Trenton, Philadelphia, and Wilmington with water. Because this is so, the upstream water supply for New York City is threatened. For as the long drought continues to lower waterlines all over the Northeast, salt water from the Atlantic presses ever farther up the estuary.

When the brine approached the water in-takes of Philadelphia in late summer of 1965, the Interstate Commission on the Delaware River Basin directed New York City to reduce by 200,000,000 gallons a day its draw from the system.

Sewage treatment has held Delaware River pollution at its 1958 level, but the drought has reduced the amount of water available to dilute and purify sewage. And it allows brackish water to move up the estuary. The experts figure an expenditure ranging between $200,000,000 and $500,000,000 by the communities and

Slaughterhouse wastes redden a ditch. Another stream carries similar refuse, domestic sewage, and storm water into the Missouri River (in the background, below).

M. Woodbridge Williams—National Park Service

Dusk on the Allagash River in Maine:
Clean water is worth keeping beautiful.

industries that line the estuary is essential if pollution there is to be controlled.

A different set of problems faces an inland body of water like Lake Erie, for here there is no appreciable flow to the sea. Fresh water is taken from Lake Erie and waste water is returned to it. In recent years this large, accommodating lake has become one of the rankest waterways in the nation.

Wastes from the big industries of Detroit, Toledo, and Cleveland, along with those flowing in from Indiana rivers, thoroughly contaminate this 9,900-square-mile pool. Contributing, too, is sewage of the 10,000,000 people living on the U.S. side of the lake and the 1,000,000 people on the Canadian side. From one end to the other, from Michigan to New York, the Erie is a receptacle of billions of gallons of filth.

DPI

Because effective local control has not been forthcoming, Federal action impends. After completing a two-year study of the lake in mid-1965, the U.S. Public Health Service held two much-publicized conferences with area political and industrial leaders. These conferences amounted to the first steps in a program of Federal enforcement of antipollution laws.

The Federal Government, some think, has entered the pollution control business with too little too late. Not until 1948 did Congress give the Government sweeping authority to deal with interstate water pollution. Importantly amended in 1956 and 1961, the Water Pollution Control Act lodges a miscellany of duties with the Public Health Service.

It was directed to:

Devise large-scale programs for eliminating or reducing pollution on interstate waterways. By late 1965, eight programs which would affect one-third of the country's land and almost half its population were under intensive study.

Promote uniform state laws controlling pollution. In 1950, the Public Health Service fashioned a model law (since updated) which has been adopted by 37 states.

Enforce pollution controls. Since the 1956 legislation which gave the PHS this power, 36 enforcement actions involving 40 states, the District of Columbia, and some of the biggest corporate names in America have resulted in programs for additional water treatment on 8,000 miles of rivers and bays.

Help municipalities build waste treatment plants. Between 1956 and 1965, more than 6,000 projects toward which the Federal Government contributed one-fifth of the $3 billion total were under way. Under this program, there's $150,-000,000 available annually, but the restrictions on how much may go to each state are enormously complicated. The net result of dollar limits, percentage limits, and population-size limits in New York's case is that the Federal Government might pay as much as $7,500,000 for projects throughout the state. PHS estimates that new treatment plants for New York City alone would cost $25,000,000.

In 1964, based on recommendations of the Senate Select Committee on Water Resources, the next important piece of Federal water legislation, the Water Resources Research Act, became law. The Office of Water Resources Research which the law established in the Inter-ior Department gives financial aid to states and individuals and to public and private agencies for water research, and acts as a clearinghouse for new water information. At the same time, it helps avoid duplication of effort.

Like the highly successful system of Agricultural Experiment Stations after which it is patterned, the program is a Federal-state co-operative effort, with a headquarters at each state's land-grant university. The 50 states and Puerto Rico have all joined the program.

On July 22, 1965, President Johnson signed the Water Resources Planning Act into law. The act created a Cabinet-level Water Resources Council, and allows the Government to make matching grants totaling $50,000,000 to the states for water resources plans.

Even without co-operation among states and communities, vigorous new anti-pollution steps will be taken soon. The Water Quality Act, signed by President Johnson on October 2, 1965, requires each state to set quality standards for interstate waterways acceptable to the Secretary of Health, Education, and Welfare by June 30, 1967, or have such standards imposed on them by the Secretary. The act also raises the amount which the Federal Government may provide annually to help cities build waste treatment plants from $100,000,000 to $150,-000,000, and upgrades the Clean Water Division of the Public Health Service to a separate Water Pollution Control Administration.

The most important feature of the law, however, is the provision for river-basin commissions with the authority to allocate water in emergencies and to crack down on contaminators. The few such commissions now in existence have not had the power to demand co-operation from their member states, and co-operation is becoming essential as populations rise and droughts shrink water supplies.

For Americans who value their hours in the outdoors, be they Sunday picnickers or hardy duck hunters, no problem bearing on recreation is of greater moment than the problem of clean waterways. Next to this problem, such questions as increasing the size and number of national parks or protecting virgin seashores are almost insignificant. Clean water is the nation's most useful, most versatile resource. If we fail to guard it, we will imperil all life in and along our waterways. Cities included.

The whole dilemma presents itself in microcosm in George Washington's favorite river. ♦

EARLY one quiet summer evening, two Interior Department aides who knew the Potomac set out with this reporter, who did not know the Potomac, to take a ride on the river in a canoe that, alas, was soon to know the Potomac all too well.

Through the woods 16 miles upriver from Washington, D.C., John Kauffmann shouldered his 70-pound canoe while John Graves and I juggled oars, cushions, and ropes. After a short hike, we emerged at the edge of the Chesapeake and Ohio Canal, a narrow waterway flanked by dirt paths. The trees lining both sides cast chartreuse shadows in the dark brown water. We crossed a footbridge spanning the canal and ducked into the woods beyond.

The aluminum canoe, the color of the Potomac's mustard-muddy water except where the river's numerous near-surface rocks had worn off its paint, banged against tree trunks and

screeched when a branch scraped the length of its 15-foot hull.

We launched the canoe in a little belly of the generally narrow Potomac. The sun was up, but no longer warm. The panorama was that of an early Dutch or Hudson River School landscape — lush, unkempt growth in varying murky shades of green topped gray rocks rising sheer out of a peaceful stream, the whole bathed in the cold late-day light. Every niche of the rocks was filled with grasses, which marched in a line down to the water, or formed a scraggly crew-cut outline against the sky.

In the quiet dusk a great blue heron's undulating wings carried it away from us. Overhead, sparrows formed an irregular, moving matrix with their flip-flip-flip, glide-glide flight. A goat on the shore regarded us suspiciously, then bolted.

Except for the steady rasping from the

A Pretty River With a Tarnished Reputation
Becomes a Vast Anti-Pollution Laboratory

The Burden of the Potomac

By Heidi Fiske

locust-filled trees—a sound that is heard but almost unnoticed—the evening was absolutely still. Not an electric light, telephone pole, road, or house was there to suggest how close civilization lay.

The men sat at either end of the canoe while I crouched in the bottom. The Potomac is very low in late summer, and at all times so muddy that one cannot see rocks more than a few inches below the surface. This gave us trouble when a submerged boulder among rapids swung the canoe around and jammed it into the rocks in front and back. When the men had pried it free, the 16-year-old veteran of the Potomac was pleated.

We paddled downstream for another hour, compensating for the new shape of our boat by all sitting to port. Functional for a change, I used a handkerchief to plug a one-inch gash below the waterline.

It was dark when we finally pulled the wrinkled canoe from the water. All gray now were the multi-green bushes, and only vaguely could we make out the birds among them. The locusts had ceased their buzzing, but the trees put forth the less regular racket of crickets, katydids, and cicadas.

We continued the trip downriver by car. It was a short ride because we had beached the canoe scarcely 12 miles from the White House, and a shorter distance still from the northern reaches of the District of Columbia. One of the fastest growing cities in the country, the 2,500,000-person metropolitan complex of Washington will soon form one terminus of an East Coast megalopolis stretching 300 miles south from Boston. Even so, Washington lies only a few miles from the wilderness country in which we paddled, and the river which flows through both is the center of an intense controversy which will determine the future of both countryside and capital. And it is a controversy duplicated in many areas of the nation.

As the population of Washington grows—and it is expected to more than double by the turn of the century — conflicting pressures on the Potomac River basin increase. On the one hand, inspiration, recreation, and health demand the conservation of the natural beauty just outside the District. On the other, clean water and an attractive river frontage for new housing and industry are needed. It is not easy for the area to have it both ways.

Allotting a river's resources is a problem facing many states and communities, especially on the Middle Atlantic Coast, where the population is concentrated heavily—and increasingly—in large urban muddles. The Potomac is not the most industrialized nor most polluted of these streams. In length, discharge, and drainage area it ranks about 25th among United States seagoing waterways. But it is getting special attention.

President Johnson, in his 1965 State of the Union message, hoped the Potomac could become "a model of beauty here in the capital," and followed through in his subsequent natural-beauty address by asking Interior Secretary Stewart Udall to draw up a program for the Potomac basin which would emphasize beauty and recreation. In late 1965, the President further pledged to re-open the Potomac for swimming by 1975, and asked that it be made a "national river," which would give it roughly the status of a national park.

The Potomac basin divides neatly into two unequal sections—the District of Columbia, and the rest of the river area. In the capital and its suburbs live two-thirds of the basin's population, accounting for four-fifths of the area's personal income. Forty-five per cent work for Federal, state, or local government, and all but one per cent dwell in nonrural areas.

In the forest and farmland which cover the other seven-eighths of the basin live the remaining one-third of its people.

The 14,670-square-mile Potomac River drainage basin (a river drains the area from which it and all its tributaries draw their water) has been compared in shape to a primitive ax. Primitive because, well, it doesn't really look much like an ax, but this is the best analogy anyone's come up with.

From its headwaters (at the blade of the ax), the basin extends from the middle of the western boundary of Virginia, and sweeps north-by-northeast to cover all of the West Virginia panhandle and a wide patch of northwestern Virginia.

Numerous Potomac tributaries cut the mountains which cover most of this western section of the basin (the head of the ax) into long strips. Not mountainous, however, is the eastern one-sixth of the ax-head (see map), where the Great Valley, bounded by the Appalachian Mountains to the west and the Shenandoah River and the Blue Ridge Mountains to the east, opens out, covered with the prosperous farms of the Pennsylvania German and Scotch-Irish who first settled here in the early 1800s.

On the axis of the Blue Ridge the basin changes direction (the handle of the ax begins), grazing western Maryland and southern Pennsylvania and becoming a narrowing sheath around the widening river as it flows southeast through Maryland and Virginia to the sea.

More of America's history is written in these waters and on these banks than those of any other river. Captain John Smith in 1608 explored 100 miles up what he dubbed the "Patawomeke" after the Algonquin word for what is now Washington, D.C., meaning "the place to which tribute is brought." Prescient, those Indians.

Smith and other early settlers rivaled each other in their use of superlatives to describe the clean air, fertile soil, beautiful scenery, and effulgent fish and wildlife.

Later on, bickering among cities along the Potomac slowed the building of the Chesapeake and Ohio Canal. The canal finally reached Cumberland, Maryland, in 1850 but never went farther, so hopes for a commercial route to the West were not realized. Thus, the District of Columbia lost its chance to become the commercial as well as political capital of the land.

In 1859 John Brown made his futile raid at Harper's Ferry, where the Potomac meets its major tributary, the Shenandoah, and the Potomac became the dividing line between North and South when war was declared two years later. Three times during the fighting the Southern armies crossed this boundary: Lee's Army of Northern Virginia came in 1862 to engage Union troops at Antietam Creek in one of the bloodiest battles of the war. In 1863 they returned, traveling all the way up the Monocacy, a Potomac tributary, to be defeated at Gettysburg. And

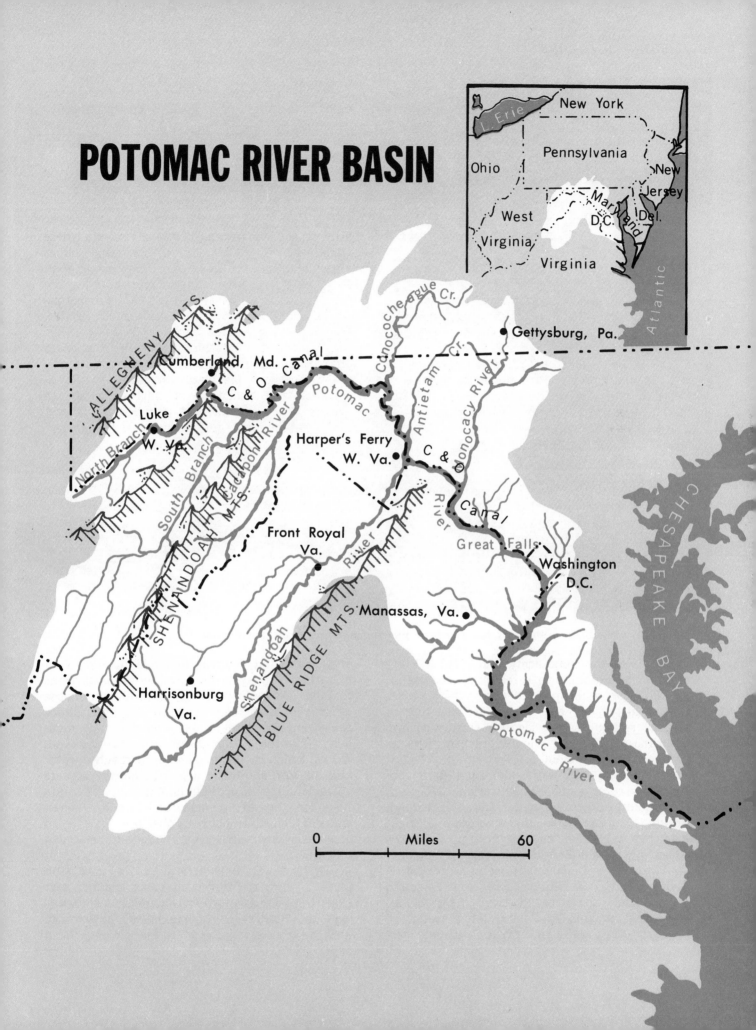

POTOMAC RIVER BASIN

Harper's Ferry, where the Shenandoah meets the Potomac.

a year later the same army under Jubal Early crossed the Potomac to threaten the capital.

Pollution—like politics and war—also has a long history on the river. The ravaging of virgin forests upstream began in earnest around the time of the Civil War, aggravating the already serious problem of land runoff. Today, some feel that the worst pollution here continues to come from sedimentation. Although the amount of farming, which frees soil through plowing, has increased, the upstream sediment load has remained about constant since the 1930s, when the Soil Conservation Service of the Agriculture Department began its education and technical assistance programs. Around the District, however, silt clogs the river increasingly as land is cleared for housing.

From the 1840s onward, coal mining west of Cumberland, Maryland, made its ugly contribution. Today, from Frostburg, Maryland, to Luke, West Virginia and beyond, hummocks of gray dust lie like scars on the green hills, tossed up by strip mines. Invisible but more deadly is the pyrite from underground coal works, which is converted when it reaches water and air into sulphuric acid. To charge anyone with cleaning up is difficult; many of the mines have been out of business for 50 years. In the water which flows between the hills, pale green and dark brown streams mingle, sulphuric acid and sewage.

"The North Branch is a sad little beat-up piece of scenery that used to be clean," says Robert M. Paul, Interior Department Potomac expert. "Now every trickle is sulphuric acid, and the trees are dying 15 to 20 feet back from the water. People's faces are drawn. This is the Appalachian problem in general; people have lost their spirit."

Unlike other badly polluted rivers, the Potomac's banks are not lined with industries belching their multifarious biles into the water. Only a few plants have contributed on a large scale to the river's filth. One, the American Viscose Company factory at Front Royal, Virginia, drew national attention when its zinc wastes caused a major fish kill on the South Fork of the Shenandoah in the 1940s.

"There just weren't any fish in the Shenandoah below Front Royal," Carl Johnson, director of the Interstate Potomac River Basin Commission, recalls. "The Izaak Walton people got very excited about it." As a result, Virginia passed antipollution laws, and the company installed a settling pond.

More important as a contaminant has been the pulp and paper mill at Luke, West Virginia, one of the first of the West Virginia Pulp and Paper Company's factories. Opened in the 1800s when the forests of the northwest basin began to be harvested wholesale, it was until recent years the major industrial contaminator of the Potomac. The mill has its own power plant, which releases hot water into the stream on which it sits. Some of the chemicals used in paper-making are recovered for re-use; others flow downstream. Cellulose fibers, which cannot be economically recovered, and which take a big oxygen load out of the river, and lignin, a cordovan-colored substance in wood, contribute their part.

But the company now treats its own and the town's sewage very effectively.

"They have the best plant in the business," comments senior engineer Harry Schwarz of the Army Corps of Engineers, "but it's still a problem."

An airplane flight over the Potomac reveals the problem graphically. The paper mill lies in a sharp curve of the river, which is very narrow at that point. In the air 3,000 feet above, one can smell the rotten-egg smoke clearly. The river as it passes the mill is a clear blue-green, but downstream, six jets of fluid suddenly erupt from underground into the river, clearly visible because what they release is a milky contrast to the earlier water. Gradually the six lines merge into a band which spreads out to make the entire river a coffee-with-cream color. This fluid is a combination of the town

Interstate Commission on the Potomac River Basin

Pollution victims near Alexandria, Virginia.

sewage and the pulp company's chemicals—*after* they've been treated by "the best plant in the business."

Today, the contributions of mining and industry to the pollution of the river as a whole pale beside that of municipal sewage, especially, of course, near Washington. As far back as the turn of the century, domestic sewage and silt forced the capital to build a water filtration plant. Since the river rises and falls with the marine tides as far above its mouth as the upstream boundary of the capital, sewage may drift back and forth in front of the Pentagon for days before finally moving out into the Chesapeake Bay.

Although Potomac pollution dates back 100 years, not till the 1930s did it come strongly to public attention. Franklin Roosevelt's inauguration brought new efforts to conserve natural resources, and local attention turned to the capital's river. An Interstate Commission

on the Potomac River Basin (Incopot) was formed in 1941 to inform the public on pollution and prod the states which were members of the compact into passing strong, uniform antipollution laws. The commission has power to influence but not to enforce. Its effectiveness is hard to measure, but it is significant that the District of Columbia and the four states touched by the basin have passed all their antipollution laws since formation of the commission, and that the four states have less pollution in the Potomac basin than anywhere else in their territories. Many close to work on the Potomac believe Incopot will soon be replaced by a body with more Federal muscle.

In the 1950s, concern for the river (described as a "microchaos" of the nation's pollution problems) came to a frenzied head. A series of television spots entitled "Our Beautiful Potomac" zeroed in on the most unattractively contaminated areas which cameras could dredge

Theodore W. Jones

up. This material, new to television, received considerable play throughout the country. Soon afterwards a film drove the point home further. "George Washington's River" painted such a relentlessly black picture of the river's condition and efforts being made to change it that the Interstate Commission refused to help distribute it or even buy a copy for its own files.

"The TV spots and the movie did such a damned good job that people are still convinced it's about the filthiest river around," says Keith Fry, assistant director of Incopot. On the contrary, Potomac experts generally agree that, as Middle Atlantic watersheds go, the Potomac is comparatively clean, thanks, probably, to the low industrialization of the basin. All that silt just makes it *look* dirty.

"As for municipal wastes," Mr. Fry continues, "when a treatment plant now being built at Arlington (Virginia) is completed, the sewage of 97 per cent of the 2,800,000 persons served by

sewage systems within the basin will receive secondary treatment, 2 per cent will receive primary treatment, and only 1 per cent will flow untreated to the streams."

But the river was dirtier when it first was criticized on television than it is now. In the late 1950s, the tide began to turn. The 1956 amendments to the Water Pollution Control Act of 1948 gave the Federal Government its first power to enforce controls where contamination of an interstate waterway might endanger health. The Public Health Service first flexed this new muscle in the Potomac River basin near Washington. The 1956 law also authorized the Government to help pay for municipal sewage treatment plants. Construction of such plants in the basin, says Incopot director Carl Johnson, began the significant reduction of pollution which has been achieved.

Until 1938 the District's sewage did not even receive primary treatment (settling out of suspended solids), and until 20 years later received no secondary treatment (biological removal of dissolved substances). Now no expansion in Washington treatment facilities is planned until the 1970s, for current capacity should take care of the growing population till that time.

Major work on pollution in the Washington area has for the last few years centered on separation of storm and sanitary sewers, of particular importance to this basin because the Potomac is a notably "flashy" river—that is, given to droughts and floods. For example, the average flow past Washington is 11,000 cubic feet per second (cfs). In 1930-32, drought reduced the flow to 788 cfs, and in 1936 floods swelled it to 484,000 cfs, or more than 500 times the volume at the nadir. The heaviest day of this flood carried enough water past the District to serve the city for four years. If storm and sanitary sewers are not separated when such floods occur, the whole works overflows, carrying raw sewage into the river. Gradually the capital is converting to a fully separated system.

Recently the District has been the setting for an experiment which promises a cheaper, more efficient method of treating sewage. The new process, developed by the Rand Development Corporation of Cleveland under contract to the Office of Coal Research in the Interior Department, uses coal in both steps of a two-step treatment. Coal has long served as a water filter, but it becomes clogged when used on sewage.

Unless you skim off a layer of sewage and coal, leaving clean coal underneath, as Rand Development proposes to do, the system is useless. Here's how the Rand Development method works:

In step one, which replaces the usual primary treatment of settling out suspended solids, the sewage is passed over a bed of finely ground coal, and the mucky layer of coal and sewage which develops on top is continually skimmed off. The coal thus lost is replaced from a second bin, to which the partially treated water from the first then flows. This second passage through finely ground coal replaces the usual secondary treatment wherein bacteria consume dissolved nutrients in the water. The coal absorbs them instead. The coal lost from the top of the bin is replaced at the bottom.

This system is superior from start to finish. The coal-and-muck which is skimmed off the top of the first bin is treated to form a solid cake called coal-sludge, an improvement over the usual non-coal-sludge because it can be used as fuel, and an improvement over regular coal because the added organic matter stores heating power. If this process were used at the major Washington water pollution control plant, 1,000 tons of coal-sludge would be produced daily, sufficient if burned to generate electricity for 700,000 to 800,000 people, or roughly one-third the current population of the Washington area.

Coal improves on the usual step two as well. Unlike bacteria, coal eliminates phosphates and ABS, the foaming ingredient in "hard" detergents. Whereas the bacteria produce ni-

The Potomac in flood at Great Falls.

Theodore W. Jones

trates in the process of eating so-called nutrients out of the water, coal absorbs these organic wastes without making what amounts to instant fertilizer. And coal, of course, doesn't grow more bacteria the way the well-fed organisms do.

After testing the process at its Cleveland plant, Rand Development demonstrated it to Potomac Basin planners in Washington. The water that flowed out of the second bin of charcoal was 88 per cent free of biochemical oxygen demand (BOD) and 80 per cent free of Chemical Oxygen Demand. (Just as the presence of oxygen is an indicator of water's purity, the presence of a "demand for oxygen" is an important measure of water's impurity.) It was also 73 per cent free of phosphates and 95 per cent free of suspended solids. Most important, perhaps, it contained no nitrates at all.

To get accurate information on costs (Rand Development estimates costs, including amortization of equipment, of $83 per million gallons of sewage) and effectiveness on a large scale, a pilot plant to take care of 10,000 gallons an hour will soon be operating in Cleveland. If this installation succeeds, pilot plants around the country will serve towns of 5,000 to 10,000 persons. One will probably be set up in the Potomac watershed, perhaps at a town in Appalachia where, ironically, a major water contaminator is coal.

The future, as well as the past, poses problems along the Potomac. The basin must provide clean water, flood and drought control, and recreation opportunities for twice as many people in 50 years or less.

The Army Corps of Engineers in 1963 published the most recent comprehensive—and controversial—plan for the Potomac. A compilation of the work of 10 Federal agencies, the report recommended improved sewage treatment, flood control, and erosion prevention, but concentrated on reservoirs as a cure-all for the various ills and inadequacies of the water supply system.

The proposed 16 major and 418 headwater reservoirs could, the report stated: Store water for use during droughts; flush out the lackadaisically flowing tidal portion of the river; provide large attractive pools along which people could swim, fish, boat, walk; and

*"If we don't do something soon,
we'll be known as the effluent society!"*

Drawing by Isadore Parker; © 1965 Washington Post Co.

Robert deGast

The river is still a principal area playground.

greatly increase fishing opportunities by impounding clean water for fish to live in.

Too, the dams would channel new water for industry. The basin's abundant water resources are the key to future expansion in all parts of the basin, said the report, but especially upriver. The Savage River Dam has resuscitated the moribund Cumberland region, but now that region is developed to the limit of its current water supply. Industrial expansion has slowed in some Great Valley communities as well, as local water shortages and pollution combine to discourage new investments.

But the plan has a major hitch: The biggest dam would rise just 17 miles from the capital (on the main river just below Seneca Creek, see map), and the water backed up would spill over onto 17,800 acres of land at normal levels, inundating, among other things, 29 miles of the historic C & O Canal.

A tremendous uproar met this proposal. Conservationists object to the possible loss of beautiful and historic sites, speculators to the flooding out of land they haven't yet sold for a profit, and small cities along the route complain about losing tax-ratable land.

"The main objection," says the Interior Department's Robert Paul, "is none of these but rather, do you want a large dam forever at the heart of your city? For soon the Potomac will be the central cord in a megalopolis engulfing the proposed site."

This chorus of nays is placidly received by Harry E. Schwarz, who directed the study for the Corps of Engineers, and who now heads a committee helping to draft a new plan for the river. The committee is part of a task force authorized by President Johnson and under the direction of Secretary Udall.

"At the time our 1963 report was written," he says, "it was the plan that could do the job. No plan is good forever. It must be a living thing, changing as it goes along. But if somebody says 'act,' I must have a plan."

The plan was selected to provide a maximum of benefits for a minimum of cost. "Certain amenities are priceless," he agrees, "but it's pretty hairy getting money from Congress to pay for them. We had to develop a plan which could be carried out—and which could reasonably be funded. It wasn't our job to say it should or should not be done.

"On one thing, however, I feel very strongly: We will need water storage in the

Theodore W. Jones

In the heart of Washington, a functional fountain.

basin. The river as it is flowing now will not serve a community of 5,000,000, which we will probably have in 20 years. (The basin currently stores about 30,000 acre-feet of water—very little.)

The Corps of Engineers plan will definitely not go into effect as is. Some of the recommendations on treatment and erosion have been adopted and one large dam has been authorized at Bloomington, Maryland. But since the President's February 1965, message on natural beauty, says Mr. Schwarz, "We want to review the plan in the light of greater emphasis on recreation in the D.C. area."

"We," in this case, are high level and technical personnel from the departments of Defense, Interior, Agriculture, and Health, Education and Welfare, formed into four subtask forces under Interior Secretary Udall. The interdepartmental group is working to update the Corps of Engineers report—or to draft a new plan. Following a preliminary memo in November 1965, the final recommendations are due in late 1966.

A fundamental feature of this report will be a basin-wide network of parks and parkways.

"This is a new concept," says Interior's Robert Paul, "trying to design river development around a system of beauty and recreation. The President is very excited about it. Interest in preserving the outdoors goes very deep with him." Mr. Paul unrolls a large map of the basin covered with yellow patches and red dots indicating present and hoped for recreation areas. "We feel there's just no way to overdesign this. We need *everything*. There is no place to swim near the District, for instance."

Most of the patches and dots denote land the Interior Department wants to develop for recreational use. Only a few important areas have already been secured. The 184-mile C & O Canal and the adjacent towpaths are already under the jurisdiction of the National Park Service, as is Shenandoah National Park, which covers one of the few large strips of submarginal land in the fertile Shenandoah Valley.

A major project for the future would wrap the Potomac in green from Harper's Ferry to the District. The Park Service wants to widen its jurisdiction on either side of the C & O Canal to provide for large numbers of visitors.

At the other end of the basin, Spruce Knobs-Seneca Rock in the Appalachian plateau offers ideal terrain for a wilderness park: Beautiful forest on land good for little else. Currently almost inaccessible by road, the region could draw new income to its impoverished inhabitants if opened up to tourists and campers.

In the middle of the basin, some rich farmland would fall into a system of parks if Interior can find the money to pay for it. Running roughly from Front Royal to Harrisonburg, Virginia, between the forks of the Shenandoah, Massanutten is a lush valley already containing some fine campgrounds. History as well as scenery suggest it for a national park. "Legend says that George Washington picked this out as his 'bunker,' the place to which he would retire if the Revolution were lost. And the Civil War was fought all up and down through here," Mr. Paul notes.

To lead the visitor from park to river to historic site, a system of scenic roadways is planned. Already completed are the Blue Ridge Parkway, running 469 miles from North Carolina to the Shenandoah National Park in Vir-

The C & O Canal in the Georgetown section of Washington.

Interstate Commission on the Potomac River Basin

At the river's edge, the Jefferson Memorial.

ginia, and the George Washington Memorial Parkway, providing Virginians who work in Washington with a most soothing and inspiring ride home. These microcosms bode well for the taste with which the road as a whole would be completed, for every trash basket and fence along them fits into their well landscaped and maintained roadsides. The first link of the "George Washington Country Parkway Loop" would join the capital with Williamsburg, Virginia. The second would run from Williamsburg through the Blue Ridge and on to Harper's Ferry. From there the road would complete the circle to Washington. If a road from Harper's Ferry into Kentucky were added, the network would open up much of the upper river which is now inaccessible.

For hikers and bikers a basin-wide system of trails is hoped for. "This is probably the handle we'll use for preservation of open spaces," says Mr. Paul. State and local parks and game refuges are essential to round out the system, and "the private sector is extremely important—the Government could never meet the need for marinas, gas stations, and farms to stay on."

The Interior Department recreation map and the 1963 Corps of Engineers report (there have been four) are but two of a high stack of programs drafted since 1900 for all or part of the Potomac. The evidence is all in, recording what the population, economy, and water supply are now and will be 50 years hence.

"We don't need any more plans," one frustrated Potomac expert commented. "We need action. It takes 10 years to plan and build a dam."

Why has action been delayed for so long?

"The problem," says Harry Schwarz, "is that people don't know what they want from the Potomac."

It's an old problem—one faced in almost every section of the country, and because it involves competing worthy values, solutions are difficult.

The current pioneering on the Potomac is not likely to provide easy answers to water-shortage and pollution dilemmas elsewhere. But these dilemmas, which bear so importantly upon outdoor recreation, are vulnerable to man's resourcefulness. And man's resourcefulness, his capacity for developing alternate ideas, is getting a thorough test on the nation's most historic river. ◆

Protecting Vistas, Visitors,

IN THE winter of 1930, forestry students at the University of Washington shuffled into their assembly hall to hear lectures by four rangers of the U.S. Forest Service. The first ranger spoke of what he considered a neglected and important consideration in the management of forest lands: The upswing in their use for recreation. During the talk, the second speaker shifted nervously in his seat. When his turn came, the reason was clear. He, too, had planned to discuss the need for campgrounds, trails, and picnic tables for the increasing number of visitors to the national forests—as had rangers three and four.

Today Arthur W. Greeley, who heard that four-in-one lecture as a freshman, is Deputy Chief of the Forest Service, and one reason he remembers the incident so clearly is that providing for recreation is now, more than ever, a problem for the agency.

Mr. Greeley is in charge of managing the Forest Service's resources, which the agency categorizes as wood, wildlife, forage, water, and recreation. The 154 national forests and 19 national grasslands on 186,000,000 acres in 41 states have a lot of each.

One-fifth of the nation's annual harvest of timber is cut from among the 990 billion board feet growing on Forest Service land. The 11 billion board feet taken from the national forests in 1964 topped the previous record, set in 1963, of 10 billion board feet. Wood—like all other resources of these forests and grasslands —is used up on a sustained yield basis: The amount harvested in a year equals the amount produced in that year. In 1964, 6,000,000 head of livestock grazed on Forest Service ranges, 3,600,000 grown animals under paid permit and an estimated 2,400,000 young pastured free. Much of the nation's water flows across Forest Service acreage, and sustaining this supply is one of the top priorities in Forest Service management.

The recreation resource is equally giant-sized.

The 150,000 miles of roads in the forest transportation system, though most were not laid down for pleasure drivers, have been planned to take vacationers by the most scenic outlooks. Through the national forests run more than 104,000 miles of trails. For those who would rather handle a paddle, there are 70,000 miles of streams plus innumerable lakes and ponds.

More than one-third of the nation's big-game animals, including over half the big game in the West, live on Forest Service lands, on which hunters in 1964 felled 663,000 deer, elk, bear, and bighorn sheep as well as many smaller game and fish. Hunting and fishing are allowed on all Forest Service land except on wildlife and game refuges and within one mile of developed recreation areas.

Winter sports developments that are all or partially on Forest Service acreage account for 80 per cent of the skiing in the West.

According to its cardinal principle of mul-

And the Companionable Trees

By Heidi Fiske

tiple use, the Forest Service tries to perform any function so as to enhance some other program. Roads cut deep into the forest for carrying fire-fighting and maintenance equipment also serve the pleasure-driver. Logging to help supply the nation with wood products creates a better habitat for wildlife by replacing a mature forest with a developing one. Timber carefully logged from a slope clears a new ski area.

At other times recreation is incompatible with other land uses. Hunters want more wildlife, but farmers want the grass such wildlife eats to graze domestic livestock; and foresters fear that overbrowsing of young trees may endanger the forests. The country's lumber needs are best answered by allowing trees to reach their full growth, but hunters want lower woods because game animals prefer it—and are easier to track—and hikers and picnickers find mature forests less aesthetic than a combination of young trees and open fields.

"Now the pulling and hauling between segments of recreational use makes battles between nonrecreational and recreational use look like child's play," says Richard Costley, Director of the Forest Service's Recreation Division. Most campers want running water, toilets, and picnic tables. Some insist on good restaurants and blacktop parking as well. Others hiking through the woods cringe at seeing these developments amid beautiful scenery. Scooter-riders want to propel themselves easily and rapidly through the woods, but bike-riders don't want the noise and the stench around them. On the Boundary Waters in northern Minnesota, water-skiers don't want to trip over fishermen, and fishermen don't want their canoes swamped by motorboats pulling water-skiers. The dispute

is hot on many other lakes, too.

"Now you're cutting it pretty fine," Mr. Costley comments. "You're only talking about boaters."

For the agency (which is part of the Agriculture Department) whose 186,000,000 acres are 94 per cent covered with forests, recreation poses a particular problem—fire. Strong campaigning against human carelessness began during World War II, in which the armed forces, interestingly, used more wood than steel. In 1944 the symbol of a bear was adopted in pleas to "Remember—Only You Can Prevent Forest Fires," and in 1950 the lone survivor of a 17,-000-acre blaze in New Mexico, a badly burned black bear cub, became the living embodiment of the famous "Smokey."

Forest fires have been cut back, though travel to the national forests has risen enormously (by more than 127,000,000 visits or 1,900 per cent since 1944). In 1961 fewer acres were burned than ever before—but that low record was still 3,000,000 acres.

As part of its program of co-operation with state agencies and private foresters, the Forest

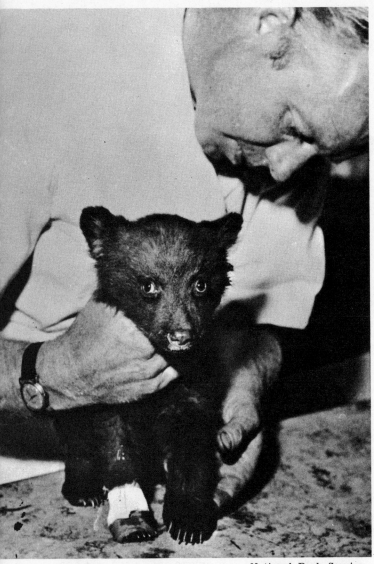

National Park Service

From out of the fire, the original Smokey.

Service encourages public recreation on private woodland as well as on its own sprawling domain. "Make your woodland pay while your trees are growing," suggest several Forest Service publications. Private foresters have responded by requesting, among other things, 115,000 copies of "Forest Recreation for Profit," a 27-page Forest Service booklet.

"To get the landowner to grow bigger trees we need time," says George Vitas, Information Officer for the Special Programs of the Forest Service, "and to buy time we show him other uses of the land. We firmly believe in helping this guy make a dollar, because if he can make a dollar, he'll stay in timber-growing. It's as simple as that."

Multiple use of private woodlands is new, and is already proving highly profitable to the landowner as well as relieving pressure on Federal lands for all forest resources. The owner of 160 acres of woods eight miles from Rehoboth Beach, Delaware, rents campsites for $2 each to vacationers in the summer; he has doubled his business each of the last two years. A farm family in eastern Ohio rents rooms to 8 to 10 guests at a time who come to enjoy the hiking, fishing, swimming, woodlands, and fresh foods their lands provide; the family has increased its income $3,500 a year.

Multiple use is a different concept when applied to the lands of the National Park Service in the Interior Department. There is no question of squaring money-making activities such as cattle grazing or timber cutting with recreation, for the national parks were never intended to help supply the nation's commodity needs. But as visits increase, (there were 102,-475,145 in 1964, a rise of 8,400,000 over 1963), the Service must decide whether to build facilities or leave nature undisturbed—to provide for maximum use or perfect preservation of lands.

"Facilities versus preservation. This is *the* pivotal question in park management. It always has been and it always will be," says a Park Service aide.

The Park Service administers everything from the Statue of Liberty to Lincoln's birthplace, from 400-square-foot patches of grass and flowers in Washington's National Capital Parks to the 2,000,000-plus acres of Glacier Bay National Monument in Alaska. The Service was established in 1916, but Congress had already created the first national park in 1872. Yellowstone is the oldest national park in the world, for the United States pioneered the idea, since adopted by 79 other nations, of preserving large tracts of breath-taking nature for public enjoyment.

Little over half the 26,102,448 acres tended by the Service lie in what are called "national parks," for to be thus dubbed by Congress, an area must have spectacular scenic or scientific value. Currently 32 in number, the national parks will never number more than 40, estimates Park Service Associate Director A. Clark Stratton. There simply aren't more than eight areas of sufficient quality left in the United States.

The Park Service administers its lands under three headings: Natural, historical, and

Monkmeyer

Jackson Lake, Grand Teton National Park.

recreational. The natural areas (which include the national parks and some of the national monuments) are "outdoor laboratories," in the words of an Interior Department official formerly with the Park Service. In contrast to the Forest Service, the Park Service cuts no primeval forest. "If a tree falls it is left there unless it blocks a road." Some Park Service administrators are such sticklers for leaving nature to its own devices in the natural areas that they have advocated allowing lightning-caused forest fires to run their course. Seriously.

The historic areas are restored as well as preserved. The Park Service leases the fields in Gettysburg National Military Park to resident farmers who grow the same crops that were trampled in the 1863 combat. The famous peach orchard still stands, and the buildings which

provided the backdrop for battle have been refaced to appear as they did in Mathew Brady's photographs.

The main administrative goal in the recreation regions (roughly 3,300,000 acres of national seashores and national recreation areas) is use, not preservation. Hunting, forbidden on all other Park Service lands, is permitted almost universally on these. (Fishing is allowed on all Park Service lands with few exceptions.) Future additions to the parklands will fall mostly into this category, both for want of suitable natural and historic areas, and because of the intensifying desire for recreation outlets.

In the more popular national parks, reservations for lodging must be made weeks in advance. The Park Service has tried to improve and increase facilities in these parks. At Yellowstone, for instance, where 9,000 people can sleep each night (plus another 27,000 in the bordering towns), a large new development will make a marina, campgrounds, and lodging for an additional 2,700 available to travelers in 1967.

But the number of structures which can be thrown up on the rim of the Grand Canyon or next to Antietam battlefields is limited by the stipulation, in what the Park Service calls its "magna charta," that the national parks be "maintained in absolutely unimpaired form."

"We can't provide more facilities without ruining the things that people have come to see," says Associate Director Stratton. "More development around Old Faithful will mean encroaching on the geyser basin. We're having enough trouble as it is digging beer cans out of the basin and keeping people from throwing detergents into the geyser." And thousands of feet tramping up to "General Sherman," largest of the redwoods in Sequoia National Park, have pounded the earth down so tightly around the near-surface roots that the life of the tree is in danger.

Even taking these difficulties into consideration, critics of the Park Service feel that it is not doing enough to help more people find food and lodging at the national parks.

But the Park Service has done more in the last 10 years than ever before in its history. "Before 1956, our construction program was practically nil," says Mr. Stratton. That year "Mission 66," timed to end on the Service's 50th anniversary, began. It was a bootstrap project to improve tumble-down visitor facilities and construct new ones. In the 10 years since, almost 18,000 new campsites have brought the total to 29,782; 1,012 miles of road have been constructed or reconstructed; the number of picnic sites has jumped from 742 to 12,393; and 3,300 new rooms for overnight guests have brought the total to 30,000, able to accommodate about 90,000 people. All of the 110 visitor centers providing information about the park in question have been assembled during Mission 66. And 48 new areas, representing almost one-quarter of the present total of 203, have been added to Park Service lands.

A five-year blitz program similar to Mission 66 began for the national forests in 1957. "Operation Outdoors" hoped to provide enough campgrounds, picnic tables, and boat ramps for the 66,000,000 visits which were expected in 1963. While that goal was reached, the visits were twice what the service anticipated.

The situation gets worse, not better. One-half the visits to the national forests since World War II have occurred in the last three years. The Forest Service recreation budget banks on a 157 per cent use of facilities, that is to say there will be half again as many visitors in 1966 as the facilities are planned to hold. And this doesn't count the many people turned away.

"Mostly we're fighting a rear guard action

Drawing by W. Miller; © 1964 The New Yorker Magazine, Inc.

Logging in Lassen National Forest, California.

The General Sherman tree, largest sequoia of all, is 273 feet tall, measures 101 feet around its base, and stands in Sequoia National Park.

Union Pacific Railroad Photo

A park naturalist explains the remarkable geology of the Grand Canyon at Cape Royal on the North Rim.

just to keep up," concedes Mr. Costley. "We're not planning where to develop, but trying to meet current use."

The national forests charge for entrance to some developed camp and picnic areas, but charge nothing to enter the forests themselves. The national parks often charge just to enter a park. The fees in either case run from 25 cents to $1 per day per person 16 or over, or two to five times that amount for a seasonal pass. Or a $7 sticker may be purchased. This will admit all the occupants of the car bearing the sticker to all parks and forests (and many other Federal lands as well) for one season.

User fees as well as entrance fees are charged at some parks and forests. Fees range from 50 cents to 75 cents for a picnic site,

$1 to $3 for an overnight campsite, or 50 cents to $1.50 for a boat-launching site.

The money earned goes not to the Forest or Park Service directly nor to the general funds of the U.S. Treasury as it did until 1965, but into the Land and Water Conservation Fund established in September 1964. The Fund provides matching grants to the states for comprehensive recreation plans, and helps Federal agencies acquire and maintain lands for recreation.

(Several Federal agencies besides the Park and Forest Services control lands used for recreation. Reservoirs built and run by the Bureau of Reclamation, Army Corps of Engineers, and TVA host more recreation visits each year than all Park and Forest Service lands combined.

The Bureau of Reclamation oversees the more than 500,000,000 acres in the public domain, more than twice as much land as the Forest and Park Services administer.)

In their efforts to preserve the wilderness, the Forest and Park Services try to acquire similar lands, and there have been some mighty clashes over who should get what. Some Secretaries of the Interior have gone so far as to try to dislodge the entire Forest Service from the Agriculture Department and bring it under Interior's roof.

When the ORRRC study report noted that "it is imperative that the Federal house be put in order," its writers may have had this ancient feud between Interior and Agriculture in mind.

On January 28, 1963, the two parties declared a moratorium. Secretaries Freeman and Udall signed an agreement "on a broad range of issues which should enable our departments to enter into 'a new era of co-operation' in the management of Federal lands for outdoor recreation." It reads like an armistice: "Mutual recognition is accorded the distinctive administrative functions and land management plans (of the departments). . . . Neither department will initiate unilaterally new proposals to change the status of lands under jurisdiction of the other department." Included in what the Bureau of Outdoor Recreation calls "the peace treaty" was agreement on who should manage four specific recreation areas.

There is a certain tight-lipped, don't-get-me-started-on-that tone in the voice of Forest and Park Service officials as they refuse to discuss the other agency. But when they do talk, there is admiration too. Park Service employes commend the Forest Service for making land productive while at the same time preserving its natural beauty, and Forest Service aides are happy to see such natural wonders as the Petrified Forest National Park in Arizona under Park Service jurisdiction, where its management is not, as it would be if it fell within the Forest Service, "cluttered up by commodity values," in the words of Mr. Costley of the Forest Service.

Basically, where recreation is concerned, the Park and Forest Services (and the Interior and Agriculture Departments as a whole) are fighting the same fight: To preserve the wildlands, to remove them forever from the reaches of developers.

But the Government can only do so much.

"I personally feel," says John Kauffmann of the Park Service, "that the U.S. is only going to keep its wilderness through education, through people cherishing it and taking care of it themselves. Otherwise it will be stamped down by sheer force of numbers.

"It boils down to the question 'What are we going to do with our environment?' We have to accept the idea that enjoyment is a use of an asset. A tree is used just as much when it's being looked at as when it's being sawed up for timber."

As the United States becomes increasingly urbanized, the wilderness becomes as strange and wondrous to most of us as the Egyptian pyramids or Reims Cathedral. The wilderness is an expensive luxury, Mr. Costley notes. It earns no money, and provides a small quantity of recreation relative to its size. But it provides a high quality of recreation.

A major victory has recently been won in the fight to save the wilderness. On September 3, 1964, Congress passed a bill which automatically includes some 9,000,000 acres of Forest Service land in a National Wilderness Preservation System. The Interior Department is considering including some of its lands in the system, too.

No roads, buildings, motorized travel, or commercial enterprises will be permitted in the wilderness system, with few exceptions.

And no electricity. Mr. Costley visited a national forest recently and watched with interest the dismantling of power saws. Forest rangers will go back to using handsaws.

Later that day, Mr. Costley returned to the lodge. In the kitchen the cook was slicing up vegetables for supper—with an electric knife.♦

AMERICA'S largest and oldest national park, which was first set aside by the Government 93 years ago—still packs them in by the millions.

It seems every year you go back the crowds get bigger, the traffic jams get longer, and the black bears get bolder.

But you've always got to go back. Its attractions never seem to jade. Where else can your children see a bear in the wild at five feet? Where else can they watch a moose, buffalo, or herd of deer feed in a plush green meadow surrounded by lodgepole pines?

Where else can they photograph an enormous elk with a trophy rack on his head? Where else can they catch a fish in one water hole and hardboil an egg in another close by? Where else can they see a waterfall twice as high as Niagara? Or a mud volcano erupt? Or friendly Old Faithful spew scalding water as high as a 20-story building?

People never tire of Yellowstone. In the first nine months of 1965, more than 2,000,000 of them visited Yellowstone National Park, breaking all previous attendance records for a single year. They came in 555,788 cars, trucks and campers, pulling 6,716 boats. They brought

twice the number of house trailers they brought in 1964.

They jammed the park's network of paved highways, crowded into its campgrounds, photographed its magnificent scenery, fished its crystal streams and lakes, and stuffed the park bears with so much bread, popcorn and candy that it was beginning to create psychological problems among the furry creatures.

And who knows how many million fish they caught? Or how many color slides were made of Old Faithful and its dramatic, nearly hourly display?

Since the park was first established by Congress in 1872, Government statisticians estimate more than 35,000,000 people have traveled through Yellowstone.

But what the average park visitor takes for granted today was considered out and out prevarication a century ago. John Colter, a member of the Lewis and Clark Expedition in 1806, was probably the first white man ever to see the wonders of the Yellowstone. He traveled through the country with a party of Indians in 1807 and returned to civilization with fantastic tales about spouting geysers, mud volcanos, hissing holes in the earth, and a "hell" of boiling springs.

But no one believed Colter. He was laughed into silence, and for many years jokingly referred to the obscure region of his adventures as "Colter's Hell."

In 1870, despite the stampede of prospectors into the wilderness in search of gold and silver, Yellowstone was still largely myth. A group of influential Montana men, however, set forth to investigate the mysterious land at the headwaters of the Yellowstone River.

Among the group were Nathaniel P. Langford—later destined to become the first superintendent of the park—General Henry Washburn, Judge Cornelius Hedges and Lieutenant Gustavus Doane of the U.S. Army.

YELLOWSTONE

By Nelson Wadsworth

It was around a campfire on the night of September 19, 1870, that the national park concept was born. The men were talking eagerly about the amazing things they had seen, and imaginations immediately drifted to how the marvels could be exploited for personal gain. Dreams of hotels overlooking the choicest geysers and hordes of tourists flocking to them with money bulging from their pockets were suddenly interrupted by Judge Hedges.

"No," declared the judge with feeling. "The Yellowstone should be made into a great national preserve for the people, removed forever by law from commercial exploitation."

His eloquence was overpowering. And before the expedition made its way back to civilization, Langford, Washburn and Hedges had pledged themselves to block any land-rush into the Yellowstone until a national preserve could be set up to protect it.

Langford kept a diary of the trip, parts of which were published in Scribner's Magazine in 1871. But still the public refused to believe. Wrote one irate reader: "This Langford is the champion liar of the Northwest."

But one man believed. He was Dr. Ferdinan Vandeveer Hayden, a geology professor at the University of Pennsylvania who later was to become the director of the Geological and Geographical Survey of the Territories, a project of the Department of the Interior now well-known as the "Hayden Surveys."

Hayden heard Langford lecture in Washington, D. C., early in 1871 and was convinced the man was telling the truth—so convinced that he changed his plans for the 1871 survey to include the headwaters of the Yellowstone.

That spring, Hayden and his men were on

Yellowstone fishing bridge: A little more crowded every year.

Union Pacific Railroad Photo

57

The Hayden expedition (above) explored many sections of the wilderness in northwestern Wyoming. Not the least of the marvels encountered was Mammoth Hot Springs (left).

their way to Wyoming. With the expedition was a talented young photographer named William Henry Jackson. Dr. Hayden reasoned that Jackson's cameras would be able to resolve once and for all the truth or myth of "Colter's Hell."

The Hayden Expedition made its way through the timber, crossed the Montana-Wyoming border, and dropped down the side of a mountain not far from the Gardner River.

"We suddenly came into full view of one of the finest displays of nature's architectural skill the world can produce," Hayden was to write later.

What he saw was the system of step-like terraces of the multicolored Mammoth Hot Springs, now near the northern entrance to the Park, where the National Park Service maintains its headquarters.

The pictures of photographer William H. Jackson (above) finally persuaded Congress to create Yellowstone National Park. His photos of the Lower Falls of the Yellowstone and other scenic splendors are remarkable for their time—1871. The following pages contain a sampling from the Jackson portfolio.

Geological Survey Photos, National Archives

Jackson unloaded his cumbersome cameras from pack mules and began preparing wet plates for the first photographs of the Yellowstone. These glass plate negatives, and others that were made during that summer, are still preserved in Government archives and in private collections. They include remarkably clear photographs of Tower Falls, The Grand Canyon of the Yellowstone, Old Faithful in Upper Geyser Basin, Lower Falls of the Yellowstone, Yellowstone Lake, and many of the mud springs, bubbling pools and so-called "volcanos."

The geology of the area fascinated Hayden. Yellowstone lies in a great basin surrounded by the lofty peaks of the Rocky Mountains. Its beauty is found primarily in the geologic turmoil that created its timbered plateaus and geyser basins and shaped its valleys and can-

59

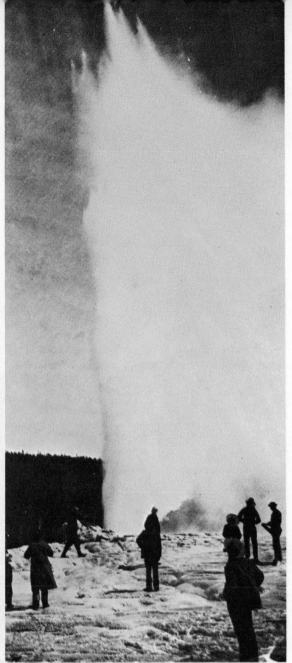

The Grand Canyon of the Yellowstone (left) remains the way Jackson photographed it. Nor has Old Faithful run out of steam.

Geological Survey Photos, National Archives

yons. Evidence of the once violent volcanic activity remains at every hand.

And to the south lie the jagged peaks of the Teton Range which rise like huge, broken fangs into the blue sky.

Early in 1872, Hayden was back in Washington with Langford, William H. Clagett, newly elected delegate to Congress from the Montana Territory, and other proponents of the na-

tional park idea. They knew they had to act fast before enterprising land speculators got wind of the Yellowstone scenic treasures and moved in to stake out claims.

Hayden and his friends lobbied intensively for the proposed bill in January and February of 1872, and at just the right moment, handsome portfolios of Jackson's remarkable photographs were placed on the desks of senators

The falls on the Right Fork of Gardner River have a cottony quality because Jackson's primitive equipment required long time-exposures. His equipment also required a strong mule to carry it.

and representatives. The pictures were neatly captioned and the name of the recipient was embossed in gold on the cover.

It was enough. The photographs clinched the vote in both the Senate and the House, and President Grant signed the bill into law on March 1, 1872.

America's first national park was established, setting the pattern for many others in the years to follow.

And today the beneficiaries come by the millions to marvel at the "unbelievable" features of "Colter's Hell."

Each year in August, a commemorative pageant takes place near Madison Junction, at the confluence of the Fire Hole and Gibbon Rivers, where 95 years ago an obscure judge, his face lit by the campfire, started it all.   ♦

The Gifts

By Edwin A. Roberts, Jr.

THE visitor stood beside the great ponderosa pine, resting his arm against the trunk to steady the camera. There in the view finder was the entrance to Zion Lodge along with the 32 young people who, with hands joined, cheerily serenaded the tourists who were boarding the big yellow buses.

Farewell to thee,
Farewell to thee,
We're glad you came to see our glorious
  canyon.
Take one last look—
The memory will remain—
Till you come back again.

With the sun streaming down Zion Canyon, with the Great White Throne sparkling off to the right of the red wall that is Lady Mountain, with white clouds moving across the small sky—clouds that sometimes stand still while the mountains move—the simple little song sent a flutter up the spine. The singers, mostly girls, swayed slightly as they sang and smiled their farewell.

So majestic is the scenery at the hub of Zion National Park, so peaceful and colorful and inspiring are the towering rocks, and so isolated is the place from the rest of the world, there seemed to be no chance that the "sing-away," as it's called, could be rudely interrupted. But interrupted—rudely—it was.

The visitor was about to snap another picture when he was startled to see an object sail in an arc from the upstairs porch of the Lodge and land, or rather splatter, at the feet of an elderly woman who was about to board one of the buses. The object turned out to be a baked potato, quite well cooked. A man behind the elderly woman picked up the remains of the potato, looked at it, then looked up to the porch. There was no one there.

The singers had stopped their serenading. All smiles faded. The mood, the moment, the memory were spoiled and the singers, who were all college students employed at the Lodge, disbanded and returned to work.

"It was like seeing a potato thrown in church," somebody said.

The culprit, a young male employe, was found and demoted. He might well have been fired because the Utah Parks Company, a subsidiary of Union Pacific Railroad, which operates Zion Lodge, is notably intolerant of mischief. The company receives 6,000 job applications each year from college students seeking summer work at Zion, Bryce, and Grand Canyon National Parks and at Cedar Breaks National Monument. Only 440 are hired and half of these are returnees from the previous summer. Thus, competition is keen.

And almost as remarkable as the natural wonders of the canyon country of southern Utah (there's no other region like it in the world) are the superior young people who spend their summers bellhopping, waiting on tables, or cleaning cabins amid more beauty than the mind can hold. This is especially true when, during a stay at Zion Lodge, one reads in the newspapers about rioting by college-age vaca-

Of Zion

For Visitors and Working Collegians,
Scenery, Serenity, Serenades, and Serendipity

tioners at other resorts or when one recalls the many analyses of campus behavior by writers who espy a "new morality."

The average person, himself perhaps long removed from the happy worries of college life, might be forgiven if he concluded that today's college men and women are phenomenally casual about sexual relations, about causing

ZION
National Park

senseless civic disorders, about asserting their independence in the adolescent manner—by breaking rules. But if such conclusions are correct as they apply to some students on some campuses and at some summer resorts, they are manifestly incorrect and inapplicable to the youths who are earning money to help pay for their educations by working at Zion National Park.

Every traveler knows that one of the drawbacks of his avocation is dealing with mindless, unpleasant persons whose job it is to provide the wayfarer with services. Whether it is a hotel desk clerk, a bellhop, a hotel maid, a waiter, or a certified car parker, the chances are at least even that the traveler each day will bump into one such functionary who hates his job and advertises it.

Thus, the traveler is especially pleased to find the college girl behind the desk at Zion Lodge exceptionally efficient, courteous, and helpful. A stay here is a bargain in any case because the cabins rent for less than $6 a night (with bath; less than $5 without bath).

After registering a guest, the girl taps a bell and a young man rushes up to grab the visitor's luggage.

"Follow me, sir," he says heartily. "Drive your car around the circle and back up toward the front. There's a parking space close to your cabin and I'll run out and save it for you."

The visitor's cabin is 200 feet from the Lodge and tucked on the side of the canyon wall. It is a steep climb up sandstone steps but the Zion bellhop takes them two at a time (he plays volley ball in his off-hours).

He opens the cabin door and sets the visitor's luggage gently on a worn wooden bench. The room is small, containing only two rustic beds and two canvas chairs of the director's

Zion Lodge: Beneath a small sky, the sun and moon are late arrivals.

type. A device called a "swamp cooler" over the door utilizes a fan and running water to keep the temperature comfortable.

The bellhop accepts his tip not only with gratitude but with obvious understanding that, when you're working your way through college, two quarters are more than two quarters.

The mattresses are magnificently saggy and, after a four-hour drive from Las Vegas (the nearest major airport), magnificently soothing. On a shelf above one of the beds is an ash tray, and behind the ash tray is a little card that reads: "Your cabin maids are Barbara Cox of the University of Utah and Judy Ritz of the University of Southern Utah. Please let us know if there's anything else you need to make your stay here comfortable." Those aren't the exact words—the visitor neglected to copy the little message down—but that's the gist of it. Immediately the guest is made aware that the maids are college students and that they will be looking for a tip. It is a pleasing way to get the idea across.

After showering and dressing, the visitor opens the cabin door to head for the dining room on the second floor of the Lodge. But he gets no farther than the cabin door.

The sun is one hour from setting and its rays slant off the sides — now rough, now smooth — of Lady Mountain only 200 yards across the greensward and rising vertically more than 2,600 feet. The mountain is so close that it blocks off half the sky, and 50-foot ponderosa pine trees look like seedlings sprouting from its upper parts.

Lady Mountain is so named because nature has sculptured the form of a reclining woman at its summit, or at least that's the story. One visitor spent the better part of an hour looking for the reclining woman, straining his eyes for a sign of what he supposed would be the identifying characteristics, and failed to make out anything that looked like a woman, reclining or otherwise. But some things have to be taken on faith.

The visitor shakes off the spell of the canyon and moves down the sandstone steps to the tree-shaded sidewalk. From there he can look across the greensward to where 40 young people are having a massive volleyball game, and beyond them is the swimming pool (admission: 51 cents per person).

It's a short walk to the Lodge but the visitor passes several young employes on their way to their respective dormitories. The employes smile as they pass and say "Hi" or "Hello" or "Good evening" to a man they never saw before in their lives. Such civility is altogether enjoyable, but for an Easterner it's hard to get used to. Extend a like greeting to a nervous stranger in New York City and he's just liable to shoot you dead.

Dinner at Zion Lodge (there's no other place to eat in the park except at Zion Inn, where there is a cafeteria for campers) is inexpensive. All dinners on the menu are $3, except for the Special Steak which is $4. The food is good but the portions are small. After an active day on the hiking trails, a man can eat two dinners with ease. No cocktails are available, but the State of Utah does permit beer to be served.

After waiting in line on the stairs to the dining room for a few minutes, the visitor is led to a table on the porch. The hostess wears a long skirt and a wide smile.

On the table is a menu and an order card of the kind used in railroad dining cars. There is also another card that says: "Your waitress is Linda Hill."

"Hello, are you a tour conductor?" asks Linda Hill.

The visitor denies it and confesses his occupation.

"Well, that's the most exciting thing I ever heard," says Linda, a pretty, 22-year-old who recently graduated from the University of Omaha. "I've always been interested in writing, poetry mostly. I love E. E. Cummings, do you? I'm going to teach in the fall. Elementary school. Do you want French or Thousand on your salad?"

After dinner the guest walks out of the Lodge and past the green wicker chairs that line the front of the recreation hall. A naturalist from the National Park Service is conducting a slide program, acquainting tourists with the plants and animals and geology of the area. The hall is crowded so the visitor watches through the window screen.

"This is a little boy flower," says the naturalist. "Notice how small he is compared to those big girl flowers on that tree. But did you know that little boy flower can fertilize every one of those big girl flowers?"

Minutes later the audience reacts audibly when the lecturer shows a picture of a rattlesnake.

"Yes, we have plenty of snakes around here," he says, "but you'll be lucky if you see one. We'd appreciate it if you wouldn't kill any snakes you might see because they help control pests. Since 1919, when Zion National Park was founded, only two people have been bit by rattlesnakes. The last time was last year when a drunk sat down on one. The drunk recovered. So did the snake."

How many times had this naturalist told the same story? Hundreds, probably. He knew all his stories by heart and he knew just when the middle-aged ladies in the front rows would sigh or giggle. If they didn't sigh or giggle right away, he waited for them.

After the lecture, it was announced that the Lodge employes would put on a vaudeville show. It was the kind of announcement that, in another environment, would have sent everyone scurrying for home. But home was hundreds of miles away for most visitors and there's not much to do in a national park at night, so the audience remained seated.

They were in for a treat. A bus boy came on stage and led the gathering in a community sing (*My Bonnie Lies Over the Ocean*). When the audience was warmed up, on came the performers in homemade costumes, singing, dancing, and gagging it up while a diminutive co-ed played a piano that had been rigged to emit a tinny tone. It was the kind of show that could have been a disaster and, in the hands of amateurs, usually is. But the Zion Lodge employes were so conscientious, so well rehearsed, and so talented that the audience stopped the show several times with applause and, after 45 short minutes, left the hall chuckling and humming.

The visitor moved away from the lodge and settled on a bench at the edge of the greensward. The patch of sky visible between the canyon walls was radiant with stars and moonglow, although the moon itself was not yet high enough to see.

"Good evening," said one of the girls who had been in the chorus of the vaudeville show. "Isn't it beautiful here. This is my third year and I never get tired of the canyon. The canyon walls somehow make me feel secure, but not in the ordinary way. They don't make me feel protected. They make me feel secure because they make me feel free."

The speaker was waitress Linda Hill. With a cheery "Good night" and a rustle of her long vaudeville costume, she turned and walked toward the girls' dormitory. Girl employes must be in the dorm by 11:30 p.m., but most of them retire earlier because their work day begins with serving breakfast at 7 a.m. There is no curfew for the men but, as one of them put it, "after the girls go in there's nothing to do anyhow."

Some of the employes were still in the recreation hall playing rock 'n' roll records and doing twist-like dances. ("No, this is not the twist," said one girl as she continued to wiggle; we're surfing." The visitor asked no more questions after that. You're either a member of the Pepsi generation or you're not.)

Sitting on the bench on the lawn in front of the lodge, with the steady hiccupping of a rock 'n' roll beat enfolding him, the visitor recalled his hike that afternoon to Canyon Overlook.

First there was the drive up the switchback roads from the canyon floor to the entrance to the Zion-Mt. Carmel Tunnel, a mile-long hole that is unlighted and black as pitch. Lodge employes, boys and girls together, occasionally take evening hikes through the tunnel where the total darkness provides an ideal

---

It is by no means easy to enjoy the beauties of American scenery in the west, even when you are in a neighborhood that affords much to admire; at least, in doing so, you run considerable risk of injuring your health. Nothing is considered more dangerous than exposure to mid-day heat, except exposure to evening damp; and the twilight is so short, that if you set out on an expedition when the fervid heat subsides, you can hardly get half a mile before "sun down," as they call it, warns you that you must run or drive home again, as fast as possible, for fear you should get "a chill."

—FRANCES TROLLOPE
Domestic Manners of the Americans (1832)

Union Pacific Railroad Photo

Zion Canyon: It encourages a long view of things.

environment for whispered promises. And what-not.

At the far end of the tunnel is a parking area where the visitor left his car to begin the trek to Canyon Overlook. The first 200 feet of the trail are very steep, and the man who huffs and puffs on the cellar stairs at home is wise to stop frequently here to regain his wind. Then the narrow trail levels out and the

grateful climber is free to marvel at the rugged slopes of Pine Creek Canyon, and the huge rock formations called West Temple and the Towers of the Virgin. Here and there the National Park Service has installed an iron railing; a misstep on the narrow ledges could mean a fatal descent.

Decorating the premises are pinyon pine, junipers, yuccas, and cacti, and the observant hiker can spot the tracks of the gray fox and the wood rat. High on the mountaintops great wild cats are said to live, but they are rarely seen by visitors.

At trail's end, a half mile from the starting point, is Canyon Overlook, a sort of natural balcony that affords an admirable view of Zion Canyon. So serene is the vista that the visitor can sit on a rock overhanging the canyon floor hundreds of feet below without being conscious of the danger of such a perch.

Now, on the bench on the lawn in front of Zion Lodge, the visitor reflects not only on the hike to Canyon Overlook, but on the manufac-

Union Pacific Railroad Photo

A glen sublime.

The National Observer

A stream subdued.

ture of the canyon itself. Zion Canyon, like all the great chasms in the area, was formed by tremendous upheavals of earth. Along the floor of the canyon runs a little stream called the Virgin River, a gentle name for so remarkable a cutting edge, for it was indeed the Virgin River that dug the canyon.

Zion Canyon was named by early Mormon pioneers, and the word "Zion," which has several meanings, was interpreted as "the heavenly city of God." It was the Mormons, too, who gave Biblical names to the prominent parts of what is now the 147,034-acre park area. Admission to the park is 50 cents per day per person, or $1 per person for a season's pass. Zion National Park is less spectacular than Bryce and Grand Canyons, but it is more intimate in that the visitor can survey it at his leisure from the lush canyon floor. Bryce and Grand Canyons are viewed by most visitors only from the rims. And while such judgments are partly subjective, at least one visitor believes Zion to be the most beautiful place in all of the beautiful canyon country of the American Southwest.

Although the park attracts many campers and tourists who arrive in automobiles, thousands of visitors see the park as part of the rail-and-bus tours operated by the Union Pacific Railroad. Two jarring noises in the canyon are afforded by the blaring bus horns used to signal tour-guests that it's time to leave, and by the helicopter that for $5 takes tourists for a ride over the park.

Both the bus horn, which sounds like the threatening cry of a Union Pacific diesel, and the clatter of the helicopter are vaguely blasphemous annoyances.

The tour buses are driven by college students who traditionally are known as gear-jammers. The gear-jammers are a little like sailors in that they usually have a girl friend at each stop on the tour—Zion, Bryce and Grand Canyon, and Cedar Breaks National Monument.

There is no liquor available in the park, and any employe caught with it in his possession is summarily fired. Cigarets are available but one visitor never saw an employe smoking. The remarkably model behavior of the college students who work at Zion was ascribed by one informed source to the careful selection of personnel by the Utah Parks Company, and also to the fact that many of the students come from Mormon homes. The Mormon Church frowns upon drinking alcoholic beverages and the use of tobacco.

Only a very naive observer, of course, would conclude that the young people who work at Zion are incapable of smuggling in a pint of bourbon, or indeed of engaging in the standard boy-girl hanky-panky that is a fact of nature. But they are circumspect, and their public behavior gives the lie to reports that college students, when they are not berating their country's foreign policy, are drawing up a new code of morality that is punctuated by permissiveness.

The visitor on the bench at night in front of Zion Lodge notices suddenly that the rock 'n' roll music has stopped. Across the lawn there is a large group of employes by the swimming pool. Then, out of nowhere and everywhere come the strains of a piano concerto. The hi-fi set by the pool booms and tinkles and soon fills the clear night air with music of the loveliest kind. The canyon is suddenly a concert hall and the big bright moon is now visible over the Temple of Sinawava.

The student-employes at Zion are not rioting or discarding beer cans or painting placards. They seem to know they are young and that these splendid canyon evenings are numbered. And once gone, gone forever.

Listening to the music and admiring their canyon, they sit on the lawn or on pool-side chairs and speak softly. Some hold hands. There is occasional quiet laughter. A couple or two walk off to the shadow of a tree for a moment of privacy.

While watching young people who seem to have learned the technique of being young, the visitor is reassured about the nation's most valuable natural resource. Then again, perhaps the visitor has been fooled and these level-headed students are not quite what they seem. Perhaps there is among the group by the pool a girl or two who misbehaves, and a boy with a bottle under his jacket. Certainly there's a boy around who thought throwing a baked potato at an old lady a good idea.

But the moonlight is in flood in Zion Canyon and music fills the night. The visitor decides to believe that these young people are here partly because they understand beauty and order. And that they understand beauty and order because almost all the girls are ladies and almost all the boys are men. ◆

Upstairs at Yosemite:
Hiking the High Sierra

By Lee E. Dirks

THE TREES of the Sierra Nevada "seem unable to go a step farther," wrote John Muir, the famous California naturalist and conservation pioneer of the Nineteenth Century. "But up and up, far above the tree-line, these tender plants climb, cheerily spreading their gray and pink carpets right up to the very edges of the snowbanks. . . ."

To ascend the western slope of the Sierra is to sample and savor an almost infinite variety of forest life. In one wilderness wonderland alone—Yosemite National Park in central California—the ascent takes the adventurer past dense groves of the stately giant sequoia and the haunting incense cedar at 4,000 feet above sea level, up to cool evergreen stands of lodgepole pine and red fir a mile and a half above sea level, and on beyond to stubborn white-bark pine breaking through the granite mountainside at more than 10,000 feet.

The adventure resembles a treadmill ride through a world's fair pavilion of the future, or a leisurely stroll through an attractive museum or arboretum. But this adventure is authentic, not simulated, and therefore it is immensely more exciting.

More and more persons are experiencing this excitement. Most of Yosemite's 1,600,000 visitors each year, like most of the visitors to the other 31 national parks, still pause briefly, admiring only the more spectacular—and accessible—sights, such as Half Dome and Bridalveil Fall in Yosemite.

But park authorities and leaders of the Sierra Club, a private organization of 30,000 members, report a striking surge of interest in the "back country" of the Sierra, the acre upon acre of wild forest, soft meadow, sculptured rock, and shimmering lake that make the Sierra Nevada one of the most richly diverse of the world's mountain ranges. Thus Yosemite National Park, older and better known than the other two parks in the Sierra Nevada, Sequoia and King's Canyon, attracts more cross-country hikers and overnight campers than any other national park with the exception of Yellowstone.

"Food. Packboards. Sleeping bags." Bob Golden, a wiry, 36-year-old official of the Sierra Club, sleepily inventoried the equipment for a three-man, backpack trip to the High Sierra. The light of dawn began to break through the garage of his suburban San Francisco home, and he displayed a trace of impatience to get under way.

The car nosed eastward over the Richmond-San Rafael Bridge, then into the lush San Joaquin Valley. When it reached the foothills of the Sierra in midmorning, Bob's enthusiasm quickened.

"Digger pine," he said. "One of my favorites. They have an ethereal, wispy quality about them, a delicate bluish cast. Usually you think of a tree as being green; this one is green in a grudging sort of a way."

He pointed out a California buckeye, a tree with a large, chestnut-shaped fruit with unusual narcotic-like qualities. "They say the Indians used to crush it and spread it in the water," he said. "It stunned the fish, and the Indians just combed the fish off the top of the water."

A herd of white-faced Herefords grazed beside the highway, their faces a tell-tale black. "That's interesting," he said. "They're grazing on tarweed. It's a weed with a pitchy, black substance. You find it here in the foothills of the Sierra."

This is the country of the famous Mother Lode, the site of frantic gold mining operations a century or so ago. In a small valley below Highway 120, a fawn pranced with a doe over a hummock of gravel churned up by a gold-dredging machine in a river bed. Only now is revegetation beginning to erase the scars the machines made in the earth.

A little farther on, a more human remnant of gold-rush days remains. Just off the highway lies the village of Chinese Camp, a community of 150 persons. Once it supplied coolie labor for the gold mines. Today its residents live a simple life, worshiping in a tiny church, educating their children in a modest school, drawing their water from a windmill-operated pump. Here, one reflects, is that rare village out of the past unmarred by the curio shop and the camera store.

The hills climb more steeply now. The

village of Priest. The village of Big Oak Flat. Hangman's Tree ("Site of many executions," the sign reads; Bret Harte wrote of it often).

Suddenly the traveler sees the first giant sequoia—but only if he knows his trees. This sequoia looks like an ordinary pine shrub in front of a handsomely landscaped home. Like the ordinary shrub, it's planted for decorative purposes—next to the brown U.S. Forest Service station in the forest east of Groveland. "The giant sequoia is a beautiful tree when it's young," says Bob Golden. "It's graceful and symmetrical. The only trouble is that if you

give it enough time, it'll displace the building." Forest Service personnel planted the sequoia several years ago; they well know that the sequoia will be there long after they and their building have gone.

The forest is not wearing its most brilliant coat on this October day. Summer's flowers have withered, and fall's leaves have not yet fully turned. But here and there a broad-leafed maple applies a splotch of yellow, a dogwood a dab of delicate pink. And the incense cedars, possessors of a beautiful reddish-brown bark and with a character all their own, wear sleeves

Picturesque America, 1874

A fallen sequoia.

of bright chartreuse, for lichen, a form of moss, covers their branches.

A haze is visible across a valley. "Forest fires probably," concludes Bob, "though they're not necessarily uncontrolled. Could be controlled burns." An endless debate rages over whether forests should be protected from all fires, or whether fires should be permitted periodically. Forest fires endanger life and property, and the Forest Service's official attitude, in Bob's words, is to "be like Smokey. Be very careful with fire." But if forests are allowed to become too dense, the chances are increased that a fire that happens to start will prove catastrophic. Moreover, snuffing out all of nature's periodic fires tends to change the forest's natural environment; some forms of wildlife, for example, find it difficult to eat if underbrush grows too high.

Around a turn just inside Yosemite, the motorist comes upon the Tuolumne Grove of giant sequoias, one of three sequoia groves in Yosemite. Located in the midst of a heavy stand of virgin sugar pine, this grove has perhaps half a dozen giant sequoias, ranging in age from 800 years to 3,000 years.

Bob leaned over to look at a sequoia cone, much smaller than the cone of the digger pine that grows at an elevation of some 1,000 or 2,000 feet below. "Strange," someone says, "that such a huge tree produces such a small cone." Bob supplies a different perspective: "It's strange that such a small cone produces such a huge tree."

The forest's hypnotism clouds one's awareness of time. Suddenly you realize you're overdue for a noon rendezvous in Yosemite Valley with the third member of the pack-trip party.

But Gosta Vogel-Rodin, it turns out, is a sympathetic individual. The managing director of the tourist traffic association for two Swedish states, Gosta is visiting U.S. parks as part of a six-week tour of the country on a State Department exchange grant. He already has spent 24 hours in the valley—more than enough time to become enchanted with its beauty and diversity.

From the valley to Tuolumne Meadows, in the "high country" of Yosemite, the road twists and climbs another 4,600 feet to 8,600 feet above sea level. First it passes El Capitan, the sheer cliff first scaled four or five years ago by mountain climbers—"ballet stars on rock," in Bob's description. Then it winds upward, through the

A "snag," or dead tree, which is reddish brown on the side most exposed to sun and wind, gives the forest of the High Sierra its most vivid color.

"Canadian life zone" (6,000 to 8,000 feet) with several varieties of pine and on to the "Hudsonian life zone" (8,000 to 10,000 feet), named because its plants and animals resemble those found near sea level in the Hudson Bay area of Canada, hundreds of miles to the north.

A "scenic turnout" on the Tioga road entices the adventurer to pause for a few moments to inspect some of the handiwork of nature's glaciers. Twice a warm, shallow sea submerged the land that is now Yosemite, and twice this land emerged, forming mountains. Today the visitor sees the hard granite rock of the last uplift, shorn of its overlying layers of sediment and carved and polished by glaciers.

A mountain chickadee chirps as you descend the path on the glacial apron, the tiny pebbles on the path giving you a footing of ball bearings. A lonely juniper or two provide

the only foliage. A dead juniper "snag," its bark stripped by the weather, displays a twisted trunk. "Twisted for strength," says Bob. "Only the strong survive here."

Still higher, the highway snakes around another curve and enters Tuolumne Meadows, a lush subalpine carpet of green before the first frost, but now drab brownish yellow. Lembert Dome, its southern flank a wall of exposed granite rising 1,000 feet, shelters a roadside area used as a take-off point for hikes through the "high country."

An hour before sundown, the threesome strikes out for Dog Lake, only a mile to the north but uphill all the way. The short hike on the first day is intentional: At this elevation, even the experienced hiker must take time to acclimate himself to the thinner air, and the inexperienced man carrying a pack of 35 or 40 pounds finds himself short of breath after only a few steps.

"This trail never was really built," says Bob. "The cavalry, which ran this area for some time, just rode its horses up the slopes, marking out a trail as they went by cutting a 'T' in some of the trees." This is woodland, but it is sparse woodland; the lodgepole pines compete for survival, and only the sturdy win.

"The highest peak in Sweden," says Gosta, pausing to catch his breath, "is only 2,100 meters—something over 6,000 feet. If we were in Sweden now, we would be walking in the air."

Yet Swedes, like persons of all nationalities, find mountains alluring. "When people ask the persons in the Himalayas why they live at such heights," says Gosta, "the Himalayans say, 'I am waiting for my soul.' In fact, this is true. When we live in the city and work in the office all day, we need to find our souls."

At Dog Lake the moon's reflection bounces off the water, and the overpowering sensation is the sensation of stillness. Squirrels would be chattering and mountain birds chirping in June or July, but in October not even the wind whispers.

By the fireside, Bob examines a dead branch of lodgepole pine destined for the fire. It tells the forest's story of birth and death. The branch lived a healthy life; its very size proves its stamina. But in the end this branch and its tree succumbed, victims of forest insects. The bark peeled off long ago; the branch's surface now displays an intricate pattern of shallow indentations and deep gouges. Bark beetles caused the indentations; flat-headed borers the gouges.

"It's the natural mechanism of the forest," says Bob. "Death and regeneration. Decay and growth." The natural inclination of the forester is to protect against decay and death—to save the life of the sick patient. But Bob, for one, considers spraying to preserve the life of trees ill-advised in national parks. "Wipe out the needle-miner (an insect that attacks the tops of lodgepole pines), and you tend to create a sameness in a forest. You'll get lodgepole pines and nothing else. With the needle-miner at work on the lodgepole, you get hemlock too, and an occasional white pine. Diversification is as important in the forest as it is in the stock market."

The stillness provokes thoughts, and thoughts provoke tales. Tales of the forest. Tales of the mountains.

Wrapped in his sleeping bag, Gosta tells of a Laplander in northern Sweden who was buried in a snowslide for eight days and survived. "He could move a little under the snow, and he put a theater ticket he had in his pocket on a long branch and raised it through the snow as a sign to his rescuers. He did not panic; he knew they would not begin looking for him for about three days. He was carrying four small fowl, and he ate them slowly. When they found him, he was weak, and his toes were frozen, but he lived."

The water's edge at Dog Lake would freeze this night; the temperature would drop below

Swedish outdoorsman Gosta Vogel-Rodin samples a stream in a high meadow.

30. But for "high country" that had tasted its first snow of the season a month before, this would be a mild evening. Back-packers who would be leaving the trails the next day and striking out cross-country through forest, meadow, and rock, would find an additional incentive to sleep in the very chilliness of the air.

In the morning light, the forest life in the "high country" blends soft greens and browns. The dramatic colors of the forest come from the dead—from the snags, with their vivid reddish brown trunks on the side exposed to the sun and wind. Occasionally a small sunflower adds a dash of yellow or lupine a touch of purple to the floor of the forest. Snow ponds—tiny lakes formed by melted snow and covered with an oily substance that has dropped from the trees—provide still another forest variation in autumn.

Bob cracks his walking stick against a boulder. "Deer," he says. In the shadow of the boulder lies a bone, perhaps eight inches long.

One-half of the day's five-mile hike penetrates woodland. Before the climactic ascent of a rock-strewn saddle between two peaks, taking the hikers to an elevation of nearly 11,000 feet, a meadow stream offers rest and refreshment.

Look southwest, down the meadow. Glacier's litter, boulders, clutter the meadow, creating the eerie appearance of a graveyard. Beyond lies Cathedral Peak, a study in Gothic architecture by nature itself. "I never weary of gazing at the wonderful Cathedral," John Muir once wrote. "It has more individual character than any other rock or mountain I ever saw, excepting perhaps the Yosemite South Dome."

Near the creek, Bob spots some flint on the ground. "Indians. Indians chipped arrowheads out of obsidian, and these are some of the chips they had left over. You can almost always predict where you'll find obsidian chips; the Miwok always chose a place of great beauty for their campsite."

The Miwok Tribe lived in the center of the Sierra Nevada, the Maidus in the north, and the Yokuts in the south. Although the Spanish explorer Juan Rodriguez Cabrillo claimed the California coast and the territory beyond in 1542, it was more than two centuries before white men discovered the mountains of the Miwok and their sister tribes. In 1776, the Franciscan missionary, Pedro Font, reached the western edge of the Great Central Valley and reported that "at a distance of about 40 leagues, we saw a great snowy range—*una gran sierra nevada.*" The missionary drew the range on a map and used the same title it bears today: Sierra Nevada.

The meadow yields still another relic of history. At its edge grow relatively young pines, half the stature of the mature pines of the forest. After the white men drove the Indians away a century or less ago, sheepherders brought sheep to the mountain meadows. Conservation experts say the "high country" still bears the scars of this indiscriminate grazing; among other things, the grazing erased the edges of some meadows and made them dry enough for lodgepole pines.

The climb continues, a sparse forest becoming a mountainside desert. Stark snags stand erect, their branches resembling the spare beauty of driftwood. Each living tree gives an instant's refreshment as the hikers savor its shade in the 70-degree heat. Heads thump, thighs ache, and perspiration trickles down foreheads and tickles the tips of noses as the sun beats against the rock between Ragged Peak and a still-unnamed mountain.

Suddenly, the reward is won. Through the saddle comes a magnificent view—a small basin surrounded by peaks. At the floor of the basin, nearly straight down, lies Young Lake. On the opposite side looms the bright face of Mount Conness, 12,590 feet into the sky. Even here, life springs to notice: On the huge patch of shade-protected snow and ice a few feet away, a rosy finch raids his "deep freeze" by devouring insects caught in the snow.

Here, at Young Lake, before an easy eight-mile hike back to Tuolumne Meadows the next day, the hiking party sets up camp for its second and final night on the trail. On the following day it would find rich additional evidence of the diversity of the Sierra—evidence of coyote and bear, of corn lilies and red heather, of single-spire Matterhorn peaks and rounded drumline domes.

But in this tiny basin nearly two miles high, they find the peace and stimulation that John Muir promised from the mountains decades ago:

"Climb the mountains and get their good tidings. Nature's peace will flow into you as sunshine flows into trees. The winds will blow their own freshness into you, and the storms their energy, while cares will drop off like autumn leaves." ◆

Young Lake and Mount Conness, from saddle next to Ragged Peak.

THE RISING GORGE

By Nelson Wadsworth

BACK in 1963 the Sierra Club of California published a book of highly artistic photographs on Utah's little-known, hauntingly beautiful Glen Canyon. In vivid color, photographer Eliot Porter recorded the magnificence of the silent, meandering canyon, and he called it "The Place No One Knew."

Since time immemorial the mighty Colorado River had flowed through the remote and lonely gorge, sculpturing finely and wending its way toward the sea. Here, man had been an infrequent visitor. First came the "Ancient Ones" of prehistoric Pueblo cultures, then the Navajos, the early day explorers and finally the handful of adventuresome river runners who sought the solitude of Glen Canyon's peaceful walls.

The picturesque canyon was named in 1869 by John Wesley Powell, river explorer and one of the founders of the U.S. Geological Survey. Wrote Powell on passing through the placid stretch of river:

"Past these towering monuments, past these mounded billows of orange sandstone, past these oak-set glens, past these fern-decked alcoves, past these mural curves, we glide hour after hour, stopping now and then, as our attention is arrested by some new wonder . . . .

"We decided to call it Glen Canyon."

The lenses of the modern-day photographer were particularly perceptive to the inherent beauty that had captured Powell's fancy: The fractured sandstone, the delicacy of green fern growing from stone, the minute detail of colored pebbles strewn on a rippled sandbar, and the golden hues of the dying sun reflected in placid pools and on the red and black tapestry-streaked walls looming on all sides.

Porter's camera saw it through the eyes of a Thoreau and left behind images of poetry.

But then the gates of Glen Canyon Dam closed in 1963, and "The Place No One Knew"

Behind Glen Canyon Dam,
Lake Powell Closes Over the Great Red Rocks

Rainbow Bridge: The best way to get there is by boat.

was no more. There arose something in the silent canyon fashioned by man.

Today, the breath-taking scenes that thrilled Powell and Porter lie under 100 to 200 feet of water, at the bottom of one of the largest man-made reservoirs in the world.

Now they call it "Lake Powell, Jewel of the Colorado," named in honor of the one-armed river explorer who found enchantment in Glen Canyon nearly a century ago. And the lake is backing up 186 miles behind the recently completed dam.

The emotion-charged argument over whether or not Glen Canyon should have been or should not have been sacrificed to the cause of U.S. reclamation will go on forever, with neither side giving a quarter.

But Glen Canyon now is gone forever, and all that remains is an ever-growing expanse of blue in the slick-rock wilderness.

Just stand today atop any one of the many sandstone mesas overlooking Lake Powell, and you will see that "The Place No One Knew" has been transformed into a boater's paradise, destined soon to become one of the most popular recreational sites in the West.

Just stand at the boat ramps at Wahweap or Halls Crossing and watch the fishermen

Glen Canyon Dam: For the wild Colorado, another bridle.

U.S. Department of Interior

coming in with the day's catch of rainbow trout and bass, or look out upon the water skiers churning up the wide bays, and you realize that the beauty of Glen Canyon has been wrested from the domain of the aesthete and placed into the hands of the American people.

In spite of the motives of those who tried to keep it primitive and those who wanted to store water in it for agriculture and reclamation, a new glimmer of grandeur has been added to the once-narrow confines of Glen Canyon. Looking beyond the government propaganda as well as the dream of the purist, one can easily see that Lake Powell has brought even more majesty to the wild, untamed, red-rock wilderness of southern Utah and northern Arizona.

And where a mere handful had enjoyed the secrets of Glen Canyon in yesteryear, today millions can look to Lake Powell as a beautiful water playground.

In a desert land where moisture is precious life itself, the azure water stands out in marked contrast to the glare of the midsummer heat. One quickly recognizes where it got its nickname, "Jewel of the Colorado." For even a teardrop of water here in Dante's July and August is like a diamond on a rockpile.

Government engineers will tell you Glen Canyon Dam is the bridle that tamed the Colorado, America's third longest and one of its most treacherous rivers. The giant concrete plug that created the reservoir is the largest of the Reclamation Bureau's dams built to regulate and control the flow of the Upper Colorado River and its tributary streams—all draining a vast basin of the arid West. The river basin includes portions of Colorado, Utah, Wyoming, New Mexico, and Arizona and drains an area equal to one-twelfth of the continental limits of the United States.

Lake Powell is much different from its downstream sister, Lake Mead, even though the designs of Hoover and Glen Canyon Dams are somewhat similar. Lake Mead, containing 31,-000,000 acre-feet of water, fills a Y-shaped basin of dark-colored rock, with comparatively gentle slopes. Lake Powell, on the other hand, ultimately containing 28,000,000 acre-feet of water, backs up into southern Utah's picturesque "Canyon Country," into the land of red rock.

When filled, the lake will have nearly 2,000 miles of shoreline, winding into a myriad of canyons on the Colorado, Escalante, San Juan and Dirty Devil (Fremont) Rivers, with innumerable fingers stretching up smaller tributary streams and draws, some of which had been uncharted and unexplored before construction of the dam.

One arm of the lake extends up Forbidding Canyon and Aztec Creek to the base of one of the greatest natural wonders in America—Rainbow Bridge. The massive stone bow spanning the canyon is the world's largest natural bridge, so immense that the dome of the U.S. Capitol would be lost underneath. Writer Weldon Heald, on seeing Rainbow Bridge for the first time, wrote these words:

"The real wonder of Rainbow Bridge is that of water carving stone; of the billions of storms which brought the water, of the stone itself, laid down ages ago as drifting sand dunes on a Jurassic desert. The wonder is the sun, the wind, the clouds, vegetation, chemical action, the forces within the earth—all working together

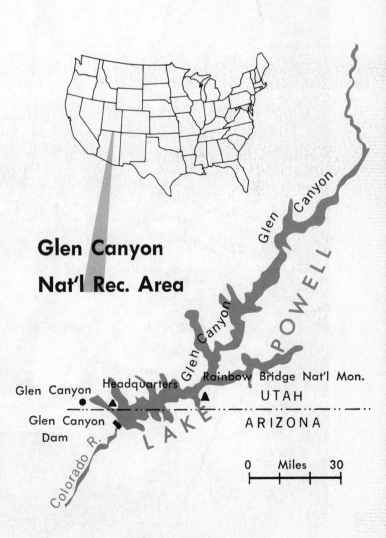

for millions of years to produce this perfect masterpiece."

And without ever having seen Rainbow Bridge, more than a half century before it was even discovered, Henry David Thoreau wrote:

"The finest workers in stone are not copper or steel tools, but the gentle touches of air and water working at their leisure with a liberal allowance of time."

Rainbow Bridge is one feature of "The Place No One Knew" that will go unscathed by Lake Powell's rising waters. However, lake water will

A burning tree a la Dante? No, just an aerial view of the Colorado River as it gives into the Gulf of California.

Aero Service Division Litton Industries

eventually pass beneath the massive bow. Already, boaters can travel to within easy walking distance of the bridge, while the controversy still rages over whether or not millions of dollars should be spent to build dams to keep water from climbing up to the abutments of the huge, nature-made colossus.

Prior to Lake Powell, only a few thousand people made the long journey down the Colorado River and up Aztec Creek to view the massive bridge. Among the first was Theodore Roosevelt who camped beneath the span in 1913, three years after it was discovered.

In its early days, Lake Powell is still a primitive waterway. Because it is a national recreation area similar to Lake Mead, the National Park Service has jurisdiction over whatever facilities are developed along the shoreline. Headquarters for the area are located at the most extensive development at Wahweap at the lower end of the reservoir, not far from the little government town of Page, Arizona. Marinas, launching ramps, rentals, concessions, and other facilities for boating, fishing, and swimming can be found in three main locations—at Wahweap, Halls Crossing, and Hite, Utah. Only Wahweap is accessible by pavement. However, Halls Crossing and Hite can be reached by improved dirt roads.

Other facilities are under development at other locations of the lake.

Fishing is excellent, especially during the early days of filling, when feed is plentiful for the millions of rainbow trout and bass planted yearly by air by the fish and game departments of Utah and Arizona and the U.S. Fish and Wildlife Service. Fingerlings grow to catchable size in less than a year because of ample feed in the slowly rising waters.

In the years to come, fishermen, water skiers, boaters, nature hikers, swimmers and sightseers will come by the millions. They will bring civilization with them to tame one of the least-known and most rugged areas of the United States.

But with their arrival, one can't help but look back remorsefully to the solitude and pristine beauty of Glen Canyon and "The Place No One Knew." The words and thoughts of Henry Thoreau come again to mind, and one wonders how the author of *Walden* would have looked upon the glittering, 186-mile-long emerald that laps these sun-bathed ledges of ageless stone.

Is it less beautiful because the hand of man and not God fashioned it?

The answer will be written by the millions who come here to see for themselves. ◆

Clouds are playing in the canyon today. Sometimes they roll down in great masses, filling the gorge with gloom; sometimes they hang above, from wall to wall, and cover the canyon with a roof of impending storm; and we can peer long distances up and down this canyon corridor, with its cloud roof overhead, its walls of black granite, and its river bright with the sheen of broken waters. Then a gust of wind sweeps down a side gulch, and, making a rift in the clouds, reveals the blue heavens, and a stream of sunlight pours in. Then the clouds drift away into the distance and hang around crags, and peaks, and pinnacles, and towers, and walls, and cover them with a mantle that lifts from time to time, and sets them all in sharp relief. Then, baby clouds creep out of side canyons, glide around points and creep back again into more distant gorges. Then, clouds, set in strata, across the canyon, with intervening vista views, to cliffs and rocks beyond. The clouds are children of the heavens, and when they play among the rocks they lift them to the region above.

—JOHN WESLEY POWELL
The Exploration of the Colorado River (1875)

A CONQUEST OF RAINIER

By Jack Wilkins

"COULD someone like me climb to the summit?"

All summer the rangers at Paradise, the major tourist center in Washington State's Mt. Rainer National Park, hear that question.

"You serious?" a ranger is likely to reply.

"No, just curious," is your answer—unless you have developed a strong desire to climb the 14,410-foot dormant volcano. You don't need much money to climb Mt. Rainier; you don't need an awful lot of climbing experience and you don't have to be an athlete—but you do need reserves of desire and determination because they ebb at an astonishing rate with each thousand feet you ascend into air that becomes increasingly oxygen-thin.

You also need time. It took me 25 years—but for most people about 10 days in the park should do it, though the actual climb and descent take only two days. The additional week or so is needed for conditioning and practice, unless you have climbed before on snow and ice and your legs are in good shape.

Paradise, with its old inn and new day lodge and nearby camp sites, is a valley of meadows and slopes chocked and blazing with heather and alpine flowers. It aprons out at the 5,500-foot level of the mountain's south side. Alpine firs that are shaped like perfect tepees peter out a few hundred feet above Paradise, and the snowfields begin. These reach up to glaciers that cling like rumpled armor to the mountain's massive shoulders of rock. On clear days your eyes keep drifting up the skeletal ridges and the icefalls to the glorious white summit that seems to fill the sky almost two miles above you.

"Beautiful, beautiful, beautiful," you hear all day from tourists and experienced mountaineers alike, but the praise never seems overdone. One good look at Mt. Rainier from a nearby viewpoint adds a new dimension to your life, unless you were brought up in the Himalayas.

That first look at the mountain can also be frightening, as it was to me in the summer of 1940, when, at the age of 19, I arrived at the park from upstate New York with a chum, eager to "conquer" the summit. When a scar on my knee from a too-recent operation caused the rangers to refuse us permission for the climb, my chagrin was tinctured with a bit of relief.

But Rainier isn't quite as tough as it looks, unless you tackle it by one of the dozens of difficult routes. You don't have to ascend that trough under heavy cornices that threaten to become avalanches. You don't have to ascend the steepest icefalls, cutting handholds and footholds up the sides of slippery seracs (ice towers) and navigating around the edges of bergschrunds (huge crevasses near the top of a glacier) which could swallow good-sized hotels. You don't have to inch up that cliff of unstable rock and straddle that knife-like ridge.

The rangers won't let you attempt such routes, anyway, unless you are highly qualified. One route—the Willis Wall, or North Face—is recognized as having been climbed only once or twice. Cold weather and moonlight were required for the ascent of this huge, icebound cliff, because pieces of the mountain fall continuously when the sun warms things up. Any others who may have climbed the wall are forced to keep their accomplishment to themselves because the route is forbidden.

Other theoretically possible routes have never been climbed. Some routes have been climbed only three or four times, and others are climbed a few times each summer by experts only. But 95 per cent of the hundreds of

The Rigors of Climbing and Something About the 'Why'

Park ranger appraises the climbers' gear—and the climbers.

people to "make Rainier" any summer take one of the four or five standard routes. Each year there are several climbers aged under 16 or over 60—and each year there is an incident similar to that of the 18-year-old chap (admittedly experienced and known for his endurance) who blithely opened his pack on the summit and took out a big watermelon, to the delight of his dehydrated companions.

The standard routes are not "technical." That is, they don't require expert techniques of aiding one another with ropes; climbers are roped for safety only, not for help in climbing. Most sections of these routes are not highly "in-teresting" (scary) though they present breath-taking views.

Immediately upon moving here 11 years ago, I sought means of climbing Rainier without a guide. I didn't have to look far—though I was not to get around to climbing the mountain until last July because I became involved with other major peaks first and I must have learned patience from the mountains.

In the Pacific Northwest are thousands of climbers, many of whom belong to such clubs as the Mazamas (Portland), the Mountaineers (Seattle and Tacoma), Slope and Summit (Tacoma) and the Washington Alpine Club (Seattle). Most of these are listed in phone books. The clubs have climbs of Rainier and major peaks such as St. Helen's, Adams, Baker, Glacier, Hood and Olympus scheduled throughout the summer.

If you have taken conditioning climbs and a bit of snow and ice instruction, you might latch onto one of these climbing parties at the mountain. Of if you are in Seattle or Tacoma for the day, phone one of the clubs or drop into the clubhouse to see if they have a climb scheduled soon; a cordial invitation is likely.

You can rent all the specialized equipment—boots, crampons (spikes to attach to your boots for gripping ice), ice axe and dark goggles—at alpine shops in either city for less than $6 a week end.

However, you will need your own lightweight down sleeping bag designed to keep you warm at zero, plus a staunchly wind-resistant parka, heavy mitts, thermal or woolen underwear and at least three thicknesses of heavy wool shirts and sweaters in any combination you like (you'll be shedding garments and put-

The way up.

ting them on again as conditions change). Tough, warm pants are a must; ski pants serve the purpose. You'll also need enough canteens to supply a quart and a half of liquid, plus a flashlight and a basic first aid kit.

Last July our party of 15 used one of the "long ways" up the mountain I had always wanted to climb. Ours was the Emmons-Winthrop route on the mountain's northeast side. Only one of two parties had been on the summit this season because the usually popular Ingraham Glacier route had become a maze of deep crevasses. That route is approached from Paradise, on the south side, from where most parties, including guided ones, start out.

The previous week end a party of 40 had been turned back from Ingraham by the crevasses. Our party gave evidences of delight that the other party's leader had been Jim Whittaker, the first American to climb Everest. "Big Jim" had been turned back by Rainier! Actually, we knew that Jim had performed tremendous feats on Rainier—had climbed it 70 or 80 times—and that he had merely exercised good leadership in not allowing such a large party, many of whom were beginners, to thread through the dangerous crevasses. They might have gotten through, but they would have fallen behind schedule and Jim wanted them down the mountain by night.

Their climb demonstrated that even the conventional routes on a major peak can become extremely hazardous when physical changes occur. Sometimes extensive scouting becomes necessary, increasing chances of slipping into a crevasse or plunging through a snow bridge or cornice. Fatigue mixed with uncertainty increases chances of accident.

Anywhere above timberline is hazardous when weather turns bad, which is one reason park officials insist that emergency rations be carried. About half the parties that start the climb have to turn back because the leader won't take a chance on there being lightning or a blizzard or a "white-out" in which the atmosphere and snow merge into the same cloudy hue and you can't tell where your next step will take you. High wind in cold weather is another demoralizer.

But with our party, everything came up

Mount Rainier National Park

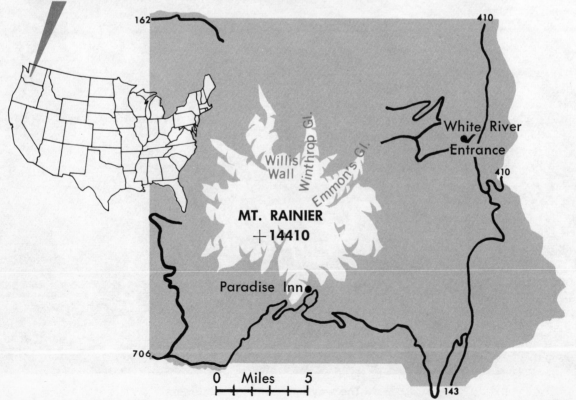

roses—or edelweiss.

We drove east from Tacoma one evening on Highway 410 and turned into the park at the White River entrance a few miles north of Chinook Pass. We parked at the White River campground at 4,500 feet and slept beneath giant hemlocks and cedars.

At 8:30 a.m. the next day, a ranger "checked out" our party, approving our food and equipment and satisfying himself that our leader was an expert and that there was a favorable balance of experienced climbers to novices in the rest of the party.

This was to be the first climb of Rainier for two of us. On this common ground, we looked each other over. She was very blond, very cheerful, a skier and a high school biology and physical education teacher, and her name was Margie.

Our warm clothing was in our packs (with the average load weighing about 35 pounds) because it was T-shirt and shorts weather. Unroped, we filed up a tree-shaded trail that climbed gradually as it followed the White River.

At noon, after lunching in an alpine meadow, we roped up in five teams of three, put on dark goggles and covered our exposed skin with protective cream, and stepped onto the Inter Glacier. The leader put Margie in front of me on the lead rope, with himself leading. We had hiked about five miles and climbed 2,000 feet. Ahead of us that afternoon was a steep 3,500-foot ascent to rocky Steamboat Prow at 10,000 feet. Just beyond it we would descend a few hundred feet—much as we would hate to lose altitude—and camp on the flank of Emmons Glacier, some of us in the rock shelter called Schurman Camp, the rest in tents on the snow or under tarps in niches among the rocks.

Climbing the Inter Glacier, our pace slowed progressively as we gained altitude. The sun had softened the snow surface "just right" so we had no need for crampons or for cutting footholds.

Praise be for the "rest step." This is a pace that must be adopted in the steeper stretches to avoid exhaustion. Slowly and steadily you eat up the distance, and you rest as you do it. A strong desire to climb Mt. Rainier, plus the rest step, are what put you on top. With one leg forward, you retain all your weight on your straight rear leg; you pause, breathing deeply

Negotiating a wall of snow.

for one, two, five or more seconds, according to the steepness and altitude; you lean forward again until your forward leg straightens and becomes a fulcrum. Then your rear leg swings forward, its boot kicks a new foothold into the snow, and you breathe again before resuming the pace.

A feeling of power—not power over the mountain; just power itself—flows into you as you do the rest step high on a glacier. You look down on peaks that had formerly always been above you. The silence is tremendous— just the sound of boots and your heartbeat and perhaps a faint ringing in your ears from the thinness of the air. You rise into clean air which holds as special a world as that beneath the ocean surface.

Sunlight bounces up to your face from the snow, bringing a mixture of heat with mountain-cold. The blessing of heat and the blessing coolness and luxury of a drink of water and a brief rest are really "felt" at high altitudes, which is one reason men climb mountains.

We gained the top of Steamboat Prow at 4:30 p.m. Before us rose tomorrow's climb— the upper Emmons and Winthrop Glaciers blending into a receding wall for 4,400 feet to the summit.

We descended to the edge of the glacier and made camp. Marge made a niche for herself in the rocks; the leader and I set up his tent; we all had a bit of supper—heavy on liquids, especially sweet tea, and light on solids because oxygen-thin air steals your appetite.

Thirst is a steady companion at high altitudes. Melting snow in coffee cans on mountain stoves is a steady chore.

By 8 p.m. we were in our sleeping bags. The camping area was silent but for the flapping of tents and the booming of distant avalanches.

At 12:30 a.m. the leader's alarm clock went off. The sound of our tent rattling returned. The wind sounded cold, but I was glad to have had a bit of sleep at least.

I reached beside me in my sleeping bag and took a sip from my canteen, which had been kept there so the water wouldn't freeze. The leader and I took aspirins for headache and oatmeal cookies for breakfast.

Despite my wearing all my sweaters and heavy shirts under my parka, I shivered while fumbling with numb fingers to attach crampons to my boots. My morale was low—but actually, the weather was ideal for that altitude on Rainier at that time of day. How would I have felt if things had been tough?

"This is it," I reflected, taking an unusually objective look at myself at the age of 44 as I tied into a rope behind Margie and the leader. "I like warm beds. I like to exercise but I don't like to suffer. After today, timberline will be high enough."

An hour later I was climbing a moderate pitch. The leader was setting a slow pace because he had to use a flashlight and find a route around and over crevasses, marking them with wands. I felt good. My headache was gone. I was warm; the wind had died; the stars were brilliant. I knew I could make the summit. It

The summit of Rainier seemed very close at hand. About two o'clock in the afternoon the clouds rolled away like a scroll; In a very short time they had disappeared, and the Cascade Range lay before us in all its greatness. The view was too grand and too extensive to be taken in at once, or in the short time we had to observe. The entire scene, with few exceptions, was covered with forests, with here and there barren rocky peaks that rose up out of the ridges; now and then a mountain lake, much more blue than the sky, and the Nesqually, winding like a thread of silver through the dark forests. . . .

We had no time, however, to study the beauties that lay before us. We had already discovered that there was no telling from appearances how far we had to go. The travel was very difficult; the surface of the snow was porous in some places, and at each step we sunk to our knees. . . .

—AUGUST VALENTINE KAUTZ
In first account of successful climb of Mount Rainier. Overland Monthly (May 1875)

Preparing to span a fissure: There's always the fast way down.

was good to be on the lead rope, above the four other teams.

At last it was beginning to get light. I was sweating and wondering why the leader didn't call a rest halt. He finally did, but it was much too brief. A damn-fool 20-year-old yodeled as the sun came up. The chunk-pause-chunk of my boots into the footholds seemed interminable. My chest and legs seemed to be squeezed by metal bands. This definitely was the last time I'd climb a major peak!

The 14,000-foot contour, the rim where the original volcanic cone had blasted away, was getting close—but the crevasse pattern forced us up the steep Winthrop headwall. The nearer we got to the 14,000-foot rim, the steeper the remaining interval.

The ascent became torture because our crampons dictated our movements. The prongs must grip the ice at a 90-degree angle, which means that on a steep slope your ankles must act like universal joints and your leg muscles must be prepared to co-operate fully. One climber slipped and fell after leaping a crevasse, but a taut rope kept him out of trouble.

For the last stretch beneath the 14,000-foot rim, handholds as well as footholds were needed in the ice.

"Congratulations!" shouted Margie as she gave me a little help on the rope while I climbed over the rim on hands and knees.

"This is the summit," I tried to tell myself, "the others can climb 400 feet more to Columbia Crest if they choose. What's the point?" But I knew I was lying to myself. Columbia Crest, the rim of a secondary crater, is the highest point of Rainier.

"Let's go!" boomed the infuriating leader.

And I arose with the others.

More than an hour later, 50 feet from the summit, I was sobbing for breath.

"Come on!" shouted the leader. "We're first on the summit!" And crazily, all three of us on the lead rope broke into a run. We fell into a heap, as high as we could get on Mt. Rainier, at 10 a.m. The second rope team rested awhile 20 feet below us and then joined us. Someone set off a firecracker to celebrate.

On the way down that afternoon, the leader confided that he had almost not made the summit. "I swore I would never climb it again," he said. "I always do that." ♦

Vacationing

By Arch Napier

IF you ever decide to vacation on an Indian reservation—as we did recently—be prepared for some questions from the neighbors:

"What's so special about Indian country?"

"Are you sure you will have a place to stay? It looked pretty empty when we drove through."

"Stay a whole week? I can see a visit to an Indian dance or a trading post for an afternoon, but what else is there to do?"

Your answers must vary according to the reservation you choose. Some could keep a family of campers entertained all summer; others are good for about one afternoon picnic. The Mescalero Apaches have a ski resort; some Utes have a fall mustang hunt; and the Navajo museums and craft centers are open the year round.

If any generalization is possible, it is this: America's Indian tribes own a lot of land—equivalent to the total areas of New York and Indiana—but because of remoteness, tribal shyness and lack of capital, and other reasons, it was largely unavailable to tourists. Now, suddenly, the tribes are opening their areas to vacationers.

They are investing millions of dollars in campsites, motels, trout lakes, and other facilities. At a time when other vacation spots are suffering the congestion of the recent camping boom, the Indians are offering a new banquet of unspoiled scenery, quality recreation, and their own individual crafts and cultures. For those who explore in depth, the reservations hold an exciting story of social change, too.

My wife and I chose the Fort Apache Reservation, high on the slopes of the White Mountains of east central Arizona, to escape city heat and hay fever. We were also told that the big change in reservation vacations started with the Apaches, and we were curious about the causes.

But anyone who starts driving toward an Indian area must first run a gantlet of pale-face-operated curio stores and "trading posts" along the highway. Some make a sincere effort to sell authentic craft items made by their Indian neighbors, but most offer a bizarre mixture of the inappropriate and phony—such as Alaskan-style totem poles in New Mexico and Navajo-type jewelry in Wisconsin and a kind of comic-book "Indian" gimcrackery that has no traceable parentage at all. Much of it comes from Hong Kong.

The signs of these stores are an incredible kind of folk art. They often tell us that we are about to enter Indian country, but somehow we never arrive. Repeatedly, we are offered a "last chance" to fill our gas tanks, buy a desert water-bag, or acquire a bullwhip. Exotic delights, like live rattlesnakes or "free shade," are promised.

Ironically, just a few miles from the highway, tourists can see a Pueblo corn dance, as sacred as any of our worship ceremonies, or watch a Navajo rodeo that is 10 times more exciting than a television special. European

Enterprising Indians Make
Reservations for Palefaces

Among the Apaches

scholars come halfway around the world to appreciate the authentic art and ancient customs of these people, and yet many Americans are so misled by this highway hokum that they ignore the real things the Indians still have to offer.

When we turned south at Holbrook, the road started climbing into the pine country. As the air became cooler, the signs dropped the Indian theme and started to promote fishing lakes, worms, pizzas, and cottage sites.

But as we finally entered the Fort Apache Reservation, the neon and billboards disappeared. We were in a forest of ponderosa pines, cathedral calm and uncluttered by man. A flock of wild turkeys—three adults and half a dozen long-legged youngsters—scooted across the road.

Most motels are built like beauty queens—they put everything possible on display. But the Apaches' Hon-Dah Motel is quite different. When we looked for it at the intersection known as Indian Pine, all we could see was a sign in front of a forest.

"Where's the motel?" I asked the Indian boy at the Hon-Dah Service Station nearby. He grinned and pointed to a house back among the trees. There, we found a door marked "Office" and a friendly fellow who consulted his reservation book and said: "You're in Number 5. Just follow the road until you see the marker. Everything's there. Ice cubes in the refrigerator."

We drove through the ponderosas, past four little side lanes, and turned into the one marked "5." Our unit—solidly built with a log-style finish—stood by itself in a glade full of red and blue wildflowers. We could barely see Cabin 6 through the trees about half the distance of a city block away.

A sassy bluejay announced our arrival and I lunged for my camera and color film. Vera took inventory; outside, a picnic table under the trees and two chairs on a shaded porch; inside, a typical motel layout, roomier than most, plus a surprisingly complete kitchenette.

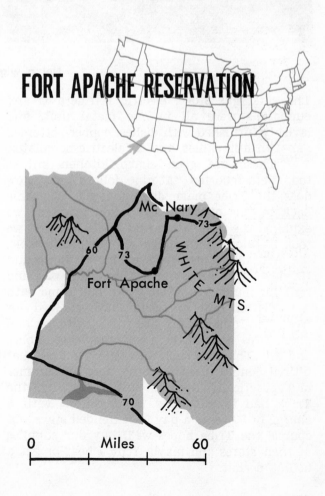

FORT APACHE RESERVATION

Photographs by Arch Napier

Not a wigwam in sight.

The sink, gas stove, electric refrigerator and cupboards were all in one metal unit, and lavishly furnished with dishes, copper-bottomed pans, an iron skillet, and an electric percolator.

"These are good sharp kitchen knives, too," Vera reported. "At nine dollars a day, how does the Tribe make any money?" We came back to this question again and again as we explored the reservation that week, but first we took it—along with coffee—to the picnic table.

Actually, some of the cabins at Tonto and Hawley Lakes are simpler than ours was and rent for much less. And, if we had come with a trailer or tent, we could have camped for free. The Indians built about 800 camping and picnic sites, most of them with fireplaces, tables, and all. This was such an attractive deal that retired couples used to camp here all summer and practically lived on trout. Finally, the Tribe had to put on a ten-day limit with a charge of 50 cents a day for extended stays. Of course, the Tribe hopes we'll buy our supplies at their stores and maybe rent a boat or get a fishing permit.

Later, we drove 27 miles south to the Kinishba Ruins and then to Fort Apache to learn something of the local history. The ruins, now partially restored, indicate the existence of two large apartment houses and a population of about 2,000 people nearly 1,000 years ago. These were Pueblo Indians, later to be displaced by the more warlike and nomadic Apaches, who in their turn were invaded by Mexican and U.S. settlers.

Today, the Tribe encourages tourists to explore the ruins and keep any arrowheads and pottery fragments they find on the surface. Digging is forbidden to anyone except members of a scientific party; in the summer of 1965, a University of Arizona "dig" was held on the reservation near Grasshopper, Arizona, and the 21 archeology students included Lynda Bird Johnson.

The Apaches fought bravely for their land for 50 years, but history generally remembers only the renegades like Geronimo who continued to shed white and Indian blood after the battle was lost. At Fort Apache, which was built in 1870 to restore order to the area (and is now a school), we learned that many once-hostile Apaches became Army scouts and helped track down paleface and Indian outlaws to maintain the peace.

The Apache clans were scattered over several states and now live largely on four reservations in Arizona and New Mexico. Those now known as the White Mountain Apaches re-tained most of their ancestral land and it is now called the Fort Apache Reservation. It covers 1,664,872 acres, which equals about half the area of Connecticut.

With a refreshing mountain climate, Al-pine meadows and forests, and 300 miles of clear cold streams (about half the natural trout water in Arizona), the Reservation had great vacation possibilities. But until good roads were built several decades ago, the Apaches lived in

Santa Fe Railway Photo

Apache Chief Deerfoot: Still a race of expert horsemen.

Fort Apache Reservation's first bid for tourists was merely an arrow in the air. Today the place offers a variety of facilities to visitors seeking some of the flavor of the Old West.

isolation and eked out a living selling timber and cattle.

Progressive Indian leaders, however, saw that lumber and livestock would not provide enough jobs for their children.

And thus began an era of discussion and decision that is still being duplicated on many other reservations today. The White Mountain Apaches opened their lands to fishing in 1942 and then, 14 years later, took the brave step of investing all their credit in camp grounds and trout lakes first and motels, stores, and other income facilities that would repay the investment.

The move took tact. Nelson Lupe, then tribal chairman, had to convince the livestock associations that the changes would not reduce grazing lands. To this day, cattle roam through camp and picnic areas, adding much local color to tourists' snapshots and, quite usefully, cropping tall grass that could become a fire hazard.

The program took courage, too. It meant sinking the Tribe's limited funds in businesses foreign to previous Apache experience. Shy young Indians had to be trained to meet the public, operate cash registers, and handle such strange items as credit cards. Dozens of policy decisions had to be made: The Tribe voted to provide the campgrounds free (and even give firewood and garbage service) and charge a nominal fee for fishing.

Courage was especially needed during the impounding of 250-acre Hawley Lake. Lawsuits were filed by downriver water-users even though the Apaches maintained that they had historic rights to the water and, in any case, were not diminishing the water supply. Albert Hawley, their superintendent at that time, ran interference and risked a jail sentence by defying a court order that was later overturned.

Located 8,500 feet above sea level, the lake's seven and a half miles of shoreline are zoned partly for public camping and picnics and partly for 500 cottage sites now leased for an average of $70 a year each.

We took our fishing poles to Hawley Lake and were pleased to see how thousands of people are being accommodated without destroying the natural beauty of the place. No motor boats are allowed on the lake, and the cottages conform to strict architectural standards. Construction of these homes from local materials created a new industry—and many new jobs—for the Apaches.

The Tribe has a marina, store, riding stables, a trailer park, laundry, and rental cabins on one arm of the lake, separate from the cottage and camping areas.

Since the opening of this first lake in 1958, the Tribe has built or improved a dozen more, and has started a second cottage area. Yet many wilderness streams remain for the dedicated fisherman. All are open except a few headwaters where the Tribe is protecting some rare native trout that may be the foundation stock for a special kind of fishing some future day.

I talked with Jim Sparks, manager of the Recreation Enterprise, at the tribal headquarters in Whiteriver. He believes that recreation will mean a job for every Apache who wants one by 1970. The success of this effort has brought visits from leaders of more than 40 other tribes and even some African nations interested in self-help projects of their own.

The Indians across the nation have gone into the tourist business so extensively that the U.S. Interior Department has now compiled a 72-page booklet titled "Vacationing with the Indians" that details the facilities and attractions on many reservations. You can order it from the U.S. Government Printing Office for 30 cents.

During our stay, we visited the two Federal fish hatcheries on the Reservation, took a tour of the lumber mill at McNary, and enjoyed an all-day ride on the White Mountain Scenic Railroad. This is the only train I've seen that stops to open and shut a cattle gate. Halfway through the trip, we all stopped to buy lunch at an Apache-owned picnic area.

I wanted to talk to Lydo Harvey, chief ranger for the White Mountain Apaches and a grandson of the famous Chief Alchesay who led his people into peace instead of war. He was away on an elk-counting trip in the mountains (the Reservation has excellent elk, dove, and javelina hunting) but when he returned, he told me:

"We like to see people come and enjoy the country here, and they create jobs for our young people. Their parents would rather see them working here than going off to the cities. But even if they do leave to find different kinds of work, it has been good experience to deal with palefaces here at home."

It is a good experience for palefaces, too. ◆

Independent Press-Telegram, Long Beach, Calif.

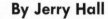

By Jerry Hall

THE lithe silhouettes perch stoically on the surfboards out beyond the breaker line and wait. Frothy curls of ocean comb between them and splash one behind the other onto the beach. Still they wait.

Tanned, bleached, muscled, and patient, that's the Young American Surfer. Fanatic, fractious, and fearless. Reviled, exiled, a man-child. That's the Young American Surfer.

Ignored and harassed and vilified all at the same time, the Young Surfer waits for The Big One, the wave that will grab him up in its foaming fury and swoosh him along on its white feathered crest as he skids, bobs, and weaves in a sun-drenched ballet atop a caroming eight-foot slice of plastic.

In the surfers' dream, the waves roll in with precise rhythm and peel off perfectly against the shore, where waits a bonfire and a pretty girl. The ocean is windless, glass-smooth out beyond the breaker line and the swells build to 10-footers as they are agitated by the rising ocean floor. As the surfer waits he daydreams that he is in the tube, racing to stay ahead of the high curl of a giant comber that crashes thunderously behind him while he skims laterally along the coastline, the taste of the salt spray on his lips.

That is the surfing dream.

But there is a stark, disturbing reality threatening surfing today.

"There is danger, real danger, that surfing will be killed," says Vincent Moorhouse, director of the United States Surfboard Championships, which are held at Huntington Beach, California.

Says Don Murray, executive secretary of the U.S. Surfing Association, "One of the best things that can happen to surfing now is utter calamity. It might wake somebody up."

What Mr. Murray means by calamity, he quickly explains, is the closing of Southern California's most important surfing beaches because of riotious conduct by surfers and pretend-surfers.

The result, says the director of the quasi-official voice of surfing, would be chaos at first

Surfing Comes of Age

but, in the end, the solution to the multi-faceted problems that are tearing apart the sport that has enveloped an estimated 1,000,000 Americans.

"Until people on both sides of the question sit down and honestly work for the answer, surfing's problems are going to get worse and worse," says Mr. Murray. "They are going to spread from the Southern California coastline to the East and Gulf Coasts. The people in New York are going to go through the same problems the people in California have, only they'll be more painful because the sport is growing so fast now that it's like a tidal wave."

The U.S. Surfing Association, a nationwide organization, estimates that there are 350,000 surfers in Southern California, a total of 500,000 on the Pacific Coast and another 500,000 on the East and Gulf Coasts. The sport has been expanding its numbers at a rate of about 20 per cent each year.

Mr. Moorhead, who directs the largest competition held in the continental United States and is chief of the lifeguard staff at Huntington Beach, explains that surfing could be choked off "simply by a few city councils passing a few city ordinances. The shoreline waters would be cleared, pushing the surfers to the next beach town which already is overburdened by surfers. So the next town would have to do likewise in self-protection, I guess. It would be a chain reaction."

Among the laws passed to control or discourage surfers have been license ordinances. Laguna Beach, California, tried this in 1960 and Seal Beach, California, attempted it in 1963. "This wasn't the answer, of course, but it was at least an attempt to do something," says the surfing association official. "Surfers are a transient bunch. They go where the (high) surf is. The ocean swells don't pay much attention to city boundaries. And it made the kids kind of angry. They didn't like being equated with dogs."

The mayors of the myriad beach communities point out that they cannot control the hordes of youths that descend upon them on a sunny summer Sunday.

The problem, to the surfer, is a simple one. He merely wants a place to surf when and where the surf is best.

To understand that part of the problem, imagine that horseback riders and golfers used the same grounds at the same time. Or that the company picnic's softball game was held in the midst of an archery tournament. Beach bathers object to trying to swim amid a swarm of hurtling surfboards, for a board that has lost its rider becomes a missile that endangers the bathers.

Mr. Murray, however, does see gains for the sport over the past few years.

"Surfing has grown in two ways," he says, "numerically and in acceptance. There are several reasons for the acceptance by the public. For one, the movies have been kinder to surfing lately. Those early movies about surfers hurt a lot. Maybe more important, however, has been the way big commercial concerns have taken to surfing. Reputable products are being advertised and promoted through pictures of surfers, so people that the sport never touched before are being touched just a little through soft drink ads or lipstick billboards or frankfurter signs. Another thing that has helped has been the organized competition."

The U.S. Surfing Association doesn't have a solution but it has a plan that it believes will

A dozen surfers on the same wave length.

lead to a solution. The U.S.S.A. believes that the problem is too large for each community to deal with separately. Lifeguard Moorhouse points out that if all the citizens of California decided to go to the beach at the same time, 90 per cent of them couldn't get their feet onto the sand, even though the state has about 1,000 miles of shoreline.

The plan calls for an over-all evaluation of the aquatics recreation on a state level, "not in terms of economics, but on a per capita basis." Since surfing is relatively new, most of its followers are under 21. "But 15 years from now today's surfing teen-agers still will be surfing," says Mr. Murray. "There is no such thing as a former surfer."

But the U.S.S.A. is not talking about setting aside public lands—or tidelands—for surfers. Good surfing is a transient thing. There are certain places where it is often good and there are places where it is almost always impossible, but the surfers roam up and down the coastline for as far as 100 miles in search of The Big Ones.

"Surfers deserve an equitable share of the beach water," says Mr. Murray. "There are places where the law prohibits surfing after

7 a.m., but nobody shows up to sunbathe or swim until nearly noon. Surfers are out in the water at sunup and the best surf is until about 11 o'clock before the wind comes up, usually. That's about the time the beach crowds begin to arrive."

Whatever the solution, ignoring the problem is not going to help. "Anybody who thinks surfing is a fad is badly mistaken," says Mr. Murray. He points out that some high schools have made a U-turn in their attitude toward the sport and have discussed including it in their intramural athletic program. The principal of one seashore high school estimates that 60 per cent of his students surf. "It's hard to ignore a statistic like that," he says.

The sport which rose out of the groundswells of Hawaii and splashed across splashy Southern California is beginning to catch hold in a big way along the Eastern Seaboard, and a major surfboard manufacturer returned from a business trip to the Gulf coast talking excitedly about the throngs of surfers that "made Galveston look like Waikiki." It is becoming an international sport with large followings in Australia, New Zealand, Japan, South Africa, South America, France, Spain and the islands of the Caribbean.

It can rightly be called a sport of kings, for it's believed the first surfers were Hawaiian rulers who had teams of servants paddle the huge slabs of wood out to the breaker line where the royalty would climb aboard from an outrigger and ride the hulking surfboard to shore. It gave the rulers a certain ethereal look and, according to opinion of historians, helped to sustain their superiority over their subjects.

Surfing first came to the U.S. mainland in about 1910 when exhibitions were arranged by land developers trying to lure Los Angeles residents to the seashore. But few took up the activity. A surfboard in those days weighed about 100 pounds.

Until 1940 the few surfers used hollow-shell plywood paddleboards for surfing, but they were still too cumbersome and too heavy for all but a few, usually oceanfront residents. In the early 1940s, youngsters began to make boards from balsa wood which were shaped much like today's models, and the craze began to take hold. But it still was confined mostly to teen-agers living near the water. Then the surfboard builders discovered polyurethane foam and the race through the waves was on.

A surfboard is a magnificent, or monstrous, piece of equipment, depending upon your attitude.

But without argument it is a complicated slab of plastic material. The finished product sells for anywhere from $69.95 to $150 and comes in lengths of 7 to 12 feet. It weighs between 28 and 40 pounds.

There are dozens of surfboard makers, from backyard producers to the major manufacturers. The largest share of the market has been cornered by 31-year-old Hobart Alter, who produces "Hobie" boards at his Capistrano Beach, California, plant. Last year he sold 4,000 boards at an average of $140 each. "We're a little high compared to the rest of the industry," says Mr. Alter, "but we don't make any more profit on a per item basis because it costs us more to make our boards.

"Since all surfboard makers can buy the same quality foam for their boards and all of them can make just as pretty designs in theirs as we can in ours, the variable is in the quality of work done by the shaper. That's why our production cost is greater. We pay our shapers more than anybody else does."

It is the shaper's job to take a "blank," a slab of foam, round its edges, slope its nose, provide the proper bow down the middle, and all the while make certain that he makes no nicks or gouges in what will become a mirror-smooth

surface after two coats of glass-fiber cloth is glued over it.

After the board is shaped it is sawed lengthwise several times and thin strips of redwood are laminated between the sections to provide strength. Then the board is glued together and covered with apoxy and cloth, and, after drying for 24 to 48 hours, it is ready to ride the briny.

As with any business aimed at teen-age buyers, surfboard manufacturing is a perilous business. A brand name that has been considered prestigious can suddenly fall from favor. But it takes a long time for a brand name to gain acceptance on a large scale. The youths are not interested in cheap boards. Production boards, those formed in assembly-line molds, have not sold well though priced far below the handshaped models. "The kids buy surfboards the way their parents buy automobiles," said the owner of a Southern California surf shop. "That's why they order all those colors and designs built into them. Those are the accessories. They won't buy an off-brand any more than their dads would buy a five-cylinder Clodmobile."

Mr. Alter, who made his first board in 1950

Jim Lyman of Torrance, California, works on a board at his factory. Precise measurements are crucial.

Independent Press-Telegram, Long Beach, Calif.

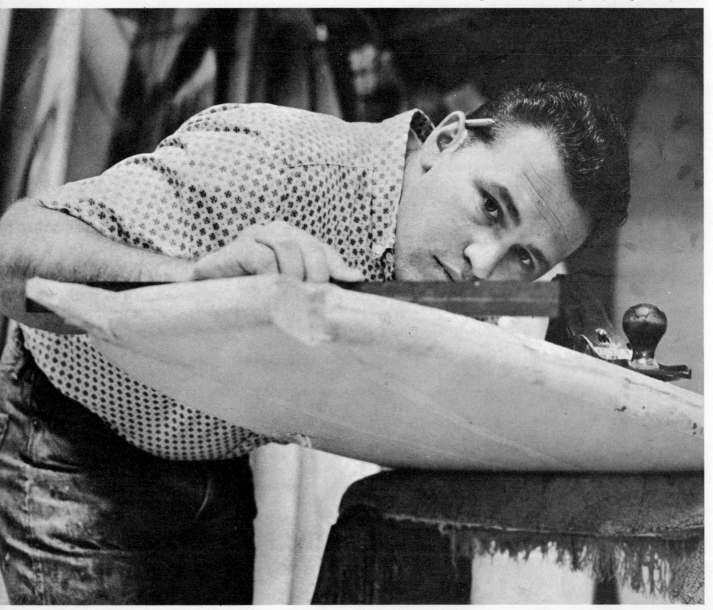

Design Photographers International

Surfing competes with many other beach uses.

in his garage, was the first full-time commercial producer. He set up his first assembly-line plant in 1954 and sold 195 boards. To date he has sold about 25,000, each one custom designed and handmade.

Surfing has a language unto itself that is totally confusing to most parents. A "gremmie" is a young, beginning surfer. A "surf bunny" is a girl who follows the surfing crowd. She may or may not surf, but she always has a bikini.

"Shooting the curl" is riding across a wave's shoulder; "hanging ten" is walking to the front of the board as the wave swooshes the rider shoreward and hanging 10 toes over the lip of the board. A "hot dogger" is one skilled at such stunts.

"But people get the wrong idea about the way we talk," says Corky Carroll, a 16-year-old Southern Californian who has won more than 50 national and international championships and recently returned from a State Department-sponsored tour to Peru. "We use some words other people don't understand, sure, but we have to have terms to describe what's going on.

Independent Press-Telegram, Long Beach, Calif.

Crash helmets are gaining favor.

We might say 'surf's up, grab your stick' (the breakers are high, get your surfboard). But we don't put all the words into every sentence the way some of the magazine stories panning us make out we do. We don't say 'Look at that hot dog in baggies doing a quasimodo hanging five in the soup; if he doesn't kick out he's headed for a wipeout.' That would be kid stuff. Just

hodads talk like that all the time."

The "hodad" is the most despicable of creatures in the true surfer's world. The hodad is the fellow who causes all the trouble for surfers, claim the surfers. He's the guy who wears the uniform—trunks and long bleached hair and a deep tan—and often carries a surfboard, but never goes into the water.

It's the hodad, with time hanging heavy on his hands, who amuses himself along the shoreline by kicking sand at sunbathers, breaking into parked autos, and stealing from liquor stores.

The true surfers, claim the true surfers, don't have time for such things. They are too busy out there 200 yards offshore waiting for the next big one.

The Song of the Surf is spreading to many parts of the land. Wake surfing is gaining rapidly. Wherever there is a lake or river, surfboards can be ridden in the churning waters behind a motorboat that is going 10 to 15 miles an hour. After the surfer is towed at the start, he can drop the line and his board will skim along behind, carried along by the swirling waters.

In New York's beach regions the Song of the Surf is getting louder. Emilio DeTurris, who has operated a snow ski shop in Forest Hills for many years, has found his surfing supply business to be such a successful summer replacement for his parka-and-boots business that he now considers himself a surf shop operator who sells snow equipment in the off-season. Mr. DeTurris sold out his entire supply of 300 surfboards in 1965, an increase from 179 sales the year before, and he believes he will double his business in 1966. He is opening a second shop at Giglo Beach on Long Island.

At Belmar, New Jersey, Virginia Beach, Virginia, Daytona Beach, Florida, and Harrington, Delaware, are other surf shops where long pasteboard crates are beginning to arrive a bit ahead of spring in anticipation of a boom year along the 1,500 miles of East Coast shoreline that is considered excellent surfing territory during the warm months. There are some 50 surfing supply shops along the Atlantic ready for the boom. Within the next three or four years there will be more surfboards sold on the East Coast than on the Pacific Coast, says one authority.

Newest twist in surfing is the safety helmet. The older heads in the sport have been trying for three years to convince the youngsters to wear them, but not until recently has there been any headway. Now helmets are mandatory in U.S.S.A. competition. There were 11 deaths from surfing in 1964, the most recent year for which full statistics are available. The most dangerous aspect of the sport is getting thrown from the board and then being smacked in the head by it—or someone else's that is being flung through the water by angry breakers. The unconscious surfer will go under, but the brightly painted helmet will keep him afloat (for it is buoyant, much as a lifejacket) until rescued.

But all the controversy over surfing licenses and safety helmets and the threat of closing more beaches is remote indeed to the bronzed youth out there at the breaker line, silhouetted against the gray water as he perches motionless, waiting, waiting, waiting for that 25-mile-an-hour ride atop a moving mountain.

When he gets back to the beach he will worry about the problems facing surfing today. But right now he's completely removed from it all. It's sunrise on a glorious day that looks like it will produce some big ones. Just the surfer, alone against the sea, alone with his high hydroxyl 100,000-pound-test polyester-base carbon dioxide blown urethane foam slab.

Appear, O' wave.　　　　　　　◆

Goodbye.

Taos: Its

By Arch Napier

I WAS STANDING in an art gallery in Taos and listening to an earnest and elegant lady expounding on her favorite topic one summer day when a large dusty mongrel scratched at the door.

With hardly a pause in the conversation, she admitted the beast and followed it over to her desk. There she opened a drawer and gave it a dog biscuit. It did not beg for a second one. This was apparently a social call.

". . . so you see," she continued with a fine jangle of turquoise and silver bracelets, "the Taos Institute of Creative Orientation should be a wonderful thing for us all."

The dog wagged its tail thoughtfully, made a casual circuit of the gallery, sprawled in a patch of sunshine near an $800 painting, and freshened up a bit.

"But you don't want Taos to change?" I said, giving the ritual friend-of-Taos question.

"Heaven forbid!" As she launched into a defense of the "real Taos," the dog yawned, stretched, and begged to be excused.

Its exit caused some confusion among an awkward huddle of Explorer Scouts who were hesitating in the doorway.

"Come on in and sign our guest book, boys," said the guide. "I'll give you a little talk on the paintings in a minute."

With a churning of sharp elbows, skinned knees, and heavy boots, they filled the gallery.

Then came a young couple carrying an infant with a wildly teetering taffy apple.

". . . this place has a unique personality, and it attracts people with imagination and independence," the lady was saying. "But fleeing a world of conformity, they come here and immediately start trying to make Taos conform to their own visions. . . ."

But why do so many people choose Taos?

Certainly, many are just vacationers who are touring the cool mountains of northern New Mexico to escape the heat of Midwestern pavements and Panhandle plains. Others are drawn by the nearby Taos Indian Pueblo. Its two five-story structures are called "the oldest apartment houses—still occupied—in the United States." Some come for fishing, hunting, or winter skiing.

But a few visitors, having read something about art colonies or D. H. Lawrence, are here to seek some new and indefinable experience that the name Taos has come to symbolize.

Taos has something for everyone, even those who want to be dismayed and disenchanted. Besides the pueblo and the scenic country all around, it offers a dozen art galleries, the photogenic old adobe church at Ranchos de Taos, the Lawrence Ranch, some indifferent cafes and curio stores, several interesting craft shops and a few fine restaurants, and enough motels—of every age and condition—to accommodate about 2,500 people a night. Loudspeakers blast out rhythm and blues, but one or two quiet cantinas provide concert-grade guitar music. Visitors can learn about the Old West in three museums: One is Indian scout Kit Carson's old home; another is that of the martyred Governor Bent; and the third has a controversial ghost story.

The village (population 2,163 at last official

Arts and Its Ages

count) periodically decides to do something "to keep the tourists a few days longer" and tries to build a swimming pool or stage a summer theater season. At times, Taos tries to solve the traffic congestion around its ancient Plaza. Occasionally, it sponsors entertainment on the low concrete platform in the Plaza. This stage, by the way, is the roof of the underground police station, a fact that led author Eric Sloane to comment: "What other village has a town hall only 36 inches high?"

But most community projects languish because Taosenos are a pleasantly individualistic lot. A few welcome tourists with neon, but many don't see any point in changing their independent style of living.

After all, in the past 800 years, Taos resisted and eventually absorbed at least four major invasions before the artists and tourists came along with onslaughts five and six.

First came the Pueblo Indians. They have resisted every foreign influence from marauding Apaches to benign U.S. Forest Rangers, and they still keep electricity and running water out of the ancient pueblo. Then came the soldiers and peasant farmers of Spain to establish an outpost 1,500 miles away from the colonial administrators of Mexico City.

Two centuries later came the American trappers and Indian fighters, typified by Kit Carson. After hard winters in the Rockies, these mountain men summered in Taos, romancing the senoritas and drinking the local "Taos Lightning" with such hilarity that the Santa Fe Trail developed a detour to see where all the fun was.

Shortly thereafter, still in Carson's time, came the U.S. Army and the Yankee traders. One merchant sold everyone some blue paint to decorate the wooden doors and window frames

Dick Kent

An elder of Taos Pueblo: No electricity, please.

of all the golden-brown adobe houses, and now the color is a tradition. You'll hear a lot of legends about the meaning of "Taos blue," but the origin is simple: The merchant had more salesmanship than variety.

When the Civil War started, the invading Texans hoped the Spanish-speaking peasants would revolt against the Union. But they did not; they nailed the Stars and Stripes to a tree in Taos Plaza and it has flown there ever since one of the eight places in the nation where the flag can fly day and night.

The fifth invasion—the artists, that is— started in the 1890s. The first two artists intended to travel farther south, but they broke a wheel near Taos and fell in love with the place. Other artists joined them, liked the color and calm of the Indians, the clear air and far vistas, and the easy Old World atmosphere of the Spanish-speaking village. Mabel Dodge Sterne (later to marry Taos Pueblo's Tony Luhan) fled Greenwich Village to start churning out books about the primitive and elemental life of New Mexico. She urged D. H. Lawrence to come, so he and his wife moved into a ranch home near Taos, and he eventually wrote: "It was New Mexico that liberated me from the present era of civilization."

Artists and writers still come to Taos, some for a summer and some for a lifetime. They like its isolation (90 miles from the nearest airline stop) and its placid pace. Very few paint the Indians and mountain scenery any more, but all admit the influence of the Taos ambience.

Painters don't grow rich in Taos, but they manage a living and enjoy a freedom from many social pressures. It is respectable to be poor in Taos County (where the per capita income of all county residents averages only $831 a year) and the village's 70 artists are held in unusual esteem. Art is the big industry of Taos. Painters have traded their canvases for refrigerators, Chevrolets, medical care, and house rent. They are welcome in the Kiwanis Club and have a good credit rating at the bank.

The artists at times rebel against signs of creeping commercialism, but they show their affection for the village, too. They enliven the midsummer fiesta with gaily decorated floats, and they brighten the long winters with parties and sketch classes open to all. When Taos started a beautification program, each artist volunteered to decorate a trash can; now the community claims it has the most beautiful trash cans in the nation. Once, when the Taos Volunteer Fire Department saved an artist's home, he donated a painting to the firehall; others followed suit, and now the Fire Department owns an art collection insured for $50,000 —against theft and fire. They have donated thousand-dollar paintings to the local school system, too.

Toward tourists, one finds as many attitudes as there are artists. In the early days,

tourists went to the painters' homes to see and buy their work, but now the galleries have taken over the initial merchandising task. The galleries screen out a lot of "lookers" but they often have to call the artist in to help make a serious sale.

The Taos tourist, often buying the first painting of his life, wants to meet the artist. Sometimes he is morbidly curious about the artist's life. "I once caught some tourists looking through my window when I was taking a bath," complains the wife of Emil Bisttram. "Some people expect artists to be having orgies or something."

Most artists like to meet the public, and some fine friendships are started this way. Art buyers in Taos generally aren't seeking "investments" or "fancy reputations"; they buy the thing that means something to them personally, and there is nothing like honest appreciation to win the friendship of an artist.

The Stables Gallery, which is owned by the Taos Artists Association, generally holds a "Meet the Artists" party twice a month to bring public and painters together. There is punch for the grownups, fruit juice for the kids, and a bowl of water for the dogs.

"Most of our paintings are sold on credit," one gallery manager told me. "The kind of

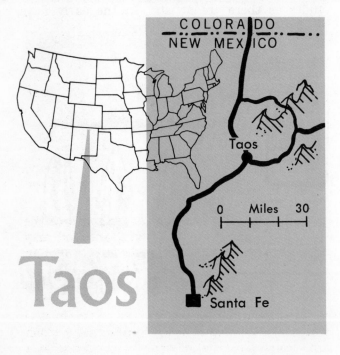

people who buy art are the best risks in the world. I don't ask a lot of questions: I ask them to send a little money every month. In seven years, we have had only two bad experiences."

The tourist season used to be about two months long in Taos, but now it is expanding fast. People come in spring, summer, and fall with their campers and trailers to enjoy the recreation areas of the 1,225,408-acre Carson National Forest that occupies the mountains around Taos. The rangers counted 796,900 "recreation visits" throughout the Carson's 37 campgrounds, two picnic areas, and three ski areas in a recent year.

The high streams and lakes of the Sangre de Cristo Mountains offer fine summer fishing, and the deep gorge of the Rio Grande is rated one of the best trout streams in the nation. The Rio Grande Box is on the Interior Department's list of "wild rivers" to be preserved for future generations.

Recently, the New Mexico Highway Department completed a $2,000,000 bridge across the Rio Grande Gorge and soon a new east-west highway will cut across the northern part of the state and link Taos with the Jicarilla Apache Reservation, and the big new lakes and parks to the west. Taos merchants are delighted, but many other Taosenos are not.

The old community has seen many changes and has weathered them all. Even if the traffic count goes up on the highways, tourists can still explore many byways where life goes on as it did under the Spanish regime. Sociologist Thomas Maloney points out that Taos farming continues as a tradition rather than as an economic operation. "The classic example," he says, "is that of a farmer in Taos county who uses his horse all summer to cultivate a field of alfalfa with which to feed the horse during the winter."

Last spring, some young Taos Indians installed electricity in their homes outside the big pueblo itself, and the elders of the tribe objected. The matter reached a stalemate, and the wires have advanced no further.

Recently, the Taos Indians won their land-claims case in Washington, and the Indian Claims Commission decided that the Pueblo owns 130,000 acres that the Government took for the Carson National Forest, plus the land that the town of Taos now occupies. But there was no panic in the village: The Indians have long

Arch Napier

In many ways, the town is devoted to the life of the spirit.

said they don't want it. They will ask Congress to return 50,000 acres of forest around Blue Lake, their ancestral shrine. To them, the sacred soil cannot be traded for Government cash.

Taos will long survive because it is an exclusive place. To some, the essence of Taos is its unchanging pueblo; to others, it is the town which, despite all, remains as easy going as ever; and yet to others, it is the rural area around Taos. This stretches as far south as the villages of Truchas and Cordova, and you may find echoes in some sunny side streets of San Antonio, Texas, and Tucson, Arizona.

But there is also the Taos of the spirit. You have to seek it and believe in it, but this kind of Taos exists wherever people pause in the business of making a living to decorate a trash can, enjoy a parade, or share a biscuit with a friend. ◆

111

GHOST TOWN

By James Cook

The Shades of Yesteryear Dwell in Silver King,
Where There Are No Living Souls Save One

GRACE MIDDLETON spotted a rusty chunk of metal in the shattered rock beside the road, and pried it out with the tip of her walking stick.

"Here's a souvenir of the Silver King." She offered what appeared to be a fist-size, hand-forged link from a chain.

"What is it?" I asked.

"I don't know. Figure out something to call it and you'll be as right as the next fellow. Look, you can see the big house now."

She resumed her deliberate pace up the main street of Silver King, Arizona (population 1).

Mrs. Middleton is custodian of a fragment of Southwestern history. The Silver King mine was one of the earliest and richest of Arizona silver strikes. Eighty-five years ago, teams of 20 mules snaked down this same thoroughfare, pulling tall wagons of silver ore concentrate. Welsh and Mexican miners stomped along its boardwalks. The street was lined with homes, stores, saloons, hotels, cafes, and an Odd Fellows hall.

But prosperity was fickle to the frontier silver camps. Half a century ago, "the King" was squeezed out by ore too poor to mine at the going price. Silver King was added to a long, long roster of Western ghost towns. Even at that, the town had enjoyed a ripe old age compared to most of its boom-and-bust contemporaries.

Today it is hard to imagine thousands of people living in the desert pocket where Grace Middleton now dwells alone. Time has reduced the King to abandoned mine shafts and ore dumps, fragments of rusted machinery, and seven battered buildings.

The buildings are scattered the length of Silver King, with acres of desert brush between. The uppermost structure is a weathered, 10-room frame house, the showplace of Silver King.

King's Crown, the abrupt, 5,541-foot peak for which the mine was named (some say it was the other way around), towers 1,500 feet above the ruins. A few weeks earlier, a summer rain had sent a flash flood rushing down from the crown. It turned Main Street into a rocky stream bed, barely passable in a Jeep, and we didn't have a Jeep. So we picked our way on foot toward the big house.

We were pilgrims questing for that indefinable kick that comes from poking through the rubble of the past. The haunting of ghost towns, or old towns, or restored towns, seems to be growing in popularity as a Southwestern pastime. We haven't found any statistics on the number of devotees, but we seldom lack for company. Southwesterners, many of them newly arrived from somewhere else to fill space-age jobs here, are enamored of the real and legendary frontier past.

We encounter historians, professional and amateur, rockhounds, photographers, collectors of all sorts of historic relics. Bottle collectors seem to get a special kick out of reconstructing the life of a frontier camp from its containers. And there are a good many like ourselves, aimless dreamers who seek a smattering of history and a touch of romance in the ruins.

Historically, the camps are not ancient. The oldest were boom towns a little more than 100 years ago, and some still roared well into this century. Their appeal seems to be in the nature of the history, the strike-it-rich days of brawling men and brassy women, of gunfight and frontier opera house. The towns sprang up around a prospector's discovery of silver, gold, sometimes other minerals. Many died almost as soon as they grew, for deceptive wedge-shaped deposits of precious ore had a way of pinching out. Their remains litter the hills in various stages of disrepair.

But other towns stayed around for the party. Such a town was Tombstone, best known in legend for its badmen and Marshal Wyatt Earp. Discoverer Ed Schieffelin, a prospector who took his pleasure in the finding rather than the mining, rode into Cochise County in the fall of 1877, in the company of soldiers. They were good company then, for this was the domain of hostile Apaches. Ed parted company with the military at Camp Huachuca to prospect some low-lying hills in the desert to the east. The soldiers joked that he would only find his tombstone. Ed was cautious, though. He still had his scalp when he found a rich outcropping of silver ore. He called his claim the Tombstone.

Miners rushed to the new find. Entrepreneurs followed with stores, saloons, cafes, gambling palaces, laundries, livery stables, gunsmith shops. Many businesses were housed in tents until lumber for permanent structures could be imported. Some mining camps never lasted long enough for the lumber to arrive, but for a time in the 1880s Tombstone was bigger than San Francisco.

There were many solid citizens among Tombstone's 15,000 inhabitants. Touring actors

American Airlines

Boot Hill at Tombstone, Arizona.

declared Schieffelin Hall one of the finest opera houses on the Chicago-Tombstone-San Francisco circuit. "Every Tombstone needs its epitaph," punned editor John P. Clum, who founded the Tombstone Epitaph to chronicle the rollicking life of the town.

As an epitaph, the Epitaph was premature. Water flooded the silver mines in the late 1880s, and the town looked as though it was doomed. But it never quite succumbed. Today, the homey little town of 1,200 sits beside U.S. Highway 80 and lures tourists with its slogan: "The Town Too Tough to Die." The Epitaph still publishes weekly, in the stilted style and atrocious make-up of frontier journalism.

The O. K. Corral, where the Earps and Doc Holliday tangled with the Clantons and the McLowerys, has been preserved. Schieffelin Hall is newly restored as a commercial tourist attraction, and so is the Crystal Palace Saloon.

The National Park Service has designated all of Tombstone a national historical landmark. The old Cochise County courthouse is a museum operated by the Arizona State Parks Board (the county seat was moved in 1929 from what appeared to be a dying town to another colorful mining town, Bisbee). Every October, the folks of Tombstone have a three-day celebration called "Helldorado." This is a frank appeal to tourists to come help relive Tombstone's garish past. Amateur actors re-enact the gunfight-at-the-you-know-what, the lynchings, the street brawls of the 1880s. There are parades and contests and parties.

For every Tombstone, or Central City, or Virginia City, a hundred lesser towns bloomed for a while and faded. Their inhabitants simply picked up and moved along to the next "strike." And there were towns that died slowly, sending sons and daughters out into the world to find a livelihood as the mines played out.

Few of these towns now look like movie-set ghost towns. One that did was Mogollon, New Mexico, one of our favorites, but we hear the entrepreneurs have discovered it. We "found" Mogollon in 1960 at the urging of natives who talked nostalgically of life there when it was a rough, bloody camp. The Mogollon Mountains grow out of the high juniper country 50 miles north of Silver City and climb almost vertically to more than 10,000 feet.

The gold in the Mogollons was first exploited in 1874 by Sergeant James Cooney, a cavalryman who left the Army to stake his

SILVER KING, ARIZONA

claim. Prospectors and miners remained Indian fighters for several years, for the range was an effective hideout for wilier Apaches. Cooney himself was killed by Apaches in 1880 as he rode out of the mountains to warn settlers of a raid by Chief Victorio. Cooney's claims were the foundation of a district that produced nearly $25,000,000 in gold, silver, lead, and copper before the last of its mines shut down in the late 1940s.

When we "discovered" Mogollon, a dirt road wound up the western face of the mountain range and dropped into the canyon of Silver Creek, where it became the main street of Mogollon. Vacant store buildings and houses crowded the unpaved street. Mine buildings and machinery rusted in the hills above the town. There were eight year-round residents, but the population rose to about 30 in the summer. Canny inhabitants of Silver City and El Paso were buying old houses for a song and using them as summer homes.

Some ghost towns are having another sort of resurrection. When the high grade ores played out decades ago, there was nothing for the miners to do but move along. Over the years, though, technology has made it profitable to mine lower grade ores. The copper industry can mine ore containing only 0.8 per cent metal. The Anaconda Company, giant of the industry, has leased old claims near the southern Arizona ghost camps of Twin Buttes and Helvetia

James Cook

Grace Middleton (right) and guest: Some say a specter treads the stairs.

(Helvetia is not far from a ghost camp named Total Wreck, and we've just got to go there someday and see if any traces remain).

I recently stood on the platform of a truck-less, wooden passenger-and-mail coach, rotting on a trackless right-of-way overgrown with mesquite trees. I tried to picture the Twin Buttes Railroad in the days when it hauled ore to Tucson. Soon, Anaconda's new open pit mine will make the Twin Buttes District hum as it never hummed before.

This has become our week-end occupation, savoring old towns. We have sought out Dragoon, Pearce, McMillenville where two hungover miners stumbled across a lodge of silver, Dos Cabezas, and Greaterville which definitely isn't. And we haven't scratched the surface; we are only apprentices.

There are in our state and other western states myriad old towns waiting to be "discovered." You can drive to some in the family sedan, some in a pickup truck, while others challenge a Jeep.

We drove to Silver King from our Tucson home on a sunny Sunday morning. Out here in the wide open spaces, it is possible to drive 100 miles of paved highway and pass through only one town. Just 102 miles from home, near the still-lively town of Superior, I turned our car off U.S. Highway 60-70. The 4.8 unpaved miles to Silver King were smoother than I had anticipated. It was narrow and twisting, and for a ways it followed beds of washes which flood once or twice a year and are dry the rest of the time. The road finally pitched up through a narrow slot in a hillside and dropped into the pocket that holds Silver King.

Grace Middleton rose from the front porch of her patchwork frame cabin and came to greet us. Not every authentic ghost town has a friendly guide built in. Mrs. Middleton has lived alone at Silver King since her husband died in 1957. We had been led to expect an eccentric recluse of the first order. We found an intelligent, straightforward woman with a sense of humor.

"You want to take my tour?" she asked. "It's a dollar apiece for you and your wife, nothing for the kids." She explained that she has not always charged for the tour. "I used to let anybody and everybody come in here, and anybody and everybody did," she said. "Now that I charge something, only the people who are really interested in the Silver King come. Once you've paid your dollar, you can come back as

often as you like."

Mrs. Middleton seated us on her front porch and brought out a collection of photos taken when Silver King was a boom town. She said she has to point out to some visitors that she was not around in those days.

As with most mineral strikes, there is an adventurous tale connected with discovery of "the King." In 1873, a soldier named Sullivan was one of many employed building a military road into the Pinal Mountains, then a refuge for Apaches. Sullivan found some heavy rocks which "gave" instead of shattering when he pounded them together. He knew nothing about rocks, but pocketed some samples. When his enlistment was up, he headed west.

Sullivan turned up at the ranch of Charles G. Mason. Mason recognized the rocks as silver ore, and formed a partnership with Sullivan. Before they could return to the Pinals, however, Sullivan disappeared. Mason figured he had been killed by Indians. Mason and friends made several attempts to find Sullivan's silver.

On a trip in 1875, Apaches ambushed their party and killed one man. The survivors detoured to bury the dead man at a known way-stop, and stumbled onto the outcropping of ore which Sullivan had described. One story says that a few years later, when Silver King was booming, a tattered man who identified himself as Sullivan showed up to see what he had forfeited, and stayed on as a ward of the camp until his death.

The King's ore was exceptionally rich, and the camp flourished until 1893 with few of the problems that plagued other mining towns. Then dwindling ore and dwindling silver prices began to put the squeeze on Silver King. Mining continued into the 1920s, though, with a flurry of business during World War I.

Twenty-five years ago, Grace Middleton and her late husband came here to mine the old ore dumps for the silver which had not been extracted by the technology of another era. Their enterprise lasted only a few years, until the price of silver again lagged behind the cost of mining it.

Grace Middleton issued us walking sticks, and advised me to carry along water for the three youngsters. She led us up the one-time main street, offering a running commentary on Silver King and its silver-bearing rock.

Mrs. Middleton led us past foundations where homes once stood, and past a couple of

James Cook

A dim memory of magnificence.

small dwellings still standing, one of stone and one of boards aged a reddish brown. She showed us a grindstone that came around the Horn and overland from Guaymas, Mexico. She showed where a stamp mill had stood, and took us to the 960-foot-deep Silver King shaft, mined in the 1880s and later supplanted by a half dozen other shafts.

But our goal was the magnificent old house at the upper end of the street. It was built sometime in the last century to house a mine superintendent, and it was palatial for its time and location. The Middletons occupied the old house in the 1940s and early '50s. Two faces of the house wear a sagging first-floor veranda and a sagging second-floor balcony. An ancient barber chair, souvenir of Silver King's busier days, sits beside the front door. The door has been nailed shut against vandals.

Mrs. Middleton led us around behind the house to a lean-to off the kitchen. A loose sheet of roofing tin flapped in a sudden gust of wind, and the house echoed its shrill complaint. As she led us through the bare kitchen, Mrs. Middleton shushed us with a finger on her lips. "You'll wake up the ghosts," she told our five-year-old. She winked at me and pointed to wasps clustered on four mud nests on the ceiling. When we were safe in another room, my wife asked: "Is this house supposed to be haunted?"

"The Mexicans around here claim it is," Grace Middleton smiled. The population of this part of Arizona is heavily Mexican-American, and the practice of witchcraft survives in some mining towns. Mrs. Middleton led us to a steep staircase with a hand-carved cherry wood bannister. "There are stories about a woman walking up and down these stairs in the night, looking for someone. I used to tell the Mexicans that my bedroom door opened when it was closed, and swung shut when it was open. I didn't tell them the ground underneath here is always shifting because of all the mine shafts."

She showed us the high-ceilinged dining room, connected to the living room and parlor by sliding hardwood doors. There is a brick fireplace in the parlor, topped by a mirror in a wooden frame. She told of finding visitors trying to stuff the mirror and its splintered frame into the trunk of their auto. A one-time paymaster's office was located beneath the staircase, its teller's window handy to the front door.

We climbed the stairs, gripping the somewhat shaky bannister. Upstairs are four high-ceilinged bedrooms, one with a cedar-lined closet that looks and smells as if it was installed yesterday. Mrs. Middleton advised us not to try the balcony, lest it collapse. "Fix the porches and the roof and this would be a solid house again," she noted. There are bathrooms upstairs and down, with chain pulls to flush the commode from an overhead tank. Sometime in this century, the house was crudely wired for electricity. "I read somewhere that Silver King had the first portable generator in Arizona," Mrs. Middleton said.

She led us back outside and wired the entrance shut. We stood for a minute admiring the battered, wonderful old house. Then we hiked back down the main street of Silver King. Mrs. Middleton's hiking stick poked and pried at rocks as we walked along. She found us samples of silver and Silver King quartz. We flipped over scraps of rusted metal and speculated about their origin.

When we straggled back to Mrs. Middleton's cabin, a middle age couple was waiting in a pickup truck. They wanted to tour the Silver King.

Our guide bade us good-by and told our five-year-old: "Come back again sometime and we'll stir up some more ghosts." ◆

Photo Researchers, Inc.

Abandoned California gold mine.

Buffs Before the Wind

By
Burt
Schorr

WITH a quick squint at his watch, skipper Ted Charles gave the order to bring Volante about. Dave Harvey, an International Business Machines exhibit designer with almost no previous boating experience, swung the wheel briskly and the bow of the 53-foot schooner began to veer to windward.

Dancing between the cat's cradle of cleated lines on Volante's deck, Ted Arnold, whose real work is repairing office machines, selected the jib sheet and hauled it in hand over hand as we settled on the opposite tack. Other Volante crew members equally inexperienced in the ways of a schooner let go the leeward back stay, allowing the big mainsail to fill away in the 15-knot southwesterly breeze. Forward, at their stations between main and foremast, handlers of the fisherman staysail pulled away on their halyards, reflying the billowing four-sided canvas between the peaks of our two masts.

"Seven minutes," shouted Ted when all lines had been secured and Volante was surging along her new course due south toward the north shore of Long Island. "Still too slow, but we're getting better."

After a half-dozen tacks requiring similar handling of Volante's varied sheets, halyards, and blocks, I was willing to agree that the words of encouragement from our skipper were more than mere flattery. All the same, 48 hours

earlier it would have been difficult to convince me that a crew such as ours could peacefully share the cramped quarters of a sailing yacht, much less acquire the beginnings of expertise in her handling.

On the Friday evening that the nine of us aboard Volante cast off from our mooring just inside the Bronx approach to the Throg's Neck Bridge crossing to Long Island, our only certain common interest was our membership in the Seven Seas Sailing Club.

The Manhattan-headquartered organization is the inspiration of Ted Charles, Volante's owner, who got it under way in early 1965 as a co-operative scheme for sailing buffs. Many would-be bluewater sailors dream of taking the helm of a big vessel when she's got her lee rail wet in a hard breeze, but they lack the money or experience to charter on their own and never had the good fortune to know a big-boat owner with a weakness for guests. Seven Seas Sailing Club aims to satisfy such yearnings and also provide a livelihood for Skipper Charles, who collects about $30 a day, including meals and drinks, from each of his paying shipmates.

The spread of co-operative sporting ventures from hunting preserves to ski clubs has been well chronicled. But similar efforts by sailors are relatively recent phenomena. One reason for this, perhaps, is that few popular American

A New Kind of 'Yacht Club' Lets Would-Be Sailors Handle Deep-Water Boats

sporting activities demand so much surrender of personal independence. The fisherman deals principally with the fish, his gear, and the weather. And it's the golfer against the course, and the skier against the slope. But aboard a vessel like Volante, co-operating begins at the lone wash basin and continues night and day in sailing the ship.

If anyone hooked by the thought of life afloat under full canvas considers this a hardship, though, it's not evident from the growing number of opportunities for amateur tars to share a deck with other learners.

One measure of the trend is the magazine, Yachting. A recent issue listed over 60 larger sailing vessels ready to carry the inexperienced where the ocean rolls. Only a few years back, by comparison, Yachting's yacht-charter advertisements were largely intended to be read by already experienced skippers well versed in such mysteries as tidal currents, compass deviation, and reefing sail in a sudden blow.

Schools teaching big-boat handling are more in evidence too. Sloane School of Sailing at Cold Spring Harbor, New York, sails students into Long Island Sound for overnight cruising aboard a fleet of 35-foot yawls. In Newport Beach, California, Ardell Sailing School expects to graduate some 2,000 blue-water sailors this year, three times the number who took big-boat instruction in 1962, the first year of Ardell's operation.

"About a year ago we began advertising a sailing-school vacation to people who live on the East Coast and in the Midwest," says Craig Cadwalader, director of instruction for Ardell. "The idea of taking a week or two off and learning to sail apparently appealed to many people because we now have a continuous flow of students from all over the country."

Ardell caters to all levels of sailing ability. A student with some experience, for example, might begin his studies with Intermediate Sailing conducted aboard 28-foot cruising sloops. The four-hour sessions costing a total of $55 review seamanship down to man-overboard drill. Advanced Ocean Sailing provides a full day's instruction aboard the 67-foot yawl, Chubasco, well known for her racing performances, for a $75 fee.

Before rushing to get his check in the mail, though, the prospective Ishmael should endeavor to learn if the vessel he's signing on with isn't a Pequod in disguise. A leading example of the shoals awaiting the unsuspecting is the impressive fleet of ships assembled by one widely advertised outfit. Sailing enthusiasts from around the country flocked in by the thousands. And some of the voyages proved as enjoyable as the copywriter said they would be. But many

of them were marked by equipment breakdowns, skimpy rations, undependable crews, and broken promises. Gauging the reputation of a boat and skipper at long range is hazardous at best; so a good rule is to invest a letter or telephone call in getting the views of previous voyagers.

So much for advice; my reaction to Volante's sleek lines pictured in the Seven Seas Sailing Club brochure was to send the $17.50 payment for initiation fee and annual dues without a single question asked. Although Volante came off the ways in 1927, her low-lying hull reflects the classic work of her designer, John Alden, one of three or four naval architects to leave a permanent stamp on the American boating scene. When Volante's berths are filled, Seven Seas members have access to other vessels ranging from a 26-foot cutter to a 52-foot bugeye ketch; a small fleet of day sailers is available for basic instruction. But Volante is the club flagship and with good reason.

Perched in the schooner's spacious cockpit as a red ball of a sun fell into the haze over Manhattan on the Friday evening we were to get under way, it was easy to see Volante would be an exciting sailer. But what would happen when nine strangers, most of them caught up in high-pressure New York careers, were thrown together in her 12-by-53-foot confines?

As my shipmates gradually were assembled from the shore by Volante's green outboard launch, our diversity was indeed plain. In addition to Dave Harvey, the designer, and Ted Arnold, the office-machine specialist, our male complement included Clark Cameron, Annapolis '45, a sometime magazine editor and the inventor of a salt-water sleeping tub with reputed therapeutic powers. On this voyage, Mr. Clark was serving as mate and cook.

As for our skipper, jazz enthusiasts might recognize him as leader of the Teddy Charles New Directions quintet. Despite his successful concert and recording career as a vibraharpist, Ted, who is 37, concluded some seven years ago that sailing vessels were his real love. His first big boat was a 43-foot yawl intended as the floating headquarters of part-time skin-diving salvage operation that he hoped to turn into a full-time occupation. This dream faded one freezing winter's day on New York's Flushing Bay as Ted was probing the bottom for the wreckage of a private plane. Before he realized what was happening, ice jammed his air valve; after his crew finally recognized his difficulties and

hauled him on board—in poor condition to play a Baltimore TV date that night—Ted decided there must be an easier way to get a deck under his feet. A couple of years later, he found the Volante up for sale and began operating her successfully as a charter boat. The schooner still carries nonmember parties but with club membership now past the 100 mark, Ted thinks it won't be long before she'll be sailing under club orders exclusively.

Among its members, the club now counts a number of physicians, two singers specializing in radio commercials, and a merchant marine chief engineer who had never held the wheel in 35 years at sea until he began cruising in Volante.

I knew about a lot of these club members but I wasn't prepared for what I saw and heard as the last boatload for our cruise came alongside: I saw women and I heard feminine chatter. Four of our week-end shipmates, I suddenly realized, would be women.

Mulling this new fact over a whisky highball (stirred, not shaken), served up as part of Ted Charles' pre-sailing mixer, I soon learned the late arrivals were a psychiatrist, a psychologist, the advertising manager of a women's apparel chain, and the sales-promotion director of a Park Avenue firm that represents a number of radio stations.

Skipper Charles dropped into the cockpit alongside me and I put my thoughts to him bluntly: "How do you know this will work?"

"I had doubts myself at first," conceded Ted, who wears horn-rimmed glasses and occasionally gives one the impression of what Peter Sellers might look like playing a role in Captains Courageous. "But almost without exception, someone interested enough to come out to the boat in the first place is someone interested in sailing—and not the social situation or husband-hunting. If I ever had any question about what members wanted, it was answered the first time I held sail drill here at the mooring. It was the middle of March, snow was falling, it was cold, and I was sure they'd want to call it off. But not those guys. They were bundled up in heavy jackets, woolen caps, and gloves when they got here. But they insisted on going through with the instruction. Later we lit the cabin stove, made coffee and had a whale of a time.

"Then there was the weekend last spring members sailed on their first overnight cruise.

Writer Burt Schorr takes his turn.

They'd been out before for the day and had some experience by then. But this was different. It began to blow hard out of the northwest with some gusts over 30 knots. My paid hand got violently seasick and couldn't move out of the cabin. So we took a poll on whether to put back in. It was unanimous in favor of staying out. I blew my foresail to shreds and opened a couple of seams in the main. But we had a great sail.

"That's the difference between club members and the average person who comes on board in a charter party. I don't mean people chartering by the week, but the typical day or week-end group. Usually they're businessmen who see the boat as a floating bar. They always want to know how fast we're moving and how long before we get there. And before the cruise is over, you can bet that each one will yell, 'Man overboard!' at least three times thinking it's a very funny joke. With club members, there just isn't any drinking problem; they don't care where we're headed or how long it takes to get there as long as we're sailing. And the first thing they learn is not to yell, 'Man overboard!'"

By now, the women safely aboard, it was 9:30. The city's lights whitened the sky to the south; but to the northeast under the piers of the bridge, the dark Sound beckoned. With a five-knot southerly breeze shoving gentle wavelets against Volante's white hull, we slipped our mooring and headed out. The change was sudden and stark. Overhead: A highway jammed with week-end traffic still moving bumper to bumper. Below: Nine people in a glistening white hull gradually isolated from urban life by a growing margin of dark velvet water. We hoisted

Photographs by Burt Schorr

Ted Arnold checks balloon jib of Volante en route to Port Jefferson.

sail and with engine silenced, glided silently northeastward, the sounds from the bridge growing fainter.

Handling a boat after dark means entirely new bearings for the landsman. It wasn't my first night passage but there were many things to recall when Ted turned the helm over to me. Those three vertical lights off the port bow meant a tug with a string of barges astern coming toward us; we would pass to the right of each other like cars on a highway, I reminded myself. A glance at the chart beside me with the aid of a flashlight confirmed that the fixed green light we were leaving well to starboard marked Stepping Stones, small rocky islands lurking just beneath the surface in wait for an ignorant keel. Ahead, our course lay between the white light flashing at precise four-second

intervals on Gangway Rock and the four-second green flasher off Sands Point on the Long Island shore.

It was almost midnight and a rusty moon was our only company when we dropped our hook just inside the breakwater of Hempstead Harbor. The sense of voyaging was well established when it came time to turn in, so it seemed hardly out of the ordinary that someone had rigged a Pullman-style curtain across the port side of the main cabin and one of our women shipmates was soundly asleep behind it. "I don't even know her full name," I mused in my upper bunk a few feet away. Lying on my back, my nose a scant six inches from the deck directly above, I had to agree with an observation of Clark Cameron, our mate, made earlier in the day. "Boats are 1,000 light years long," he had said. "You never realize at first how many places there are for privacy." He was dead right, I mused, and fell asleep.

A popular body of water like the lower end of Long Island Sound may float a hundred hulls per square mile on a summer week end. But more often than not, the sailor cruising its length can count on a degree of privacy and solitude a motorist would consider luxurious.

Within a semicircle drawn on a 10-mile radius of our anchorage off the town of Glen Cove, perhaps 500,000 suburbanites were beginning to stir under the climbing sun the following morning. Yet the only sounds were an occasional gull's cry, the breeze in the rigging, and the gurgle of small waves on the hull—scarcely 10 miles from our starting point.

By 8 a.m. we were crawling lazily up the Sound before a flickering southerly breeze. Presently servings of tomato juice, stacks of French toast and bacon, and steaming cups of coffee began to issue from the galley forward.

"Once you've lived on a boat, you can't understand why anyone wouldn't want the luxury of getting up in the morning and participating in enjoyment as soon as he opens his eyes," observed our radio advertising careerist, Inez Aimee, as she balanced a paper plate on her knee in Volante's cockpit. As a child, she explained, she had spent eight idyllic summers aboard her parents' motor cruiser moored on the Hudson River below Albany. Today, her work and vacations have carried her to sleek entertainment palaces from Las Vegas to Puerto Rico. "In a hotel, you always seem to be getting dressed for the swimming pool, cocktails, or dancing," Inez said. "And of course you couldn't think of going for breakfast without putting on your face." Inez' comely features struck me as rather well maintained at the moment and she seemed at ease in white deck sneakers, white corduroy pants, and a pink print shirt with sleeves rolled above the elbows. "I really don't care about sailing," she confided. "What I really enjoy is being lazy." And with that she popped open a copy of *Invisible Horizons*, a collection of true sea tales, and began to read.

The day proved to hold charms for the sailors as well as those who shared Inez' penchant for reading. By 11 a.m., there was enough wind to set a fascinating sail nicknamed the gollywobbler, but more technically known as the main balloon staysail. Not quite double the area of our mains'l, it stretched from the peak

Britain's 12-meter Sceptre: Another kind of sailing.

United Press International

of our foremast to the end of our main boom, casting a cool shadow on the foredeck as it filled away in a majestic expanse to leeward.

Our skipper ordered the remaining open space above our decks filled with canvas in the form of a balloon jib that we hoisted and set to windward on the opposite side from the golly-wobbler, a pattern known as wing-and-wing. With but 5 or 6 knots of breeze astern, our speed through the water was only some 2½ knots (calculated with the aid of a paper cup dropped at the bow and clocked as it passed astern). But our tricks at the wheel were made pleasant by our graceful appearance as we moved over the placid green water to the distant blue headlands.

The enjoyment in moving at speeds slower than the pace of a walking man demonstrates how cruising under sail reduces the scale of life. Ordinarily commonplace events take on importance. Take Port Jefferson, our destination. It's some 90 minutes by car from the New York City line. But to arrive at the white lighthouse marking the harbor entrance and drop anchor behind stony Mt. Misery Point is to journey much farther than the 40 miles or so on the chart.

A purple thundersquall crashing in from the distant Connecticut shore precisely at the hour of our planned steak-and-corn cookout ashore scarcely mattered. We were snug in our protected harbor and there was plenty of grog for all hands—specifically a No. 10 can full of Martinis. The consensus of the main cabin: A great cruise and a great crew.

"We've got big plans," Ted Charles said the following day as we beat our way homeward against a spanking breeze. "There's an old 12-meter sloop in commission at City Island. You know, that's the class they've been racing in the America's Cup competition off Newport, R.I. I figure that after the club members have more experience, we can charter her for a few weeks. Maybe we can get another 12-meter and have our own race. I've always wanted to sail one of those big sloops. And you can be sure those America's Cup people aren't going to invite me or any of the club members to join them."

It's a crazy dream, I told Ted. But count me in. I've never been aboard a 12-meter sloop. And those America's Cup folks certainly aren't going to invite *me* either. ◆

To take a book on deck on a fair day is to get miles away.

Volante beds down for the night: Eight bells and all's well.

Canoe in the Rapids by Winslow Homer. Fogg Art Museum, Cambridge, Massachusetts.

THE RESPONSIVE CANOE

By James R. Dickenson

A Man and His Narrow Boat
Carry Each Other Into the Quietude
Of the Northern Minnesota Wilderness

WHEN there is no wind and the water is perfectly still, paddling a canoe is easy, pleasant, and probably healthful. The canoe slides easily through the water, so easily that it gives the paddler the illusion of strength and competence. It is probably no wonder, therefore, that the craft has traditionally been a young man's romantic prop. Any fool with a mandolin and moonlight can play King of the Waves to his uncritical companion, and there are obviously more strenuous ways to pass the time.

But paddling a heavily loaded canoe in a high wind on a large lake deep in the U.S.-Canadian wilderness is something else again. It is not a particularly romantic pastime, except in the safety of hindsight, and while it is not exactly the same thing as being a galley slave it does afford some insight into what that life was like.

One problem is that you generally encounter wind on a large body of water where there is no sheltering lee shore and there's a long way to go. The wind whips down the channels of the lakes from the northwest, and by afternoon it seems that it has spent all day coming across Canada, building up momentum just for your benefit. Another is that when the wind is pushing waves across the lake and you're a long way from shore, it is difficult to believe that you're making any headway. A third is that wind makes steering difficult, particularly for the inexperienced.

The lightest end of a canoe tends to swing into the wind. It is theoretically possible to make the wind work for you, the experts assure us, if you so load the canoe that its bow tends to move in the direction you want, given the direction of the wind and your direction of travel. It actually works out at times, mostly by accident, but the major problem with canoeing in a wind is that you generally have to paddle on the same side all the time to compensate for the wind and when you can't change sides frequently, paddling a canoe rapidly becomes a dreary form of manual labor.

But these things work out with practice. After a while you learn how little time it takes to cover what appears to be an immense expanse of lake. For one thing, to the inexperienced, distances appear exaggerated and, for another, being out in the middle of a large lake with the wind whipping up whitecaps provides a motivation that is considerably more basic and direct than we're accustomed to in our normal society. It's all up to you out there, baby, and no doting parent, paternalistic employer, or benevolent government is going to bail you out of this one.

This cold rush to the heart is not often come by in the regular course of our society. The hand-to-hand confrontation with the elements, plus great mobility and independence, accounts for the appeal that canoeing affords. It is easy at first to envy those people with motors who zip around so rapidly and easily, but spend three or four days or a week or two weeks paddling a canoe, all on your own, and you'll soon share the feeling that all real sportsmen feel for these gasoline-fumed clowns: Opprobrium and contempt. In the end, the gas babies are tied to their sources of supply and their range is limited by their size, weight, and fuel requirements.

A canoe, however, can navigate in water that wouldn't drown a kitten and can be carried

The National Observer

Bon appetit.

from lake to lake when there is no connecting waterway. The only limits to a canoeist's range in this wilderness country are his energy and imagination.

There is no limit to the space available to him in the Superior-Quetico canoe country, which lies northwest of Lake Superior. There are 5,000 lakes and 3,782,-932 acres in the Superior National Forest in Minnesota, about 1,000,000 acres and 5,000 lakes in Canada's Quetico Provincial Park, plus millions more acres and thousands of additional lakes north and west of that.

There are three major points of entry to this area where the canoeist can be outfitted and sent on his way: On the east there is the Gunflint Trail from Grand Marais, Minnesota, northeast of Duluth on Lake Superior; Ely, Minnesota, is the central starting point; and on the west is Crane Lake (which is northwest of Ely on the way to International Falls).

About 10,000 people a year now leave from Ely, according to Jim Kerntz and Jim Pascoe, the owners of Wilderness Outfitters, which has been operating since 1922 and is the oldest of a dozen canoeing outfitters in Ely. The number of canoeists pushing out from Ely has doubled in recent years because this part of Superior National Forest is now the Boundary Waters Canoe Area, a wilderness area as defined by the Federal Wilderness Act. So the big commercial fishing lodges used to operate in the big lakes near Ely, such as Basswood Lake, have been forced to shut down.

The purpose of the Wilderness Act was to make it possible for those who are so inclined to see what this country originally looked like. No airplanes, which once used to carry fishermen into the lodges, can fly over this area any more (except for Government patrol planes) and there's no hunting—firearms are illegal. We have come full circle; for 300 years this area has been the object of various forms of commercial exploitation—furs, timber, minerals—but now it is to be exploited for solitude, which, like fresh air and pure water, is increasingly scarce in this country.

All this stirs mixed emotions in the people of Ely, who refer to the Federal Government as the "Great White Father." Most are as devoted to the principle of a wilderness area as anyone else, but shutting down the fishing resorts cut into tourist trade considerably. Wilderness Outfitters operated one of the resorts, which maintained a payroll of about $50,000 a season, largely college kids working on their summer vacations. "Restricting the area to canoeists means, in fact, that the area is being set aside for young people," Jim Kerntz observes. "Older people can't go canoeing, but they could fish at the lodges."

It has resulted in an increased number of canoeists, but the outfitters doubt that they compensate for the difference. And, ironically, the increased popularity of canoeing has cut its profitability for the outfitters. For $7 per day per person they will outfit you with everything you need to canoe around the wilderness except personal clothing and fishing gear. Canoes, packs, sleeping bags, tents, food, shovels, axes, whatever you need—they can provide it. They'll also partially outfit you if you want to bring your own food or some of your own equipment, but this is less profitable so they've raised their rates on partial outfitting. "People try it once and like it and then they get in the habit of giving outdoor equipment as Christmas and birthday presents," Kerntz says. "It's natural. I do it myself."

At any rate, you'll need such personal items as a first-aid kit, a sharp knife or two, a flashlight, sunglasses, waterproof matches (a cigaret lighter and fluid are good insurance and can be carried in your fishing tackle box), sharpening stone, and camera if you so desire. Clothing should include two or three changes of underwear, two pairs of wool socks, two pairs of long trousers, a pair of shorts, a light cotton shirt (old Army shirts are good because of the handiness of the two breast pockets), a wool shirt, sweater or sweat shirt, bathing suit, and rain gear. Unless you plan to do a lot of hiking, boots aren't necessary; two pairs of sneakers or

moccasins are best for canoeing—one for during the day, the other for evening when the others are drying.

As for food, eggs, bread, slab bacon, pancake flour, canned meats and vegetables, dried or condensed milk, coffee, tea, and condiments are staples. Fresh butter keeps nicely in a quart fruit jar wrapped in cardboard. Dried dinners, such as beef and chicken stew, sold by the outfitters are delicious (and so is leftover pancake batter, made into dumplings).

The chief advantage of supplying your own food is the fun in planning the menus; it doesn't save much money. If you provide it, you can rent everything else for $5 a day per person, but this isn't all the expense. If you go into Canada there is a canoe tax ($1 per canoe) and Canadian customs charges on food (about $1.35 on $25 worth, calculated on a formula that baffles the ordinary mortal), and Canadian fishing license ($6). It also costs $2.50 per person to ride by boat and bus up to Hoist Bay, and another $2.50 each to be boated into Canada up to North Bay where the wilderness area really begins. Return charges are the same, except, of course, that you can paddle down for nothing. All in all, it shouldn't cost two people much more than $100 to stay out a week.

The boat drops you off in North Bay amidst more solitude and quiet than most modern people have ever known. It calls to mind Huizinga's observation about the Middle Ages: That modern man can hardly imagine the dramatic impression of a single, solitary light or sound in that comparatively dark and silent age. The wilderness is not hostile at first, as it's often described—merely indifferent. What puts the human ego into its proper place is not the enormous expanse of the area, but its timelessness. The trees, for instance, are in various stages of their long life cycle from saplings to rotting logs. Man may conquer space, but not time.

It is in the process of making a campsite and using the available resources to make yourself as comfortable as possible that the wilderness begins to seem more familiar. It is quite easy to be comfortable and happy in the wilderness—if the weather is nice. If it isn't, as any Army veteran knows, then you're likely to be miserable; only those people who write books on camping stay dry when it rains.

The ideal campsite is on a rocky point sheltered by Norway pines on the windward side of a lake. It must, of course, have a landing for canoes. The pines protect you from too much wind and provide wood and a soft humus of pine needles that is conducive to sleeping and loafing, not that many canoeists need help along these lines.

Camping on rock on the windward side of the lake keeps the insect problem at a minimum, which is important in Canada, particularly at night. By all means avoid camping in inlets. They are tempting to the inexperienced because they are sheltered, but insects breed and congregate in them, particularly because the wind doesn't get in to disperse them. Insects weren't bad in the summer of 1965, but the poison from even a few bites by deer flies and those northern mosquitoes will bother you for some time, often two or three weeks.

There are a few basic rules that help make camping safer and easier. First, although there are bears, wolves, deer, and moose in the wilderness, the only problems they present are (1) that the nature-lover won't get to see them because they are so shy, and (2) that the timid and ignorant will unnecessarily lose sleep worrying about them. Food packs left on the ground unattended will attract bears. They (the food packs) should be hung on a pole suspended between two trees about eight or nine feet off the ground. If you're really nervous about bears, keep a couple of metal plates in your tent to bang together to scare them off (or, more precisely, to allow you to get to sleep) and put a couple of metal dishes on your canoe (which should be hauled out of the water every night). If a bear stumbles into camp and knocks that over the noise will scare him off. Whether bears scare humans more than humans scare bears is an unresolved question; there are no known cases of bears ever attacking campers up there.

Modern tents are remarkably light and compact and satisfactory for summer camping. The best are the small wall tents that sleep two, are about five feet high at the ridge pole, and have a floor and mosquito bar that pretty well solve the insect problem. The floor also helps with rain, although there is probably no way to keep from tracking mud in. They are easy to pitch and roll up to the size of a sleeping bag.

There are no poles or pegs; pitch it between two trees and cut your own pegs. And save them. The improvident will foolishly throw them away on the grounds that there is plenty of wood for pegs at the next campsite, and, of course, there is. There is also plenty of work converting it into another set of tent pegs. Whether the tent opening faces into the wind depends on the temperature and wind velocity.

Sleeping bags, air mattresses (which are well worth the small amount of space they occupy), cooking equipment, and other camp gear are compact and efficient. Three packs should suffice for two people—one for clothing and personal items, one for tent, sleeping bags, mattresses, ax, and shovel, one for food and utensils. Ideally, the food pack should be lined with a waterproof bag or at least such items as bread that are susceptible to water damage should be waterproofed. Getting other things wet is not fatal; clothing and sleeping bags will dry out. If you stow your packs under the thwarts and strap them to the thwarts, they won't fall out if the canoe turns over and, being lighter than water, will add to its buoyancy.

There is, however, little danger of capsizing a canoe unless you really work at it, or run the rapids. It is difficult to fault the aluminum canoes now in use. They are sturdy, stable, and lightweight—between 60 and 70 pounds—and they don't increase in weight, as did the old wood and canvas canoes, by absorbing water. A bulkhead seals off the point at each end, creating air compartments that add buoyancy and prevent it from sinking if you do manage to capsize it.

After you establish your first campsite and begin exploring, you really begin to appreciate the mobility of the canoe, which in turn means that the wilderness becomes less awesome and overpowering. And, the urge to explore and master it is impossible to ignore. You will find little lakes not shown on your map, often the result of beavers damming up a creek, and it is tantalizing to think that you may be the first human ever to see them (which is the inevitable reaction, the ego being what it is) although the chances are that you're not even the first there that summer.

The urge to head farther north, farther into the wilderness, also becomes overpowering The entrance to the next big lake always seems to be just around a bend or masked by rushes, which gives it an air of mystery. Also, you become impatient if you see too many people.

For instance, we spent a day fishing the inlets of the east side of North Bay and saw more people than fish. First were two worried Scoutmasters looking for three lost Explorer

Scouts. Then, in the most remote and unlikely inlet we fished, along came three fugitives from a teen-age camp on Cigar Island. They were out of gas, but not beer, and were not too concerned. We gave them cigarets and our best wishes for the future. Then along came the three lost Scouts.

It is not difficult to get lost in the wilderness, but it doesn't appear to be fatal. The people you encounter are a testimony to the number of inexperienced that are taking to canoeing in the wilderness. On our return to Hoist Bay, on our last day, we met two canoeists who had already been out for several days and were headed further north. They had lost their map, so we gave them ours. One looked at us rather sheepishly and explained: "We're city boys. From Cleveland." They were likely to find a lot of congenial company in their travels.

From the way their canoe was staggering around the lake and their obvious difficulties in getting together on the paddling, it seemed unlikely, however, that they would get too far north before the first frost. Canoeing, of course, is a matter of muscle power plus the simple principles of physics of lever and fulcrum and action and reaction. The ability of some minds to confuse these basic concepts is truly impressive, however.

Normally if there are two paddlers, they paddle on opposite sides to offset each other's torque; the only time this is not true, as has already been noted, is in a heavy wind. The sternsman tends to push the canoe to the opposite side that he's paddling on, even with a strong man in the bow, and he compensates for this by using either the pitch stroke or the "J" stroke. The pitch stroke is the mark of an expert and it involves changing the angle of the paddle blade so that it acts as a rudder during the power stroke without creating a drag. The "J" stroke involves a slight hook away from the canoe at the end of the stroke to bring the bow around.

An experienced canoeist steers with a minimum of drag, but a beginner can botch it pretty well. The bow soon has swung around much

U.S. Forest Service

Boundary Waters Canoe Area: A land of peaceful passages.

too far and, losing his temper, the neophyte will dig his paddle and push one way or another to bring it back. This tends to invite long and detailed analysis on the part of the bowsman of the sternsman's mental competence, family background, and all-around fitness for this planet. There is, moreover, ample time and stillness in the wilderness to conduct these critiques. Another maneuver that often excites comment is the draw stroke, which is simply perpendicular to the canoe and is used in turn-

The National Observer

Heavy going.

ing and docking. It is also easy for the beginner, confused about which side to draw in order to turn in which direction, to botch this one. Among rocks this precludes life from becoming dull.

Portaging is an integral part of canoeing and enables you to roam from lake to lake, and to traverse the entire wilderness area if you wish. Most portage routes are old and well-traveled and many were discovered long ago by Indians. They are mostly wide, well-packed routes, and are measured in rods although light years might be more apropos.

There's nothing particularly complex about the process: Any ex-infantryman who has ever carried a machine gun or 81mm. mortar already knows about it. One man gets the canoe on his shoulders the best way he can (most are fitted with pads on one of the thwarts that fit on the shoulders and are appropriately called the "yoke") and off he goes. The other takes one of the packs and then they both go back for the other two. It's quite simple; just equal parts of masochism and brute force.

Fishing is another large part of the wilderness tour and while it is less taxing physically, it is an emotional strain when the fish aren't biting. The fishing was bad on our trip in 1965, and my companion and I tried two theories. He has had best luck in shallow, heavily reeded sand bars, but bad luck caused us to try the deeps at the base of steep, rocky bluffs. There was at least one big, tantalizing, beautiful Northern pike that followed my lure almost to the canoe but didn't take it. I have long regarded fishing as a good way to waste time, but this can make the importance of catching fish suddenly loom large. Also, the prospect of dining on fresh fish cooked over a wood fire provides a powerful motivation. On our last night out, our luck changed and—in shallow reeds— we caught a mess of wall-eyed pike, which are esthetically less appealing than the Northerns, but better eating.

There are a few drawbacks to outdoor living. Food cooked over an open wood fire is wonderful, but the chef's skin tends to get a bit smoke-cured after a while, and semiblindness becomes an integral part of the cooking process. And, the smoke is almost impossible to get off the pots, although a number of correspondents have informed me that the way to handle that problem is to coat the outside of the pot with liquid detergent before putting it over the fire. Then the soot washes right off.

But these are minor matters. In an age of specialization, there is great satisfaction in being able to perform all the functions necessary for survival. Given our civilization, it is difficult to feel much nostalgia for neon, gasoline fumes, Herman's Hermits, funeral parlors, and 19-cent-hamburger stands. In a time of cynical sophistication, it is something to shiver at the infinite sorrow and loneliness of the loon's call, or to watch a moose make a silvery wake as he swims across a lake at dusk, or to wake up

to find the dainty, delicate tracks of deer around your tent.

One final note. In the process of learning to get in and out of a canoe, there will inevitably be someone who says something like: "Tippy-canoe," and others who chime in with: "And Tyler, too." By the Code of the North it is permissible to destroy these creatures on the spot, the act being only a misdemeanor carrying a $15 fine. Do not hesitate to dispatch them. They have infiltrated the world of canoeing and are on the verge of taking it over. ♦

Approaching the rapids: One mistake and the canoeist may be well rinsed.

THE EVERGLADES

By Edwin A. Roberts, Jr.

THE car entered the parking area with apparent reluctance. Its speedometer must have shown no more than five miles an hour as it passed the six or seven autos that were angle parked near the brown pond. The car came to a halt at an empty space but then moved on. Inside, the four passengers were talking anxiously (their faces were set and their eyes bright with anxiety). When the car was almost at the exit of the parking area, the driver stopped, stepped on the emergency brake, but left the motor idling.

The driver opened his door and got out. With his hand on the top of the door he squinted at the brown pond and the thick trees behind it. He looked off to his right across the roadway to the sea of sawgrass extending almost to the clouds that hung over the horizon. Poking his head back into the car, the driver said something to the woman in the front seat and to the two young boys in the back. Quickly, those three climbed out of the car and walked to a spot in the middle of the parking area. The driver reached into the car, turned off the engine, and pulled out the key.

He was moving swiftly now. He walked to the rear of the car, opened the trunk, and took out a baseball bat. The woman and the two boys fell into step behind him as he marched toward the brown pond. He held the bat like a club and his eyes darted from side to side.

"Where are you going with that?" said a voice. The voice belonged to a park ranger who had been watching the foursome with interest.

The man with the bat didn't smile. "I'm just ready in case," he replied.

"Ready for what?" asked the ranger.

"Anything you got here—snakes, alligators, and things."

The ranger removed his broad-brimmed hat and ran his hand through his hair. "You won't need the bat," he said, "unless you want to have a little pepper game in the parking lot."

Most first-time visitors to Everglades National Park don't know what to expect, and because they don't know, they assume the worst. But visitors who are careful, who don't go tramping about at night and who make plenty of noise in the daytime, are unlikely ever to see a snake, a bear, a panther, a crocodile, a wildcat, or any of the other dangerous local fauna. The only exception is the alligators that are on display in a pond at the Royal Palm Area, three miles from the park's east entrance. But even these alligators are kept behind a stone wall so there's no danger to a visitor unless he deliberately jumps into the pond.

"We've only had two cases of snake bite since the park was opened in 1947," says the park's chief naturalist, Ernest T. Christensen. "The park is a very difficult place for humans to get about in—that is, once the main trails are left—but it's an error to think of the place as dangerous."

It is not an error, however, to think of the place as weird, curious, unique, vast, and fascinating. Comprising 1,400,533 acres of land and water at the southern end of mainland Florida, Everglades National Park—third largest in the National Park System — is 25 per cent bigger than the State of Delaware. It is characterized by hundreds of square miles of waving Jamaica sawgrass and, near Florida Bay and the Gulf of Mexico, an eerie labyrinth of mangrove swamps interlaced by a maze of placid, serpentine waterways.

The Everglades form the largest subtrop-

From a Land Alien to Man,
Little Stories of Life and Death

ical wilderness in North America, and provide a refuge for a startling number of birds, reptiles, animals, fish, and plants. They are startling both in their nature and their variety.

Some 800,000 tourists and sportsmen visited the park in 1964, most of them entering the park by auto at Florida City, although some arrive by boat or via auto by way of the town of Everglades on the park's northern border. The only visitor not welcome in the park is the poacher who comes by boat at night to hunt alligators, which bring six dollars a running foot on the open market.

Alligators had been hunted so vigorously prior to 1947 that when the park was opened in that year, the reptile was all but extinct in the area. Now under the protection of the United States Government, the alligator is back in numbers. But poachers remain a threat because there is a good payoff for alligator hides, because there are only 18 rangers to police the huge park, and because convicted poachers have been let off with reprimands and small fines.

At various observation points throughout the park are signs urging visitors not to feed the wildlife, including the alligators. It seems that if an alligator is thrown a fish often enough it will lose both the inclination and the knack of hunting its own dinner and eventually will starve to death.

Alligators have rarely been known to make unprovoked attacks on humans, but are very dangerous when cornered. Females with young also are dangerous—almost as dangerous as bull alligators in mating season. The big bulls (they usually reach a length of 12 feet) roar their heads off when they are in love, and anyone who interrupts them at such a time

National Audubon Society

The National Observer

The mangrove swamps: When a man wants to lose himself. . . .

must contend with an absolutely, and understandably, furious alligator.

There are two seasons in the everglades, wet in summer and dry in winter, and it is this cycle that is the dominant fact in the lives of all the animals. Big alligators dig ponds for use in the dry season and these ponds, called 'gator holes, are the last places of survival for many fish and frogs during periods of drought.

Since 1963 there has been a marked reduction in rainfall in the park and this, together with man-made drainage systems north of the park, has caused crisis conditions for many aquatic creatures. The water shortage in the everglades, in fact, is threatening the $6,000,-000-a-year shrimp industry of southern Florida, as well as all sport fishing in Florida Bay.

Whereas alligators are found throughout the American South from South Carolina to Texas, crocodiles, their narrower-snouted cousins, exist nowhere in the U.S. except in southern Florida. Generally speaking, alligators are fresh-water creatures and crocodiles prefer salt water. Crocs are shyer, are rarely seen, and build nests of sand and shells on the narrow beaches of Florida Bay.

A summer visitor to the park is frequently distracted from his observations of wildlife by the peculiar beauty of the place itself. It is not the beauty of snow-capped peaks and tall forests, nor of rippling streams and red cliffs. It is a kind of Patagonian beauty, flat and unending, filled with swamp smells and the suggestion of creatures watching but unseen. In the summer, when electric storms strike with little warning and when the rain falls in torrents as thick as gray wool, it's possible to see fantastic cloud formations. Great glaciers of clouds pile on top of each other, often reaching 20,000 feet in height, and form shapes which each man must define for himself.

Summer rains permit the wildlife to disperse over vast areas of the park and thus many creatures are not readily seen. When the land dries up in winter, the park's inhabitants retreat to ponds and sloughs and become "exhibits" for visitors. In winter there are few mosquitos; in summer they are painfully abundant, especially in the mangrove swamps and

Diamondback rattler.

National Audubon Society

along the shores of Florida Bay. Here they team up with green-and-brown horse flies to lap up insect repellent like nectar, bite through clothing, and totally distress wildly slapping humans.

Park rangers say many visitors expect the everglades to resemble the Louisiana bayou country, with Spanish moss hanging thick from live oaks and perhaps several lengths of snake coiled in branches above stagnant black lagoons. Instead, most of the everglades resemble prairies, although there are plenty of snakes in 23 slithering varieties. And of the 23 varieties, 4 are poisonous.

The most common of the four is the pygmy rattler, a miniature rattlesnake that grows only to a length of two feet. The pygmy's famous uncle, the diamondback, is also present, however, and grows to lengths of six feet and more. The diamondback, while not as aggressive as the big rattlers of the American West, packs a large charge of venom and is considered one of the world's most dangerous snakes. The water moccasin, or cottonmouth, lives around sloughs

National Audubon Society

Loggerhead turtle.

National Audubon Society

Coral snake.

and canals. The famous, multicolored coral snake is seen occasionally in "hammocks," which are islands bearing clumps of trees amid the Jamaica sawgrass.

There are several kinds of harmless snakes in the park that resemble the water moccasin and the coral, so park rangers urge visitors not to kill any snake (or anything else in the park, for that matter). But there's a chance that, when walking through thick vegetation, the visitor may find himself suddenly introduced to a beady-eyed viper whose intentions and capability are not immediately discernible. It is then that the visitor may lean toward civil

disobedience and have at it with a stout stick. Such a confrontation, however, can normally be avoided if the visitor makes plenty of noise as he proceeds, thus warning local reptiles to make themselves scarce because a clumsy human is slogging about in the neighborhood.

On the southwestern shore of the park is Cape Sable, a strip of narrow white beach that is a favorite shell-hunting place for shell hunters. Reachable only by boat because thick mangrove forests block an overland entry, Cape Sable is serene and desolate. It is a small beach but there are those who love it, and among these are the great sea turtles that waddle ashore to deposit their eggs in the sand.

These turtles, called loggerheads, grow to be more than twice as big as manhole covers but not twice as smart. Although they live to be more than 700 years old, they don't seem to learn much in that time. Their eyesight is bad and they go around snapping at anything and everything, including their stupid relatives. They even go after rocks and pieces of wood, discovering only after hurting their powerful jaws that they made a mistake. Loggerheads are useless to man. Their shells have no value (unlike the green turtle of the Florida Keys whose shell is used to make eyeglass frames), and their meat is considered inedible (again unlike the green turtle which was created with soup in mind).

Loggerheads deposit eggs the size of table-

Anhinga.

tennis balls above the high-water mark when there is a full moon in spring. If the eggs aren't stolen by bears, panthers, raccoons or people, they hatch in two months, whereupon the two-inch-long hatchlings plunge immediately into the sea. If they escape being eaten while they are tiny and vulnerable, they can look forward to a very boring 700 years of life. Probably some loggerheads are ready to throw in the towel after 200 or 300 years, life being what it is, but there's no way to know that for sure.

Sea turtles, by the way, are different from other turtles in that they cannot retract their heads under their shells. Their heads must remain outdoors in any weather; nevertheless, their heads are rarely bitten off, either because of the loggerhead's powerful beak or because marine predators find the big turtle no more appetizing than do humans.

Everglades National Park is one of the best places in the world to watch birds, especially wading birds such as the great white heron, the great blue heron, the common American egret, the pink-winged roseate spoonbill, the snowy egret, and the wood ibis—the last being a stork, and the only stork found in the U.S. The famous flamingo is rarely seen in the park, but there are many squadrons of pelicans. All these birds are expert fishermen, although their

angling techniques vary with their equipment.

The anhinga, for instance, is a kind of pelican that looks vaguely like a turkey (it's sometimes called a water turkey) and is adept at swimming under water, stalking its prey. It catches a fish by spearing it with a quick thrust of its sharp-pointed bill. Then the anhinga rises to the surface, shakes the fish off its bill and into the air, and catches it head first in order to swallow it.

The anhinga lacks the large oil glands common to most waterfowl and thus gets soaking wet every time it goes fishing. The bird must then climb out of the water and spread its wings to dry in the Florida sunshine.

The brown pelican, for its part, takes its sightings of fish while high in the air and then power-dives into the water, trapping its prey in its great pouch.

The man-of-war bird, which measures seven feet from wing-tip to wing-tip, is especially well constructed with regard to the dynamics of flight and can hang almost motionless in the teeth of a gale. So fast is this bird it can snatch a flying fish in mid-flight. When flying fish aren't around, the man-o-war harasses pelicans until they drop a fish from their pouch. It performs similar acts of extortion upon gulls.

Several hammocks in the park interior and a few islands in Florida Bay provide rookeries for the waterbirds. In the summer one can see 100,000 wading birds in convention on Duck Rock on the park's west coast. It's a sight not only to remember, but almost to disbelieve.

In the former fishing village of Flamingo, on the shore of Florida Bay, there are a motel, cottages, and marina for the use of park visitors. A nonpaying but frequent visitor to Flamingo is a great white heron which walks around thoughtfully, mingling with tourists, and, while never getting close enough to pet, stays near enough to keep a stern eye on them. The heron stands more than three feet high, postures regally, and hugely impresses those Northerners who tend to think of birds in terms of backyard robins and sparrows.

The everglades are, by the map, in the Temperate Zone but they are very close to the tropics. Thus, the wildlife they contain tends to be a mixture of species found in the West Indian islands as well as in northerly sections of the U.S. Along with tropical birds, for instance, such as the mangrove cuckoo and black-whiskered vireo, there are the familiar cardinal,

National Audubon Society
Man-of-War birds.

bluejay, and woodpecker. Also present, mostly on the little keys, or islands, in Florida Bay, are 30 pair of bald eagles.

A recent visitor searched in vain for a bald eagle, with wings outspread, clasping arrows in one talon and an olive sprig in the other. The only thing everglades bald eagles seem too clasp is fish. While less patriotic, the practice is more practical from the eagle's point of view.

As far as fish are concerned, there isn't a better place to be than in Everglades National Park. Within the park, in the myriad streams and backwaters, there is every kind of environment from sweet rain water to extra-saline sea water and all gradients in between. Because of this, there are fighting black bass for the fresh-water angler, snook, redfish, and weakfish for

THE EVERGLADES

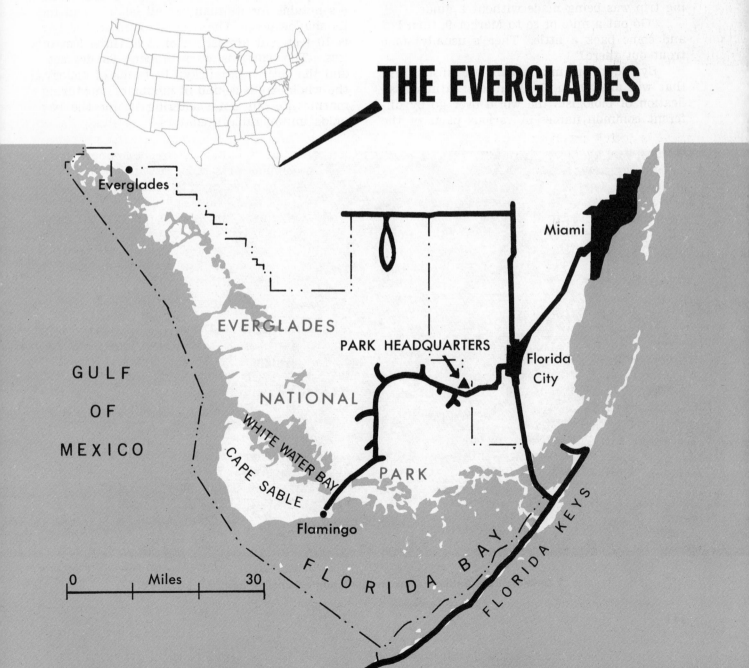

the salt-water man in Florida Bay, and, of course, the great silver tarpon that swim between the Gulf of Mexico and the rivers of the Florida west coast.

Not long ago, a visitor decided to see for himself how good fishing is in Florida Bay (most of which lies within Everglades National Park). All-day rental of a 16-foot skiff, a low-powered, worn-looking outboard motor, a fishing rod, extra hooks, and three dozen shrimp cost $19.01. That odd sum results from inclusion of the ubiquitous Florida state tax.

"Where's the best place to catch fish in Florida Bay," the visitor asked the man behind the counter in the Flamingo marina store, which sells everything from bait to cold cuts. It was necessary to ask the question because the fishing trip was being made without a guide.

"Go out a mile or so to Marker 9, turn left and come back a little. There's usually some trout out there."

By trout the man meant weakfish. Fish that will answer to the identical Latin classification of biologists the world over go by different common names in various parts of the country. What is known as a weakfish in the Northeast is called a sea trout in Florida. One state's croaker is another state's strawberry bass. One man's porpoise is another man's dolphin (although a true dolphin is only a dolphin and is no way related to the porpoise).

The visitor stowed a two-quart bottle of water and a box lunch under the forward seat of the roomy skiff. The shrimp were dumped live and perturbed into a well under one of the center seats. The rip cord was pulled, the motor clicked into forward gear, and the boat nosed out of the marina and into the canal that gives into Florida Bay.

Florida Bay is a remarkable body of water. It is that area of blue on the map that separates the Upper Keys from the Gulf of Mexico, and it's notable for its many small islands and for its shallowness. The deepest point in the bay is 10 feet, but almost all of it is three feet or less. The water is warm (about 88 degrees) and the bottom is mucky. In terms of biology, the whole bay is a kind of incubator, nurturing marine life but not sheltering it, for the bay holds innumerable predators.

National Park Service

Desolate Cape Sable: Turtles and shell hunters know it best.

The visitor pointed the skiff toward Marker 9, staying all the while in the channel that permitted larger boats to come in from the Gulf and tie up at Flamingo. Dotted about the bay were other rental skiffs from Flamingo, identifiable by the large numbers on their bows and by their hulls, which are the color of red clay. The water was very still and the sun was the length of an extended pencil above the eastern horizon.

It's odd, the visitor thought, that the fishing skiffs are scattered about so. On most lakes and bays there are a few fishing holes where small boats can be seen clustered. The wide dispersion of boats on Florida Bay indicated that the fishing was either very good everywhere, terrible everywhere (and thus the boats kept moving about), or that the man back at the marina sent customers to various parts of the bay quite arbitrarily.

As it turned out, the fishing for snook and weakfish that day was unusually slow in those shallow places where the action normally is good. The visitor found the place near Marker 9, dropped the anchor, slipped a hook into a panicky shrimp, let out the line—and waited.

Hours passed and there was nary a nibble, and passing boats reported equal luck. The inactivity seemed all the more odd because dozens of mullet, a bait fish favored by many species of game fish, jumped happily about all around the boat.

The visitor was sitting in the bottom of the skiff getting a bit bored when he noticed a long shadow in the water. He looked again. It appeared to be a four-foot shark meandering along in the shallow water by the boat. The creature would make an interesting catch if it would go after the hooked shrimp—and if the small hook could hold the shark.

The shark may have had many things on its mind that day but one of them was not shrimp. Nevertheless it stayed close to the boat. The visitor decided to catch the black shadow with his bare hands.

This was neither so foolish nor so heroic as it may seem. The creature was a nurse shark, a comparatively harmless variety whose teeth never grow to more than a quarter-inch in length. And this one was a young one. Too, if it looked to be four feet long in the water, it was probably a foot shorter than that.

The nurse shark is the most common kind in southern Florida and around the Keys. It

Monkmeyer

Who says?

U.S. Department of Interior

A walk on the wild side.

is so named because unlike other sharks it remains close to and protects its young. Protruding from its jaw are a pair of "feelers" that give it an acute sense of smell, which it needs because its eyesight is weak.

By reaching into the water quickly, the fisherman caught the shark's tail in his right hand and the back of its neck, if it had a neck, in his left. In one easy motion the shark was in the boat surprised and annoyed. The creature's tail pounded on the floor of the plywood skiff with a resounding thud, thud, thud.

Because sharks have only two bones in their body and are built almost entirely of cartilage, they are extraordinarily flexible and can be twisted into many unlikely shapes. This flexibility gives them great power in their tails. A swat from the tail of even an adolescent shark is a swat to remember. Too, the sandpaper-like texture of the shark's skin can leave a painful abrasion.

The shark the visitor had plucked from Florida Bay was a three-footer. Some hardy souls have caught five-footers with their bare hands, but that can be a dangerous sport, even when dealing with a nurse.

When the three-foot nurse showed signs of losing interest in tail-thumping, it was returned to the bay with a gentle flick of the broad end of an oar.

The bottom of Florida Bay is crawling with life. Shrimp burrow there during the day en route from the Dry Tortugas, 70 miles west of Key West, to the waterways of the everglades in their peripatetic life cycle. There are also blue crabs, stone crabs (with claws that are almost lobster-like), crawfish (which are lobster-like but lack claws), skates, barracuda, groupers, jewfish, salt-water catfish, minnows, killifish, redfish, bonefish, snappers, oysters, fiddler crabs, and many other varieties of marine life. These creatures are not only present in the bay; they are almost all present in abundance.

Had the visitor decided to head

his skiff north from the marina to Coots Bay and White Water Bay, instead of south to Florida Bay, he might have brought back a sack of black bass. Other notable fresh-water fish in the everglades are the garfish, which is the alligator's favorite food, and the sunfish, which are preferred by herons.

One of the most unusual sights awaiting the visitor to Everglades National Park is the two-inch-long tree snail, whose beautiful, multi-colored shell comes in more than 50 patterns. The tree snail is just that—a snail that lives in a tree, feeding on bark fungi. The large type of tree snail of southern Florida is found nowhere else except in Cuba and Hispaniola.

In summer, especially, insects abound in the everglades. Near Florida Bay mosquitos and horse flies are a serious problem, particularly since the recent drought has killed many of the tiny fish that ordinarily feed upon mosquito larvae. Beyond these common pests, however, there are hundreds of other insects Northerners never see at home (there are even some bugs that haven't been translated into Latin yet).

Along with palm and cypress trees, plus several varieties of tropical hardwoods, the everglades contain a generous share of trees that are quite weird. There is, for instance, the strangler fig which springs up around a host tree and eventually chokes it to death. Perhaps of more concern to humans is the manchineel or tree of death. This plant exudes a milky sap that can cause a severe skin rash. It also produces a little growth that looks like a crab apple but isn't. To eat this fruit is very likely to eat one's last.

Another itchy bit of Florida flora is the poisonwood which grows little orange berries and has the same effect on people that poison ivy has. But not every pesky plant in the everglades is so exotic. There is also a generous supply of common poison ivy.

In 1960, a hurricane roared across the everglades and destroyed a large part of the great mangrove forest, the hoary remains of which are still visible along the main road between Florida City and Flamingo. Mangroves are able to survive in areas overflowed by sea water. Their trunks, limbs, and strange root growths look like old bones, and on a bleak day they are chilling to the eye.

The south Florida buttonwood tree is in-

National Audubon Society

When (alligators) clap their jaws together it causes a surprising noise, like that which is made by forcing a heavy plank with violence upon the ground, and may be heard at a great distance. But what is yet more surprising to a stranger is the incredible loud and terrifying roar, which they are capable of making, especially in the spring season, their breeding time. It most resembles very heavy distant thunder, not only shaking the air and waters, but causing the earth to tremble; and when hundreds and thousands are roaring at the same time, you can scarcely be persuaded but that the whole globe is violently and dangerously agitated.

—WILLIAM BARTRAM
Travels (1791)

teresting because its curling branches provide most of the inventory of dealers in "driftwood." The branches are often ornamental but they are sold under false pretenses. They acquire their weather-beaten look from the weather and not from the sea. They are collected where they fell when uprooted by storms. They never "drifted" any place.

All these trees, insects, fish, birds, and land animals make the everglades unique. Such a teeming combination of temperate and tropical forms of flora and fauna is found nowhere else in the world. Unfortunately, this whole boggy, mysterious place may go down the drain in a few years because of an already near-disastrous shortage of fresh water.

There was a time, 40 years ago, when abundant fresh water was the least of the everglades' problems. The rain that fell mainly in the plain around Lake Okeechobee in south-central Florida flowed naturally southwestward across the broad grasslands into the streams and rivers that wandered out to the sea.

But in the late summer of 1926, a hurricane whirled across southern Florida. At the height of the storm, wind instruments spun crazily after registering gusts of 125 miles an hour. Power lines snapped like kite string, stout buildings broke and fell, the shacks of migrant farm laborers were blown sky high, and hundreds of people were drowned in the swollen waters of Lake Okeechobee or were crushed to death by tumbling trees and falling buildings.

When it was all over, outraged citizens demanded that dikes and canals be built around Lake Okeechobee to contain the water should another storm strike. Over the years, too, the resort towns on Florida's east coast became concerned about their fresh water supply and demanded access to Okeechobee. The demands were met, and more than met. A huge complex of levees and drainage canals was erected south of the lake and vast areas of the northern everglades were drained for agricultural use. The sweet water that for centuries had flowed across the grasslands into what is now Everglades National Park was detoured.

Still, the plants and creatures of the everglades are hardy and resourceful. They managed to survive with less water until the early

146

1960s when the area came upon a period of sharply reduced rainfall.

In the winter, or dry season, of 1964-65, park rangers were forced to blast out holes to create ponds for alligators, and for the fish that are the food of the great birds. The rangers were kept busy hauling protesting alligators to water and, all the while, keeping an eye out for the swamp fires that regularly burn out the brittle, tooth-edged sawgrass in the dry season.

The shortage of fresh water has had other effects. The salt content of the water in the everglades estuary rose, killing those creatures that were not made to live in sea water. At the same time the meandering waterways that had for centuries supported only fresh-water species, began to attract predatory marine fish. Some creatures live best in water that is part fresh and part salt. As the sea water worked its way farther into the everglades, numberless delicate life balances were disrupted and numberless tiny organisms, which form the beginning of the food chain, were destroyed. Nature was thrown out of whack. Almost all the rare and odd and beautiful creatures of the everglades were threatened with extinction—*are* threatened with extinction.

Nor is it just a matter of the well-being of scientifically valuable and esthetically interesting birds and reptiles and fish. The water shortage in the everglades is shrugged off by many people as being of importance only to animal life, to bird-watchers, nature lovers, and people like that. Better that the water from Lake Okeechobee is flowing to Miami, where it can be used by people, than merely running down to the sea by way of the great swamp— this is a sentiment heard often in Florida.

But it's not an either-or proposition. According to scientists at the University of Miami's Institute of Marine Science, too much water has been redirected to the east coast from Lake Okeechobee. There is talk now of tapping some Okeechobee water for the everglades but the problem has become more complicated by the building of highways, the growth of towns, and the expansion of farms south of the lake.

The area just north of the park once had the same character as the sawgrass prairies inside the park. But since Fidel Castro came to power in Cuba, forcing Uncle Sam to look elsewhere for sugar, thousands of acres of marshland have been drained and planted to cane. How then can the needed water be brought from the lake to the everglades? There are ways and all of them are expensive. Engineering studies are currently under way.

"See you later."

Associated Press

Time, unfortunately, is short. Another two or three years of drought and it may be too late. And if the everglades are left to die, it won't be just the scientists and conservationists who will be unhappy. Southern Florida's $6,000,000-a-year shrimp industry could very well be ruined. Why? The reason is as curious and wondrous as any tale in a child's naturebook.

In 1964, more than 19,000,000 pounds of pink shrimp were caught in the waters off the Dry Tortugas, a tiny group of islands 70 miles west of Key West. The dockside value of that amount of shrimp is $6,000,000.

Here is how C. P. Idyll, a biologist at the Institute of Marine Science, explains the connection between shrimping off the Tortugas and the shortage of fresh water in the everglades:

"The shrimp caught by trawlers are adults. Spawning occurs here, on the Tortugas grounds. The fertilized eggs are cast free in the water, hatching in about half a day to tiny larvae. In the space of about three weeks the shrimp pass through 11 larval stages, during which time millions of them have travelled from the Tortugas grounds to the mainland of Florida.

"They enter the brackish water estuary through the Buttonwood Canal and the many streams which drain this area (in the everglades). For about half a year they live in the estuary where large quantities of fresh water exclude marine enemies, and where warm temperatures and rich supplies of food favor their growth and survival. Then the migrating urge hits them and in great numbers they reverse their route and head to sea once more, to spawn and to be caught by the commercial fishery. . . .

"In the period of the shrimps' life from postlarvae to young adults they are one of the principal foods of a very long list of fishes and invertebrate animals. But for the shrimp the danger of being eaten seems to be very much less in the estuary than it is in the ocean. This is because the kinds of fishes most abundant in the estuary are those which, generally speaking, do not eat shrimp—fishes like anchovies, mullet, and young menhaden.

"Outside the estuary on the other hand, the shrimp face fish like the spotted sea trout, red drum, snappers, grunts, groupers, and a host of other predators. Inside the estuary small shrimp are eaten by the young of some of these predators, but even these enemies are largely left behind when there is sufficient fresh water to dilute the sea water by half or more.

"As the salinity rises in the estuary following droughts or artificially created freshwater shortages, the predator species move further into the estuary, consuming shrimp in areas which formely were refuges. . . .

"Presumably if the shrimp can live in the low salinities of the estuary throughout their whole juvenile existence they will have a better chance of survival, and more of them will make their way back to the fishing grounds to improve catches."

What's more, says Mr. Idyll, young shrimp appear to thrive on an upbringing in the everglades rather than at sea—predatory dangers aside. He notes: "It has been estimated that some of the regions where fresh and salt water mix are often 1,000 times as productive of life as either fresh water or sea water."

Mr. Idyll concludes that without the healthy environment provided in the natural order of things by the everglades estuary, there can be no shrimp industry 150 miles away off the Dry Tortugas.

The threatened shrimp crisis, oddly, turns out to be a boon for conservationists. Politicians who must authorize any expenditures for diverting fresh water back to the everglades are likely to listen more earnestly to spokesmen for the Southeastern Fisheries Association and the Shrimp Association of the Americas than they might to a delegation of bird-watchers, however articulate and sincere.

Aside from fishing and observing wildlife, the visitor to the everglades can take advantage of facilities for boat launching at the Flamingo marina. The National Park Service, too, conducts "boat caravans" through the winding waterways. Dozens of small pleasure craft, after their skippers have been briefed on the rules, form a long convoy and enter the bewildering everglades labyrinth—there to explore the park in a manner too dangerous for one boat alone. The chances of a lone boat getting lost are excellent.

An area similar to the everglades in many ways is the Okefenokee National Wildlife refuge in southern Georgia and northern Florida. This mysterious 600-square-mile swamp abounds in exotic flowers, reptiles, and more than 200 species of birds. The entrance is at Waycross, Georgia. There are boat tours and trestle walks

National Audubon Society

American egrets: "And his wife doesn't dream, poor dear."

for tourists but, because it is not a park as such, it does not have facilities as extensive as those available to the everglades visitor.

The everglades—that is, the natural everglades—extend beyond the boundaries of Everglades National Park. And while such craft as airboats (flat-bottomed boats mounted with an airplane-like propeller engine) are prohibited in the park, various entrepreneurs on the park's outskirts operate speedy and exciting tours of the surrounding grasslands.

But Everglades National Park is not en-tirely a sanctuary for wildlife and for people who appreciate it. Inside the park is a missile base, built after the 1962 Cuban crisis.

Declared one park ranger: "Military missiles are the only firearms allowed in the park. We want to protect the everglades and its creatures for our children to enjoy. Here is one of the few places left in the country where the scenery is beautiful because it is subtle, and where the numberless birds and animals can show man what it's like to live in alert tranquility." ◆

A Certain Lake in Maine

By Mason Philip Smith

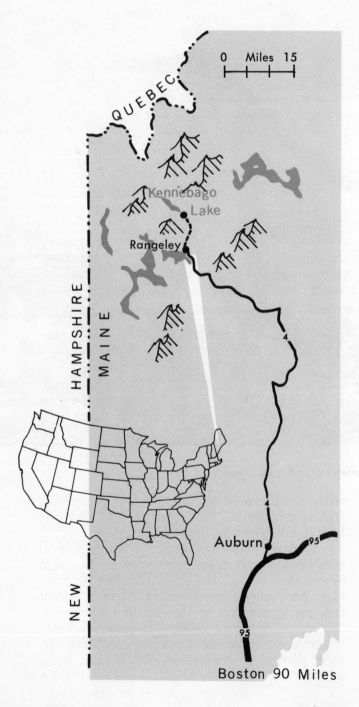

S PORTS fishermen have been coming to Maine's Kennebago Lake for over a hundred years to catch the prime brook trout and landlocked salmon found in the cool lake waters. It was here that Charles Bradbury, a Maine guide, caught 213 brook trout in one seven-day period several years ago. More significant than the number of fish caught is that Bradbury returned all 213 fish to the lake. That's sportsmanship as practiced at Kennebago.

Once it was possible to reach Kennebago, located in northwestern Maine in the Rangeley Lakes region, by overnight sleeper train from New York's Grand Central Station. But today, with the demise of the passenger train as a means of transportation north of Boston, it is possible to reach the lake only by car or private plane. A fisherman coming by plane lands at Rangeley's 2,000-foot airstrip, nine miles from Kennebago. If he should come by float plane, he lands on the lake and taxis right up to the sporting camp dock.

The fisherman can drive from New York to Kennebago in 10 or 11 hours by following the Interstate Highway System north until he reaches Auburn, Maine, where he leaves the Maine Turnpike and drives the last 100 miles over Route 4, which winds through some of the best farmland in the state until it begins to climb through the hill country to Rangeley.

A small village of 1,087 persons located at the edge of Rangeley Lake, Rangeley caters to fishermen. It is the jumping off place for fishing trips to Kennebago, Aziscohos, Mooselookmeguntic, and Parmachenee Lakes.

Almost every other store on the wide main street sells some sort of outdoor equipment, ranging from complete camping outfits to non-

Kennebago Lures 'Sports' With Salmon, Trout, And Salt Pork Apple Pie

resident fishing licenses ($8.75 for the season or $3.75 for three days).

Many lakes and ponds in Maine are so far back in the wilds they can only be reached by hiring a float plane or by a long, difficult canoe paddle. Kennebago is in the wilderness, but is made accessible by a nine-mile private road maintained by the Kennebago Lake Club, one of Maine's best sporting camps.

Happily, you can't get lost. There's only one way to go after you leave the main highway a mile outside Rangeley, and that's straight ahead, past Loon Lake and Cow Pond, around Spotted Mountain and over Tipcart Hill until the lake and West Kennebago Mountain lie before you. It's best to drive carefully over this hard-packed gravel road so that you save wear and tear on your car's springs and so that you can keep an eye open for wildlife. Frequently deer are seen on the drive to the lake and occasionally a fisherman will spot a bear with her cubs lumbering up the road ahead of him.

Big Kennebago Lake, usually just called Kennebago Lake, almost five miles long and three-quarters of a mile wide and surrounded by mountains, is one of the most beautiful lakes in Maine. Its shores are thickly wooded and in several spots sandy beaches break up the timbered shore line. "The Caribou," a small steamer, plied the lake before the turn of the century carrying fishermen and tourists.

Twenty-five miles to the north, on the edge of the Kennebago Divide near the Maine-Quebec border, the Kennebago River begins its flow southward to the Rangeley Lakes. Winding past Sable, Cow, and Sol Ridges, it comes out of the deep woods at Little Kennebago Lake, then flows south another two miles to Big Ken-

nebago, where it turns west for the ten mile white-water run to Mooselookmeguntic Lake at Oquossoc, 10 miles west of Rangeley Village.

All Kennebago waters are limited to fly fishing and the daily limit is five fish. Only one fish may be taken below the second of two power dams on the Kennebago River after it leaves the lake. It is illegal to take a trout under 6 inches and a salmon under 14 inches from any of these waters.

Some fishermen stay at a Rangeley motel and drive in to Kennebago every day, but most stay at one of the two sporting camps on the lake, either Grants or the Kennebago Lake Club.

A sporting camp is the traditional deep woods resting place of fishermen, called "sports" by the camp owners and Maine guides, while the fishermen's wives are called "sporting wives."

Built in 1871, the Kennebago Lake Club is a typical Maine sporting camp. Twenty-eight shingled or log cabins are strung along the lake's edge.

One rambling house serves as the lodge and dining room. Each cabin has a living room, bedroom, and bathroom. Several of the larger cabins have more than one bedroom, so that an entire fishing party can be accommodated in one cabin. A fireplace or Franklin stove heats the cabins, once the cool Canadian September air begins to edge down across Kennebago. It's a comfortable place to gather for spinning fishing tales and playing poker into the wee hours of the morning.

Kennebago Lake Club, owned by Bud Russell and his wife Ooie, sits on a 1,000-acre lot leased from the state. Unorganized towns in Maine are designated by township and range numbers for tax purposes, and Kennebago is located in Township 3, Range 3. The law says lots must be set aside in each township for a church, a school, and minister's house. These lots cannot be sold, but may be leased from the state. Russell's camp occupies the school lot.

Mr. Russell, now 59, ran a seaplane base at Rangeley for six years before World War II. His rugged face bears the weatherworn marks of a man who has spent the greater portion of his life in the outdoors.

An expert bush pilot, he flew fishermen deep into the woods so that they might dip a fly into rarely fished waters. Besides guiding sports into the interior and doing a little fishing himself, Mr. Russell ran an airlift to isolated camps deep in the woods. In many cases his small float plane was the only communication between an isolated camp and the outside world.

During World War II, Bud Russell flew for TWA as a contract pilot. He led the first flight of B-17s to England as a TWA ferry pilot and recalls proudly that all 84 planes in the mission made the hop successfully.

After the war he stayed with TWA as chief check pilot. In 1949 he left the airline to return to Rangeley to buy the declining Kennebago Lake Club. He repaired the aging cabins and shortly word began to filter through fishing circles that "Kennebago is coming back."

If you ask a sportsman or Maine guide who is the best outdoor cook in the state, nine out of ten will answer "Bud Russell up at Kennebago." An expert outdoor cook, Russell has won many professional outdoor-cooking contests for guides and sportsmen.

He is at home with a frying pan in the "back hall" or kitchen area of a sporting camp, as he is over a small open fire at the edge of a lake. One of his favorite "back hall" recipes is his salt pork apple pie, a mouth-watering collection of Maine apples and diced salt pork.

Good food is important to the fisherman, but good fishing is even better. The average salmon found in Kennebago waters, including the lakes and the river, ranges from 1½ pounds to 2½ pounds, with the bigger ones tipping the scales at three to four pounds. The brook trout, called squaretails in the region, weigh in at 1½ to 2 pounds, with the biggest ever caught at Kennebago reaching a record 6⅞ pounds. Occasionally brown trout are taken from the lake, but they are rare. They are not

Photographs by Mason Philip Smith

Bud Russell: He knows where they are.

native to these waters and were placed there by the state in a stocking error.

It is not necessary to have a guide to fish Kennebago, but it helps. Masters of their craft, guides know where the fish are in all sorts of weather and know which flies are apt to attract them. Many, like Ralph Philbrick, 63, have guided sports in the Kennebago region for over 40 years.

Several years ago, during the harsh winter months, Mr. Philbrick and Bud Russell, using the Russells' float plane to reach inaccessible lakes and ponds, ran a beaver trap line through the wilderness. Many nights they returned to Rangeley so late that they had to make difficult landing approaches over the mountains guided only by the afterglow of the sunset on the lake. Recently they have had to abandon their trap line because the price of beaver pelt is now so low that it does not cover the expense of flying into the woods.

Experiences like this have hardened men like Ralph Philbrick to the outdoor life and made them crack woodsmen who understand the wilderness. They know where the fish are, in good weather or in poor, in early summer and in September. They know in which season one pool in the river is better than another, and whether to fish it with a dry fly, which floats on the surface of the pool, or with a wet fly, which must be kept moving below the surface. If a sport has never cast a fly, the guide will even take him out behind the cook shack and teach him the fundamentals on the lawn.

Kennebago guides charge $15 a day, plus the $4 expense of their meals at the sporting camp, a small fee for what the fisherman obtains in return. Most guides are conservationists at heart, with respect for the mountains and lakes and the fish and animals that live there.

It is largely due to the teachings of men like Bud Russell and Ralph Philbrick that Kennebago has never been fished-out. They have urged the fishermen to return their catches to the lake rather than take them to the frying pan. To the Kennebago guide, it is not the size and quantity of the catch, but the manner in which the catching is done that is important. Ninety-nine per cent of the fish caught at Kennebago are returned to the water to fight again.

Many Kennebago sports, lured by the excellent fishing, return year after year, hiring the same guide each season.

In many cases, after years of fishing together, the guide and the sport will develop a relationship almost like that of two brothers in a close-knit family. They are united by the common bond of love for the outdoors and of fishing for the sport, rather than fishing for the "meat."

In other cases, however, the relationship between a sport and a guide will fall apart after several days fishing. The guide will never say anything to the sport, but he will quietly take the sporting camp owner aside and tell him not to assign him to that particular sport again. This usually happens when the sport has completely disregarded the guide's advice and has selected his own fishing spot and lures instead. Usually the sport doesn't catch any fish at all and the guide has a very frustrating day, one he doesn't care to repeat. None of this would have happened if the sport had listened to his expert guide and used him for something other than just rowing the boat.

The first sparrow of spring! The year beginning with younger hope than ever! The faint silvery warblings heard over the partially bare and moist fields from the bluebird, the song sparrow, and the redwing, as if the last flakes of winter tinkled as they fell! What at such a time are histories, chronologies, traditions, and all written revelations?
—HENRY DAVID THOREAU
Walden (1854)

Most Kennebago guides are not only master outdoorsmen, they are also master open-fire cooks. At noon time, the guide will either catch and fry a trout, or prepare a chicken or steak brought along from the camp. Often the meal consists of both a trout chowder and a steak with all the trimmings, including handmade french fries.

Kennebago guide Cleon Corrow loves to relate the tale of how one sport, watching him prepare a cookout, asked him what he was doing as he chopped up a potato. Cleon replied he was making french fries. The sport then exclaimed, "Why I always thought you had to freeze them first!"

The main room of the lodge is the favorite gathering spot of sports and guides in the evening after a hard day on the lake. There, pulling on their pipes and chewing their plug tobacco, guides and sports dissect the day's fishing. One subject which always arises is that of the state's policy of stocking lakes and streams to provide fish for the fisherman.

Every year the Maine Department of Inland Fisheries and Game stocks lakes, ponds, and streams with thousands of salmon and trout. Kennebago was first stocked in 1880 and was last stocked 10 years ago. The guides say that fish raised in the state hatcheries are not as crafty as are the fish native to the lakes and streams. Men like Ralph Philbrick feel that the stocking program is "just feeding sheep to the wolves."

Philbrick feels the state should create natural breeding pools on streams feeding into a lake. There, the trout and salmon would spawn and grow in their natural environment, unharmed by the fish diseases which often sweep through hatchery fish.

However, if it were not for the fish hatcheries, landlocked salmon found in Kennebago and many other Maine lakes would have been extinct years ago. This fighting fish, *Salmo sebago*, named for Sebago Lake in southern

Kennebago Lake Club: Comfortable beds, comfortable talk, and a good 'back hall.'

No fisherman with a healthy sense of anticipation is ever alone.

Maine where it was discovered, was originally found in only four Maine waterways. Through an active hatchery program it has been introduced into many lakes and ponds and has been exported to lakes as far away as Argentina.

Today the landlocked salmon population in Maine is growing, aided by the hatchery program maintained by the state as well as by the natural propagation advocated by men like Ralph Philbrick and Bud Russell.

For a few years, Bud Russell kept his camp open late in the fall to accommodate deer hunters, but now he closes before the hunting season. Sitting around the lodge one evening after a day's fishing, I asked Russell why he did not want hunters at Kennebago. Puffing on his ever-present pipe, he replied, "People just don't know how to handle their guns any more. You would think professional people like doctors and lawyers would know how to handle their rifles, but after I saw a lot of foolish things happen I just decided that I would close before the hunting season."

I then turned to Ralph Philbrick, who had been listening, and asked him what he did when the fishing season was over and all the sports left. Thinking a minute before answering, he replied, "Why, I go up on top of the hill near Blanchard Brook and sit and listen to the sounds of the woods. I smoke a little, sleep a little, and think a little. I sit all day, or get up and walk through the woods, depending on the mood. Sometimes, I just sit and watch the clouds spin by and watch the leaves turn, then I get up and go home." ◆

HAWAII

Pix

A pretty part, but a pretty small part, of the famous islands.

Hiking on Growling Mountains

And Beaches the Color of Coal,

Along Trails Best Taken by Goats

THE bubble-shaped helicopter rose off its royal-palm-enclosed landing pad at the tiny village of Haena, where the road and the houses end, and we began beating our way down the majestic Na Pali coast of the Hawaiian island of Kauia. Na Pali, a rough, uninhabited stretch of hanging cliffs, leaping waterfalls and long beaches, is only 120 miles northwest of Hawaii's capital of Honolulu, but it is centuries away in mood and pace.

We were on our way to remote Kalalau Valley and its long, golden beach, 50 miles north of Kauai's county seat and single landing strip at Lihue and the same distance away from Nawiliwili, where resort hotels and glittering beaches lure the tourist. Kalalau ("kah-lah-low") is about midway on the 25-mile Na Pali coast. It is inaccessible except to hardy hikers who backpack in over a high, narrow, twisting 11-mile trail; those less hardy who don't mind paying $30 for a helicopter ride in and out of the valley (from Haena; it costs more if you fly from Lihue); or those with sturdy boats which can drive through the sometimes choppy waters off the Na Pali coast.

My companion (Ron Loftus, editor and publisher of a Hawaii sports magazine) and I had decided to drive from Lihue to Haena, take the helicopter into Kalalau with our full packs, spend a week end exploring the beach and valley, and hike out with our packs, lightened by the absence of the food we would eat during our stay.

The trail is the same today as it was hundreds of years ago when Hawaiians, living in Haena, walked it to and from lush Kalalau Valley where they grew taro and other food crops in terraces. Since the Na Pali coast is a continuing succession of ridges, valleys and streams, the trail lifts the hiker high above the ocean on narrow, open ledges, then plunges him down steep switchbacks across cliff faces into valleys dense with jungle growth. On the floor of each valley is a stream, to be forded, and then the trail lifts upward again to cross the next ridge and traverse the next valley wall.

It is no hike for the amateur or the faint-hearted. Only expert hikers complete it in much less than eight hours, and most prefer to make it a two-day hike, staying overnight in a Hawaii Forestry Division cabin at the trail's halfway point.

From the helicopter the ledges of the trail were in open view, but it was hidden from sight when it dipped into the verdant valleys. It was a bright, warm, cloudless summer day, and we scanned the blue waters below us for sharks, porpoises or whales—all common to Hawaiian waters—but saw only a trim boat, bouncing along on the kick of its outboard motor. It was filled with a family, off for a day of fishing for succulent, brightly colored reef fish in the Na Pali coves.

We also saw rifles in the boat, for the high valleys of Na Pali are home to the mountain goat which may be hunted during July, August and September.

Goat hunting, available in Hawaii only on the wild slopes of the Na Pali valleys, is hardly hunting at all. It is no more difficult than scaling the cliffs to the goat pastures in the high valleys, for goats are abundant, and they have a great sense of curiosity which, in hunting season, makes them easy targets. Each hunter gets a bag limit of four goats per season.

Our helicopter turned inland at the mouth of the wide Hanakoa Valley, a neighbor to Kalalau, for an inspection of the magnificent Hanakoa waterfall. The slender ribbon of water plunges 500 feet from the Na Pali summit, pools, plunges another 500 feet, pools again, and drops another 200 feet to the valley floor. The 'copter paused at the summit and then fluttered downward the length of the falls, leveling off 100

157

feet or so above the treetops before it swung seaward again. The pilot showed the waterfall to us from the top down; later, during the hike out, we saw it from the bottom up.

Rearing over the Na Pali coast is Mt. Waialeale ("wy-ollie-ollie") whose 5,080-foot summit wears a continual garland of fluffy rain clouds. Its 476 annual inches of rainfall give it the name, perhaps accurately, of "the wettest spot on earth," and it waters all the Na Pali coast and feeds a waterfall at the head of every Na Pali valley.

It is by no means Hawaii's highest volcanic peak. On the island of Hawaii—called "Big Island" by most residents of the state—are the extinct volcano, Mauna Kea (13,796 ft.) and its neighbor, the active volcano, Mauna Loa (13,680 ft.).

Maui Island's extinct volcano, Haleakala, reaches up to 10,025 feet. Its crater is the home of a unique and exotic plant, the silversword. There are trails to the tops of all these volcanoes, but the Mauna Kea and Mauna Loa hikes are gruelling climbs. Ropes and Alpine equipment are not necessary, but stamina is. Both Mauna Kea and Mauna Loa wear snow on their tops from November to May, so hikes to their summits are easiest in summer.

Haleakala sometimes gets winter snow, but it is a national park and the visitor may rent horses for the climb and exploration of the crater and may stay in any of three 12-bunk cabins in the crater or on its rim. They're open the year around and may be reserved ahead of time from the National Park Service.

Also open the year around is the Big Island's most famed attraction—live volcanoes. From the Big Island's county seat of Hilo, it's an hour's drive to the eerie land of smoking volcanoes. A new 22-mile highway takes the driver past the chain of craters of Kilauea Volcano which rumbles into life and eruption on an average of twice a year.

The road goes by Kalapana Beach, formed of black sand. The sand is the product of live lava pouring into the cold sea water. It explodes into granules and washes up on the shore. Kalapana is no good for swimming, but it is a vivid sight when the white foamy surf runs hissing up on the coal-black beach.

Also along this 22-mile drive are fields of petroglyphs, the "stick picture" writing of the ancient Hawaiians. Anthropologists are still

Mauna Loa on the island of Hawaii: Old but still active.

Associated Press

trying to unravel the meaning of the petroglyphs. Just off the road at one point is one of the strangest sights of all—huge lava boulders with holes drilled into them. Each hole was the burial place of the umbilical cord of an Hawaiian infant, another custom that anthropologists are unable to fathom.

The road climbs upward to the smoking mile-wide crater of Kilauea Volcano with the deep hole of Halemaumau firepit in the crater floor. An unusual hotel, Volcano House, sits on the crater rim, and the hotel wall facing the crater is almost a solid pane of glass. Guests at Volcano House may keep an eye on Halemaumau from their rooms or from the hotel dining room. The hotel is small (37 rooms) and cozy, its rates are $16 a day double, European plan, and it has a steam room provided by nature—water and steam heated by underground lava is forced upwards through tiny cracks in the ground.

Not far away from Volcano House is the U.S. Geological Survey's Volcano Observatory, perched on the Kilauea crater rim. Here visitors may watch the seismographs in action as they trace the underground movements of lava, called "magma," to see where the next eruption will likely be. There is no season for eruptions. They occur when the underground lava finds a weak spot in the earth's crust to push through and become a fountain of fire that is a thousand Fourth of Julys rolled into one.

Monkmeyer

On a smaller island, a quiet corner.

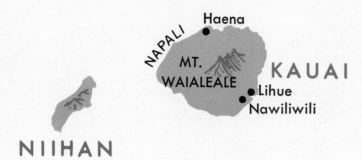

NAPALI

Haena

MT. WAIALEALE

KAUAI

Lihue
Nawiliwili

NIIHAN

OAHU

Waianae

Honolulu
Waikiki

THE HAWAIIAN ISLANDS

To most nonresidents, Hawaii means tropical beaches, and beaches there are. Perhaps the most perfect beach in Hawaii is on the Big Island—Hapuna Beach on its northwestern shore—but wide beaches are on every island. Hapuna Beach is a wide stretch of fine sand, unmarred by a single rock, and it slopes gently far out into the warm waters of the tropical Pacific.

Within walking distance of perfect Hapuna Beach is Laurance Rockefeller's ultra-plush resort, Mauna Kea Beach Hotel. The hotel beach is almost as perfect as Hapuna, and the hotel offers the vacationer many things, although rates are high. A double room on the "modified American plan" is $43 to $48; a double on the European plan is $33.

The resort has a championship 18-hole golf course with Hawaii's top professional golfer, Ted Makalena, resident pro. Jack Nicklaus carries the Mauna Kea colors on the professional golf tour; Jackie Pung is the women's pro. There are also tennis courts with a teaching tennis pro, Henry Kamakana, and the lovely tropical grounds of the hotel to wander in.

The nearest airport to Hapuna Beach and Rockefeller's hotel is in the Wild-West-styled village of Kamuela, 12 miles away. Kamuela is the Hawaiian word for "Samuel" and refers to Samuel Parker, a seafaring man who jumped ship in Hawaii to found the Parker Ranch, second in size in the U.S. to the King Ranch in Texas. Its cowboys are called "paniolos", and

Monkmeyer

Hawaiian cowboy: That hat would have emptied every saloon in Dodge.

riding enthusiasts can find several stables to choose a mount from. The rolling, grassy hills of the Parker Ranch (actually they are cinder cones formed by small volcano eruptions centuries ago) remind one of the cattle country of Colorado and Utah.

There are excellent beaches on the small, sparsely populated island of Molokai, but they are undeveloped and, for the most part, uninhabited. The island of Maui is not especially known for its beaches, but the one good one it has is a beauty. It is called Kaanapali ("kah-ah-nah-pah-lee") and is the fastest growing resort area in the state.

Many persons rate Kaanapali Hawaii's best beach, but I think Hapuna has a slight edge. Sheraton has a big new hotel at Kaanapali and there is another just opened, another being built and a fourth about to be started. An excellent golf course, the Royal Lahaina, adjoins the hotels, and the course is designed for championshhip play. Both the Royal Lahaina and the Mauna Kea course were designed by noted golf-course architect Robert Trent Jones Golf and indeed all outdoor sports are year-round activities in Hawaii.

The most beaches are on the capital island of Oahu, where nearly three-fourths of Hawaii's people live. There are swimming beaches (Waikiki), picnicking beaches (on Oahu's eastern shores) and surfing beaches (on Oahu's northern shores).

The north shore is surfing country, and Makaha is the best. It is the site of the annual International Surfing Championships in January, when winter storms, tides and currents throw up 20-foot waves on the Makaha beach. A half-dozen days a year in the winter, waves as high as 40 feet roar into Makaha, and I have seen surfers "wipe out" (lose control and have the wave break on top of them) in 40-footers, their long surfboards snapped like match sticks and the pieces hurled high into the air.

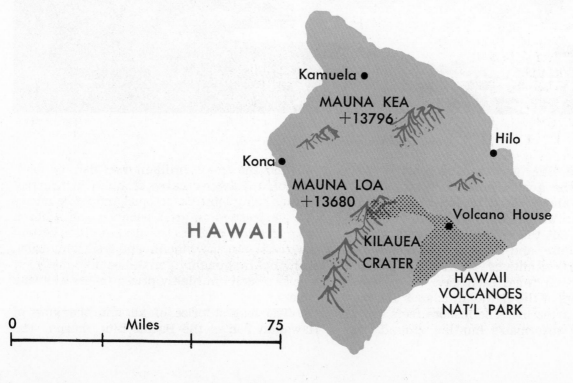

0   Miles   75

Monkmeyer

Oahu coast sculptured in volcanic rock.

There are other good surfing beaches—for experts—on the north shore, such as Sunset Beach and Waimea. Most beginners and amateurs find the waves right off Waikiki Beach high enough, but the serious surfer goes where the big waves are, and Honolulu radio stations broadcast surf conditions (wave heights and intervals) several times each day.

The waters of the Hawaiian Islands abound in fish and marine life. The inshore reefs are a skindiver's or spearman's hunting ground. He will find the small, brilliant reef fish, or denizens of underwater caves or holes in the reef such as spiny lobsters, octopus and fierce moray eels. Surfcasters go after bonefish and a dozen other species, and in the deep waters beyond the reefs live the bluefin and yellowfin tuna, and the mahimahi ("mah-hee-mah-hee"), a species of dolphin highly prized for its exquisite flavor.

The biggest prize of all and the king of Hawaiian fish is the Pacific blue marlin. The sleepy, cozy village of Kona, on the Big Island's western shore, is the headquarters for the deep-sea sport fishing fleet. Each July the International Billfish Tournament is held in Kona, and the world record Pacific blue marlin, a 1,095-pounder, was caught off Kona.

In September 1965, a California angler hooked and landed a new world-record blue marlin weighing 1,148 pounds. He will not be listed in the record books, however, for a crewman on the boat touched the tackle and dis-

qualified the catch. The rules require the angler to hook and land the fish himself. In this case, the monster marlin was the first deep-sea fish ever landed by the angler (Sherwyn M. Woods of Sherman Oaks, California), and the crewman didn't want him to lose it, so he gave him a helping hand. Veteran fishermen think the fish is the largest Pacific blue marlin ever landed with rod and reel.

Hunting in Hawaii attracts only a small but devoted following compared to other out-

Other products of the islands are sugar and pineapples.

Monkmeyer

Three and a half miles from Honolulu on the island of Oahu . . .

door activities, although a good variety of game is offered. Kauai has goat hunting, wild pig and pheasant; there are wild pig, Mouflon sheep, pheasant, quail and chukkar partridge in the mountains of the Big Island. Molokai's mountains are home to the axis deer, wild pig, pheasant and quail. Maui and Oahu are not fertile ground for the hunter.

The hunter's favorite island is Lanai, a tiny island near Maui that is owned by the Dole pineapple firm. Its level land is a huge pineapple field, but much of Lanai is too dry or too hilly for pineapple. In these sections are axis deer, antelope, a few sheep, pheasant, quail and partridge.

Hunting is carefully regulated, especially deer hunting. Lanai hunters draw for hunting days, for not all who want to go hunting are permitted. The deer and antelope herds are counted by state game wardens, the "harvest" determined, and exactly twice the number of hunters for each deer and antelope are permitted to go after the game. In 1965, the Lanai season ran from August 29 to October 17. On Molokai, the deer season is normally May and June.

All these things are available to the sports

enthusiast in Hawaii, but Kalalau Valley offers the remoteness that none of the other islands do, and that's why we were making the trip.

Through the helicopter's bubble front we could see the long, golden beach of Kalalau ahead, and our pilot prepared to put us down on it. "If you get into trouble or want to fly out, just write a message in the sand," he said. Since Kalalau's beach is about a half-mile long and several hundred yards wide, one could write him a long letter if loneliness set in.

The cliffs at Kalalau are pocked with deep, dry caves with sand floors, and after we had swung our packs off the helicopter and watched it fly away, we began looking for a campsite.

Until recently, perhaps until the helicopter flights began, the valley was the home of a Virgin Islands physician, Dr. Bernard Wheatley, who renounced civilization to lead an idyllic life as "the hermit of Kalalau." We found his abandoned cave and lived in it for the week end, secure in our solitude and its shelter.

We shared the long beach and deep valleys only with Pat and Dot Rigg, a California couple who are veteran campers and backpackers. They were living in the ideal cave on the beach, because it was nearest the 200-foot waterfall that

Pix

. . . the last of the day's surfers loll on their boards at Waikiki.

is both fresh water supply and shower bath for Kalalau campers. They also hiked out of the valley when their month's vacation was over.

The valleys of the Na Pali coast are called "hanging valleys" and that is just what they are. They sweep down from the Na Pali head-wall and end at sheer cliffs anywhere from 250 feet to 1,000 feet above the beach. Kalalau Valley is the single exception, for its waterfall-fed river has, in centuries, carved through the cliff. One may begin where the Kalalau River rushes into the ocean and climb up the river canyon to the high valleys and plateaus.

All other valleys along the Na Pali coast can be reached only by scaling the cliffs. Kalalau's other neighboring valley — Honopu — may be reached—after a 200-yard swim around a rocky point—by climbing up a knotted rope that goat hunters have tied to the clifftop. The swim, through mild currents, is a challenging one, and without mask, fins and snorkel, is only for the strongest swimmers, and then only in summer.

At the end of most valleys, the stream plunges over the cliff and leaps into the ocean. Motorists or non-hikers may see the Na Pali coast from a point on the summit rim called

Kilohana Overlook. An excellent highway leads to the overlook. It is at the head of Kalalau Valley, but one may look into many of the Na Pali valleys from that vantage point.

The most breath-taking views of Na Pali, however, are from its beaches, where one looks upward to great shafts of lava rock, eroded by centuries of wind and water into huge spires resembling a giant pipe organ.

They are not the bare granite of the Rocky Mountain West, but are festooned with great growths of greenery—grass, creepers and shrubs—which change into dense, luxuriant tropical jungle growth along the streams.

For the first mile of the trail out of Kala-.lau, these vistas are easy to see, for the trail skirts the edge of the beach. It is wide and grassy and is like walking through a well-tended lawn. The lawn is, in fact, the taro terraces of the Hawaiians, now filled up with earth and grown over with a carpet of grass. On the edge of the Kalalau River, the trail comes to the remains of a heiau, the temple of worship of Hawaiians.

At the heiau, the trail turns up Kalalau Valley, goes through some scrubby jungle growth and comes to the bank of the river. It is the first of many fords that come on the trail. You tie your boots around your neck, hold your camera and wade gingerly through the swift, waist-deep water, trying to find solid footing in the stream bed of round stones that roll under your foot the moment you put any weight on them. The 20-pound pack on your back makes the crossing no easier.

The trail zigzags upward from the stream and finally emerges from the thick brush onto a small, grassy plateau about 300 feet above the ocean. From there it goes up a bare slope at such a steep angle that we were gasping for breath after a hundred feet. It kept climbing steeply upward until we finally leveled off at about 1,000 feet above the water.

Here the ledge skirting the cliffside began, only there was about a 30-foot section of the ledge missing. It had been eroded away by the weather, and only the bare, nearly vertical cliffside was left to walk on. We debated about crawling across this danger zone on hands and knees, but we tested the footing carefully and found that our rubber-soled boots did not slip on the granular lava surface.

My companion edged across—5 feet, 10 feet, 20 feet and onto the solid ledge. A cold sweat broke out on my forehead and a pulse began beating in my throat. I edged out onto the cliffside, carefully avoided looking down at the pounding surf far below, and slowly walked across to the ledge. There, driven into the hillside above the ledge, was a sign that said "Kalalau."

There were no other places where the ledge had fallen away, but often it was barely a foot wide where it skirted a high ridge or ran around a windswept point. It was not the best weather for a hike. Frequent rain squalls blew in from the ocean, drenching us as we inched along the exposed ledges and dripping on us when the trail dipped into the valley floors and under the heavy foliage.

At several points along the trail we quenched our thirst by eating a pear-like tropical fruit called "mountain apple" which is not very flavorful but is very juicy. At other times we drank from the streams we crossed.

The trail went on in this manner, zigzagging up the ridge from the valley floor until it reached the ridge shoulder, then becoming a ledge with the cliff falling away steeply below, then skirting the point of the ridge and dipping downward into the next valley and across the next stream.

After four hours of this, we reached the forestry cabin, the halfway point in the trail. It was raining heavily at the time, and the extra clothing in our packs was soaked. We had nothing dry to change into, so we examined the cabin briefly, found it in good condition and resumed the hike.

The sun came out not long afterwards, dried us off somewhat, and we stopped on the ledge at a point some 1,500 feet above the sea. Off to our right, down the coast, we could see a ribbon of water plunging 500 feet into the sea. A mother goat and two kids, twitching with curiosity, came within 20 feet of us and questioned us with nasal "baas."

They kept pace with us, even when we came to a spot where the trail ended and became a series of stepping stones on outcroppings of rock from a vertical cliff. It was heart-in-mouth time again, and we carefully stepped from rock to rock.

The trail gradually became easier. It maintained the pattern of upward zigzag, skirting ledge and downhill switchbacks, but the ledges were getting wider and the hills not as steep. From the forestry cabin to Haena, milestones have been posted every quarter-mile along the trail. They are morale boosters, and as the quarter-miles came and went, both packs and spirits seemed lighter.

The last half-mile of the trail is over a paved waterway, handmade of lava rocks fitted together by ancient Hawaiian hands. It is as solid—without any form of mortar—today as it was when they built it to divert fresh water to their village at Haena.

We stepped off the end of the trail at Haena just 8 hours and 20 minutes after we had started that morning. Our car was waiting for us where we had left it, and it was a welcome sight. So was the blue-water bathing beach, and we had a quick, satisfying dip before we drove to Lihue and caught the plane for a 35-minute ride back to Honolulu.

This is something that I can't get used to even as a longtime Hawaii resident—how close the pleasures of the more scenic, more restful, more sparsely populated outer islands are to the Honolulu resident.

Honolulu now has a population of nearly 600,000 out of the state's 800,000 total. It is a growing city with the same problems of any

Pix

Boat basin at Honolulu: Plenty of ocean in every direction.

growing city in the U.S. It has crowded high-ways, too few parks and too few schools. It needs improvement in urban renewal projects, sound planning for the future, and better control of the urban sprawl.

But the Honolulu resident and visitor can fly to the volcanoes, the open ranch lands, the hiking and hunting grounds of Mauna Kea or the serenity of Kona on the Big Island for $20, in 62 minutes. Next year when both inter-island airlines convert to short-haul jets, the flying time will be halved.

Maui is 37 minutes and $13 away. Kauai is 35 minutes away and air fare is $10. Molokai and Lanai are a half-hour away at a cost of $12.

Beautiful resort hotels are on all the islands except Molokai and Lanai, but soon they'll have them, too. For a maximum of $28, one can get the best double room in a new resort hotel overlooking Kauai's Nawiliwili Bay, or Maui's Kaanapali Beach, or the harbor at Kona. Excellent accommodations in new or nearly new resort hotels are available for much less, if you can forgo a panoramic view from your open lanai (porch).

If you're the sleeping-bag or tenting type, the outer islands have wide, empty beaches where you can sleep under the stars, at little more than the cost of renting a car to drive there.

Hawaiians are a friendly people, too. They know how much fun it is to live in a place full of sunshine and natural beauty. They don't mind at all sharing it with others. ♦

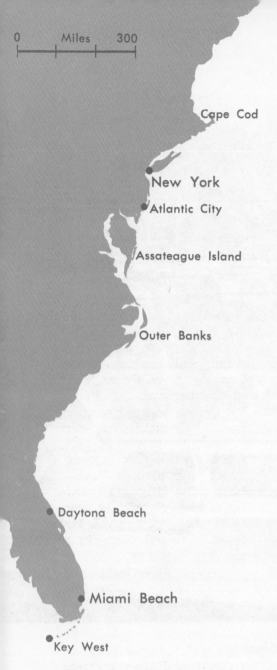

FISHING

that great ocean river which pours through the Florida Straits, hugs the East Coast to Virginia, and then bends out into the mid-Atlantic. The Stream warms the coastal water for bathers, moderates the climate of the American East, and carries an abundance of fish for food and sport.

Just as the edge of the sea is indefinite because of rising and falling tides, so the area we call the seashore is indefinite because its opportunities for recreation extend as far out into the ocean as sailors and fishermen are inclined to venture.

There was a time when Key West fishermen thought nothing of leaving the shelter of Garrison Bight and heading for the waters off the coast of Cuba, trolling most of the way across the Florida Straits, the 90-mile-wide passage between Key West and Cuba. But no more. Today the Florida Straits are intensively patrolled by the U.S. Navy, which warns fishermen against straying too close to Castro's island. Nor have the Cubans themselves always encouraged casual visits by small craft.

International politics has thus given Key West fishing a singular character; it is practically impossible to troll the Straits without sensing the presence of the Navy—on, under, or over the sea.

And the Navy is just part of the U.S. defense complex in Key West. The Air Force, Army, Coast Guard, and Marine Corps also have bases there, and they all are keeping an eye on the Straits. Most of the time this surveillance is unobtrusive, but when the Navy stages war games things get lively—as a pair of fishermen discovered during an outing on Captain Ted Smits' 34-foot charter boat, Floalong II.

The Floalong, together with several dozen

SIXTY-FIVE miles north of the Tropic of Cancer, it begins. It is America's Atlantic seashore, extending from Key West to Canada in a serpentine line that is perforated by countless inlets, estuaries, and coves, and punctuated by capes, reefs, and headlands. It was cast by the great glaciers of the Ice Age and it is continually polished, and occasionally altered, by the battering sea.

The Eastern seashore of the United States is mostly a rim of sand, and as such it is a favorite playground for Americans. The Gulf and Pacific Coasts are admirable in many ways, but the Gulf of Mexico lacks the great Atlantic surf and, except in Southern California, the Pacific Coast is not known for sandy beaches. Too, the Eastern seaboard is washed by the Gulf Stream,

THE FLORIDA STRAITS

By Edwin A. Roberts, Jr.

other charter fishing boasts, is berthed at the edge of U.S. Route 1 in the little harbor known as Garrison Bight. The run from there past the Naval base and on to the fishing grounds takes an hour and a half. A short leg of the trip is made through a canal posted with signs prohibiting picture-taking. These signs went up during the Cuban missile crisis. The banks of the canal are lined with private homes, so it's not immediately clear why Uncle Sam doesn't want anybody taking pictures of the place, especially since Key West shops sell five-cent postcards bearing very sharp aerial views of the island, including its Naval installations. But then perhaps the signs were put up by the postcard manufacturer.

The Floalong is equipped with three fighting chairs and three outriggers, and the deckhouse is simply furnished with two wide bunks and an icebox. The two passengers on this day's trip were J. B. Palmer, a Memphis cotton planter who had done all his prior fishing in the lakes of the Tennessee Valley, and a newspaper reporter.

The day that was to turn out to be unusually eventful began serenely enough at 7:30 a.m. when Captain Smits started the Floalong's two 115-horsepower engines. By 9 a.m. the bright green coastal water had been left behind and the Floalong was well into the clear, blue Gulf Stream. The mate, a blessedly taciturn teenager, affixed spoons to the lines and the trolling for bonito began.

The bonito is a well-styled fish of the mackerel family that, while quite edible, is too bloody for many tastes. It is frequently caught for use as marlin bait. Two bonito were quickly hooked and boated. A third bonito was hooked but only two-thirds of it was boated. A barracuda had shot across the wake of the boat and snipped off the bonita's hind quarters.

Although the first goal of the day was sailfish and the second goal dolphin, Captain Smits was intent upon providing his customers with a certain amount of variety. A heavily weighted line was dropped over the stern and the skipper idled the engines. J. B. Palmer took his position in the center of the fighting chair and, with some misgivings, grabbed the stout rod with which he was to do some fierce bottom fishing.

When 200 feet of line had been paid out—straight down—Captain Smits directed Mr. Palmer to throw the brake on the reel. As soon as this was done, the rod lurched forward. Mr. Palmer lurched forward. The rod bent like a horseshoe and line spun off the reel.

Mr. Palmer, who was accustomed to the gentler fishing of the Tennessee Valley, was awed. "What do we have here?" he asked.

"You've got a monster on the line. Wait till you see it," said the skipper.

Mr. Palmer put his back into pumping the rod, raising the tip slowly and then lowering it quickly and reeling fast, gaining on the fish in three and four-foot bursts. But progress was slow. Mr. Palmer would bring the fish up 10 or 12 feet, and then the fish would make a run, undoing all the fisherman's hard work. After 20 minutes Mr. Palmer's tan sport shirt was dark with perspiration, his face was taut and red. Then, in a second, it was over. The line eased, the fish was gone.

"He's off. You lost him," said the skipper. "He probably cut the line on the bottom."

The line was refitted and baited and the newspaperman took a turn in the center fighting chair. Again the line was let down to 200 feet, again there was an immediate hit, and again the long pull to the surface began.

Such fishing does not require skill. It does

169

not even require a knack. Just strong arms and a healthy back. The fight was long and very hard. Every inch of line was bought with sweat. Each pumping motion brought a holler from protesting muscles.

After half an hour, the fish began to tire. The newspaperman was practically numb. There was never a time when both fish and fisherman could rest because the fish was not darting about just below the surface, occasionally causing a slackening of the line. It was dangling and pulling far down beneath the boat.

There is no sea water in the world clearer than the water of the Gulf Stream as it pours through the Florida Straits. A man can look down into the ocean for 80 feet, but he cannot always *see* 80 feet. The topside of a fish at that depth will be invisible; only if it turns so that the white of its belly is exposed will it be visible from the surface.

The fish was coming up steadily now, if still slowly. When it was just 50 feet from the surface, the mate sounded the cry that tears at the heart of an embattled fisherman.

"Sharks!"

There were three of them, their black hides plainly visible 50 feet down, and they did their work quickly. The line eased suddenly as all on the boat knew it would, and no one said anything as the newspaperman brought in his catch. Just the pink head of what must have been a 50-pound amberjack was left.

The mate held up the head briefly and then dropped it into the fish box. The newspaperman was silent as physical aches were forgotten. The pain of losing so stout a fish was enough to deal with for the present. Inadvertently, he touched the metal rim of his fishing reel and leaped out of the chair. From the friction of the fight, the reel was hot as fire. Thus, the fisherman was muscle-sore, sweaty, blistered —and burned. And the sharks had got his fish.

"Let's catch us some dolphin," said J. B. Palmer. Captain Smits was already at the roof controls revving up the engines.

Throughout the morning the sea had borne a variegated traffic. Along with a half dozen other fishing boats were U.S. submarines, destroyers, and Coast Guard cutters. Overhead were twin-engine Navy planes, each with what looked like a large pool cue poking out from under its tail. And far higher, pressed against the sky, were the delta-winged jets, appearing and

disappearing in seconds, leaving only a disintegrating line of chalk across the blue.

"We don't see much of this sort of thing back on the lake in Tennessee," said Mr. Palmer.

Captain Smits headed toward the southeast horizon at about 20 knots, and soon the Floalong had the ocean pretty much to itself except for a destroyer and a pair of those planes with the pool cues. With the armada thus reduced the fishermen began to lose the feeling that they had somehow blundered into the Battle of Leyte Gulf.

The water was very calm and the passengers aboard the Floalong began opening lunch bags and beer. In the distance a tanker which plowed low in the water cast up a thin ribbon of black smoke. The sun was high, the breeze was cool and tangy, and there was easy talk about world-record fish, the way to play a blue marlin, the best season off Panama, the tuna situation at Bimini, and the rigors of camping on the Dry Tortugas.

Baroooom!

Not 50 yards from the Floalong there was a huge explosion of water, a great, splashy up-

heaval that put one in mind of a detonated depth charge. Mr. Palmer and the newspaperman immediately thought the worst: For some reason the U.S. Navy had become unhappy about the Floalong and had decided to blow her out of the sea. As it turned out, the Navy was not attacking, but the reason for the explosion was only slightly less interesting.

The destroyer that had been cruising in the Floalong's vicinity most of the day was engaged in Naval exercises with two submarine-spotter planes (those with the sonar-equipped pool cues) and with a submarine somewhere beneath the waves. It was the planes' job to detect the location of the submarine and relay this information to the destroyer. The submarine, for its part, was trying its best not to be discovered.

To this end, the submarine decided to hide itself under the Floalong, thereby confusing the planes above. When the exercise was over the submarine indicated its exact position to the planes by blowing out one of its water ballast tanks, thus causing the eruption on the surface. Then the planes could check to see how near or far their estimates were from the mark.

This information, which was deduced by Captain Smits, was greeted with great relief by his guests. "Too bad we didn't know the sub was down there," said the newspaperman. "What's the biggest submarine ever taken on a rod and reel?"

After that, the Navy went its way and the Floalong went hers—at least for a time. The

lines were baited with ballyhoo and the trolling for sailfish and dolphin began. Two hours went by without a strike. Mr. Palmer fell to discussing a profitable venture into the junkyard business when a brownish hump appeared near his bait.

"Dolphin!" yelled the newspaperman.
"Dolphin!" echoed the captain.
"Dolphin!" re-echoed the mate.

The dolphin hit the bait like an express train. When its charge was partially braked by Mr. Palmer's reel, the fish used its momentum to leap completely out of the water, flashing like some great marine jewel. It was not brownish now for the sun was on its wet sides, bringing to life the brilliant greens, blues, yellows, and pinks of its body. The dolphin has a blunt head and its face might be thought to lack character, but its rainbow flanks make it the dandy of the sea.

As the fish was brought next to the boat, the mate grabbed the wire leader and hoisted it aboard. Soon the fish would die and its colors would fade, but now, captured, angry, and fresh from the sea, the dolphin was a thing of beauty. Mr. Palmer, who had been tiring of the long trolling without a hit, perked up remarkably and regaled his listeners with an account of the battle.

"He was a tough one," Mr. Palmer said, and one suspected the boys back in Memphis would be hearing a good deal about this catch.

Minutes later Mr. Palmer caught another dolphin of equal size—about four feet long— and there was no doubt that the Tennessean who heretofore had confined his fishing to lakes and streams was won over by this more spectacular kind of angling.

By 2 p.m. there was a barely noticeable air of discouragement aboard the Floalong because no sailfish had been sighted. Then a remarkable thing happened. The water near the boat became a kaleidoscope. The sea around the Floalong was filled with young, or "chicken," dolphin. Quickly the lines were brought in, the

large hooks removed, and small hooks fastened in their place.

It was an orgy. As soon as a baited hook touched the water it was attacked by dozens of chicken dolphin, about 18 inches long. A slight yank set the hook and brought a fish aboard. The skipper set the controls so the boat turned in a tight circle and then he and the mate tried to keep up with the activity, unhooking fish and rebaiting as fast as possible.

The trick was not to lose the school. When a fish was hooked it was left in the water until another line had snared another fish. Thus there was always one hooked fish swimming about by the boat, serving to keep his friends in the neighborhood.

For more than 30 minutes the Floalong went around in circles as dolphin after dolphin was brought into the boat. It was an exciting half hour. But what was exciting to the fishermen was just peculiar to the U.S. Navy.

While the party on the Floalong had been preoccupied with the chicken dolphin, a destroyer with a large "470" on its bow had been heading straight for the scene. A destroyer is not, of course, a large ship. Even sub tenders are far larger. But when one is in a 34-foot fishing boat looking up at a destroyer that's right next

door, well, in that case a destroyer tends to bulk.

The good ship "470" had apparently become interested in the Floalong's curious round-and-round behavior and had come by to see what was what. The newspaperman was tempted, briefly, to shout something in Spanish, but decided against it.

A couple of people up on the destroyer's bridge peered at the Floalong through binoculars, and 20 or 30 sailors along the rail watched the fishermen intently. The fishermen tried a friendly wave, in the manner of sociable yachtsmen, but nobody on the destroyer waved back.

This often happens, even when the U.S. Navy isn't involved. Passengers in a little boat will wave at passengers in another boat, and the passengers in the other boat won't wave back. This is always a disappointment because the passengers in the first boat then feel they have wasted a wave.

The destroyer finally sailed away without one of its crew even giving the Floalong a friendly nod. But then the destroyer was many times the size of the Floalong and this could account for it. Big boats almost never wave at little boats. This is the first unwritten rule of the sea, practiced everywhere from Oyster Bay to Puget Sound. There is a lot of class consciousness in the world of boating, and it's

well for every boat to know its place. The destroyer's crewmen knew their boat was bigger and more costly than the Floalong, and they reacted accordingly.

It was 3 p.m. and the fishermen were 25 miles at sea. In the east a storm signaled its approach so the Floalong headed home. With three miles to go and with Key West in sight, the storm struck. It was a rain squall accompanied by fog and, after getting a final land bearing before the mist closed in, Captain Smits turned the bow part way into the wind and used the engines just to keep the boat steady.

The skipper, the mate, Mr. Palmer, and the newspaperman huddled in the cabin as rain and wind rattled the windows. The wind made the sea choppy and the Floalong bounced hard. Water streamed off the cabin roof and into the cockpit. In the distance the bong of buoys and the groan of foghorns began their ominous cacophony.

A fog at sea is curious. Within its misty folds a boat lies hidden yet vulnerable, like a child with a blanket over his head to thwart the specters in his darkened bedroom. Only a child can fully appreciate the dawn. Only a seafarer knows how to love a lifting fog.

"Can't see much out there, can you?" said Mr. Palmer.

Then the occupants of the cabin fell silent for a few minutes. There wasn't much to say. There was nothing to see and remark about.

"Where's that destroyer 470 now?" the newsman wondered. "Destroyers are all over the place except when you need one."

But the Floalong didn't need a destroyer—only patience. Soon the rain stopped and the fog thinned. Thirty minutes later the boat was snug in her slip at Garrison Bight, and two dozen onlookers were admiring her fish as they were mounted on the spikes of the display wrack. The total: 2 sharks, 2 big dolphin, 34 chicken dolphin, 2 whole bonito, 1 amputated bonito, and 1 amberjack head. A fair day.

The National Observer

Monkmeyer

Fair days are frequent in the Florida Keys, and more and more people each year visit the low-lying little islands, including Floridians from northern sections of the state. All of south Florida, in fact, has more visitors in summer than in winter, because in summer motel rates are less, the beaches are no less enjoyable than in winter, and because children's summer vacations often dictate when the family will take its annual holiday.

Florida varies so widely from section to section and city to city that generalization is impossible, even if the subject is restricted to the Florida seashore. But some small facts about Florida beach areas are worth noting.

Key West beaches are occasionally littered with a variety of seaweed that is most curious. The seaweed, when drying in the sun, gives off a gas so powerful it removes the paint from wooden buildings. This gas has few rivals in the natural world when it comes to pungency. Even the assault of a long-continent skunk can produce no odor to match it. And, when the wind is right (or wrong), when the seaweed gas rolls upward over the island, it is no exaggeration to say that Key West then, at that time, smells to high heaven.

The Florida Keys offer, along with fishing, boating, and swimming, a distinctive delicacy called key lime pie. The Keys support a particular species of lime trees that produce a fruit quite different from the ordinary lime. And from this little fruit, the natives make a tangy pie that's available at many restaurants in the islands.

Visitors to the Keys first pass through the small city of Homestead, near the main entrance to Everglades National Park. Homestead is noted for its bicycling. Dr. Paul Dudley White, the heart specialist, has visited Homestead frequently because of its ideal terrain and many paths for bike riding. People who don't know how to ride a bike, however, will find Homestead short on alternate activities.

Miami Beach is the best known of Florida seashore resorts, largely because of its long row of modern hotels and motels that offer an exciting night life. Relatively few Miami Beach visitors seem to care for the ocean or the beach. Mostly, they prefer lounging around swimming pools, where the amenities of bar and kitchen are close at hand. Restaurant food in Miami Beach is uniformly good. Hotel and motel rooms are generally expensive, although lower rates can be found in the older establishments at the southern end.

Farther north is Palm Beach, a town of seaside estates, perfectly landscaped homes, and many smart shops. The shops are indeed smart. Whether their customers are smart is another matter. Prices are high.

Many people who go to the beach are anxious to forget for a time the rigors of civilization, including auto traffic. No such respite is afforded visitors to Daytona Beach because cars are welcome on the strand. That Daytona, which has a very wide, hard beach, should permit autos to mingle with sunbathers, seems unfortunate. Although the beach traffic must move very slowly, a sunbather still has the feeling he is reclining at the side of Route 66, scantily clad and altogether vulnerable. Even so, the beach at Daytona is a marvel.

It is often the smaller, less publicized beaches that are the best and most reasonable for families, and it's worth a trip along Route A1A, the ocean highway, to do some firsthand exploring. Most chambers of commerce respond

Miami Beach News Bureau Photo

Miami Beach.

quickly to inquiries; indeed, the inquirer is likely to be deluged with pretty pamphlets, many of them bearing a picture of a girl in a bikini holding a beach ball. The theory seems to be that the average father is anxious for his family to vacation at a place that allows beach balls on the beach.

The seashore along America's East Coast is a varied place. From Key West to Cape Cod the shoreline is chiefly sand, but it is sand with an inconstant composition. Because the mineral make-up of sand is different from place to place, even within the same state, some beaches are covered with several inches of soft sand while others are hard as concrete.

North of Cape Cod are the rocky edges of New England and here the water tends to be much colder. Swimming is often possible only in August. But the cliffs and the evergreen forests that come right down to the ocean's edge, the warm summer days and nippy summer nights, the excellent sailing facilities and the seasonally good fishing, continue to entice millions to Maine's seacoast every year.

The rocky coast of Maine becomes less rocky and more sandy in the southern part of the state, and from there the rim of sand extends along New Hampshire's modest seacoast and on south to Cape Cod.

The sweeping, bending beaches of Cape Cod, marked as they are by rolling dunes and coarse dune grass, form one of the most popular recreation areas in the crowded Northeast. While veteran Cape vacationers lament the

The Atlantic surf can be a churlish companion when the wind comes in from the southeast.

New York State Department of Commerce Photo

Cape Cod National Seashore.

growing commercialization of the peninsula, it still retains a Colonial, seafaring flavor and numberless examples of charming architecture. There are even Cape Cod houses on the Cape, although they don't much resemble the so-called Cape Cods that modern real estate developers are responsible for. A large tract of beachfront has been reserved as the Cape Cod National Seashore, and this beautiful strand is a favorite of fishermen, shell collectors, and beach strollers.

No type of real estate is disappearing more swiftly than unspoiled beachfront, thus the preservation of national seashores at Cape Cod, at Assateague Island, Maryland, and elsewhere represents a valuable legacy for future generations. It's possible, too, to see what can happen to a beautiful seashore when it becomes almost entirely commercialized. New Jersey is Exhibit "A".

Before World War II, most of the New Jersey shore, from Sandy Hook in the north to Cape May in the south, was sparsely settled and little built upon. Except for Long Branch, Atlantic City, and Cape May, which were fashionable resorts in the Nineteenth Century, the Jersey coast was largely duneland, accessible mostly by yellow-pebbled roads. There were boardwalks at Atlantic City, Asbury Park, Sea side Heights, and Wildwood—boardwalks lined with the usual concessionaires—but between these places of carnival-like amusements the coast was quiet.

An occasional house stood atop the dunes facing the ocean, but for every house there

were usually several vacant lots, which could be bought for a few hundred dollars, if anyone cared. Few did.

But after the war the buying and building began. Cottages were erected only four feet apart in many places. Speculators made for-tunes by erecting tiny plywood shanties, identi-cal and in row after row running from beach-front to highway. And the highway was no longer a pebbled road, but a four-lane express-way.

The problems caused by rapid growth were

not really the problems of progress. They were the result of municipal indifference to the kind of zoning restrictions that might have preserved some measure of beauty. The town of Manasquan, for instance, after its modest boardwalk was washed away in a hurricane, decided not to replace it. This was an understandable decision, considering how many times the town had lost its boardwalk to the sea. But Manasquan decided to defy the ocean by pouring an asphalt walkway where the boardwalk used to be. Strolling upon it is like strolling on a tarred roof. Two decades ago the Manasquan beachfront was lovely. Today a different kind of adjective must be found.

Some unpretty construction along the Jersey beaches was essential. With the ocean threatening to reduce the size of several towns, it was necessary to build jetties which, resembling bulkheads, were extended oceanward perpendicular to the beaches. They are ugly, but they have helped save the beaches.

As additional highways were built, connecting the Jersey shore more directly with New York and Philadelphia, the summer crowds increased not only in size, but in noise. The one-day visitors, the week-end party people, and the affluent teen-agers wanted more than a beach to romp on and an ocean to play in. They wanted action and they got it. Night clubs multiplied, tavern licenses in some towns were dispensed with alacrity, dazzling neon tubes heralded hundreds of catch-penny businesses, and on the crowded boardwalks strollers continually bumped into each other, occasionally jamming a candy apple into somebody else's frozen custard. And all around were the noises of the summer throngs. It was like vacationing inside a mammoth pinball machine.

Several Jersey seashore towns are not this bad. Some are quiet, expensive, and well cared for. But enough are so poorly zoned and overcrowded that more and more vacationers are eschewing them; instead they are camping on the dunes of Island Beach State Park, a 10-mile strand that has been spared the tawdry fate of so much of the Jersey shore.

Just as that woman is blessed who knows how to grow old, so is the resort town that knows how to grow up. One area that is in the process of being tested lies midway between rocky Maine and sandy Key West. Unlike the New Jersey shore, the development of North Carolina's Outer Banks is only beginning. ♦

Monkmeyer

Bruce Roberts

Cape Hatteras Lighthouse.

Where Wind-Driven Dunes Confront

A Contentious Corner of the Sea

THE CONVOYS of vacationers searching for respite from the neon's bright glare and the cacaphonous U.S. urban life used to drive through Waves, North Carolina, at 45-minute intervals. They sought solitude. They sought the frothy spectacle of an ocean battling itself. They sought the sudden singing of a fishing reel as a drum charged toward open water. They sought the barren, beautiful Outer Banks of North Carolina.

For this they had to travel long distances, over generally poor roads, to the easternmost tip of North Carolina. There, at Whalebone Junction, they drove south for a few miles and, exhaust pipe scraping, eased aboard the rusty deck of a small ferry. Three-quarters of an hour later, after the ferry had twisted through the narrow, continually shifting channel crossing Oregon Inlet, they had left much of one kind of civilization behind them in temporary exchange for a quieter variety.

Now the transition can be made at 55 miles an hour.

A curving, three-mile bridge now spans Oregon Inlet. The state-operated ferry has been retired from duty. And the once remote Outer Banks are within reasonable reach of anyone with an automobile—a reach shortened considerably for the millions of residents of the populous Northeastern United States by the Chesapeake Bay Tunnel and connecting interstate highways.

"A shame!" say veteran Outer Banks vacationers, a bit selfishly. "Hurray!" shout most Outer Banks natives, who feel they have been isolated from the world long enough.

The Outer Banks buff, who fears that this new, easy method of ingress will doom the peculiar character of this strip of sandy islands, really does not have a great deal to fear. In the first place, many persons who visit here for the first time go away disappointed. The first

North Carolina's

OUTER BANKS

By Ken Clark

impression is one of lifeless desolation. And the National Park Service, determined to keep things that way, is preserving about 45 square miles of beachland in its original state of wildness, or almost so. And this considerable deterrent to creeping commercialism is accepted philosophically by the natives, since the Government left enough private land around the numerous small villages along the Banks for the construction of motels, marinas, and other commercial ventures.

Thus the visitor to the Outer Banks will be able to choose for himself between the wildness of the area and the comforts of home—to a point. Posh hotels, championship golf courses, and bars are nonexistent. Area restaurants, while serving their purpose, are mediocre at best.

But the veteran Banks vacationer never sought these attractions. For him, contemplation of the crashing Atlantic Ocean off Cape Hatteras, where the Labrador Current battles the Gulf Stream over shoal sand, beats contemplating the ice in a bourbon and soda.

He is the sort who finds joy in watching the glee of his children as they scamper across the beach after an outraged little ghost crab. Or he feels a fleeting kinship with the past when he discovers the century-old hulk of a schooner, suddenly uncovered by the ever-shifting sands of the Banks.

The Outer Banks are made up of several slender islands beginning just below Norfolk and extending southward to near Morehead City, North Carolina. In some places the islands are so narrow it is said that one can spit across them in a high wind.

Physically, the Banks are of considerable interest to geologists. They are, it seems, nothing more than mounds of sand upon which vegetation has taken root, and which are continually moving landward as the ocean winds lift millions of the tiny grains from the seaward

side of the dunes and deposit them to landward. These dunes are among the highest in eastern America. One, Jockey Ridge, soars more than 135 feet above sea level.

Primary vegetation consists of yaupon (a form of holly that doesn't look much like holly), myrtle and beech trees, with occasional forests of live oak and loblolly pine on the landward side. Marshy valleys and occasional freshwater lakes lie along the wider parts of the islands, surrounded by ferns, vines, and a considerable variety of wild flowers in season.

This terrain supports a few white-tail deer, a number of wild ponies (descendants, it is said, of a shipload of Arabian horses that sank off the Banks), and more than 300 species of birds.

But it is the sea, not the land, that dominates the Outer Banks. The battle of the ocean currents off Cape Hatteras has shaped the geography, the history, and perhaps the future of the area. During the past 400-odd years, these currents have brought more than 2,600 ships to sudden death within sight of the Cape—ships whose captains, taking advantage of the momentum offered by one stream or the other, suddenly found themselves adding another chapter to the scores already written about the "Graveyard of the Atlantic."

These same currents brought settlers to the Banks when a large portion of the civilized world still thought the earth was flat and ended somewhere just east of the Azores. Roanoke Island, lying just westward of the main thread of islands comprising the Banks, was the site in 1585 of the first, abortive English attempt to colonize the New World. A second try, no more successful than the first, was notable because of the birth of Virginia Dare, first American child born of English parents—and because the entire colony vanished without trace. This disappearance of 150 men, women, and children gave rise to the story of the "Lost Colony."

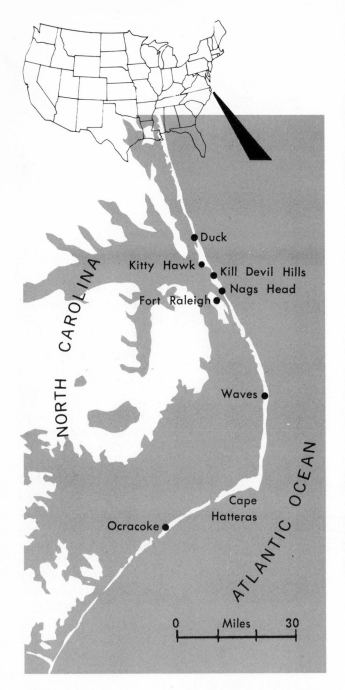

Fort Raleigh, the site of these two colonization attempts, has been preserved as a national historic site, and partial restoration has been made. Visiting is permitted daily except holidays. Paul Green's famous outdoor symphonic drama, *The Lost Colony,* is produced each summer at Waterside Theater adjoining Fort Raleigh.

Many of the small villages along the islands boast houses made largely from the timbers of sunken ships—and the houses in turn often are occupied by persons whose ancestors became

Banks residents rather suddenly as a result of these same shipwrecks. (The accent of the natives, in fact, still is more than vaguely reminiscent of the dialect of northern England. The nearest motel, you will be told politely by the native, is "noine moile, roight down the baich, and you'll make it in toime for hoigh toide.")

These villages were named "Duck," "Rodanthe," "Salvo," and the like long before tourists found such names cute. They are interspersed at fairly regular intervals along the single paved highway that runs down the is-

Bruce Roberts

Silver Lake Harbor, Ocracoke Island.

lands.

One of the most picturesque, Ocracoke, lies across unbridged water and can be reached only by ferry. This hamlet of 500 persons is nestled haphazardly around a large natural harbor near the southern tip of 18-mile-long Ocracoke Island. The remainder of the island is uninhabited, and much of it is included in the Cape Hatteras National Seashore. Motels, food, tourist information, and hunting and fishing guides are available in the village proper.

Ocracoke once was considered home for the pirate Edward "Blackbeard" Teach, who apparently wasn't quite the villain legends sometimes make him out to be. When a ship manned by Virginians surprised Blackbeard's vessel at anchor in Ocracoke Sound in 1718 and sailed away shortly afterward with his severed head displayed at the bowsprit, civil war almost broke out between the two states.

Many Ocracokans claim to be direct descendants of Blackbeard, and few years pass that do not find mine-detector-equipped treasure hunters sifting the sands of the island for

183

buried loot the pirate reputedly left behind him.

And it was at Kitty Hawk, on the northern end of the chain, that brothers Orville and Wilbur Wright flew their first airplane in 1903. A reproduction of the plane, two earlier gliders, and the original Wright camp now form part of a visitor's center set up at the site. The center, and the nearby 60-foot Wright Memorial Shaft, are open to the public year-round. There is a 3,000-foot airstrip at the center and visitors are invited to use it, but no gasoline, oil, repair facilities, or hangar space is available.

South of Cape Hatteras, down the island from Kitty Hawk, is the beach where Colonel Billy Mitchell took off to sink two outdated U.S. battleships with aerial bombs in 1923 to prove that the Wright invention could rule the sea as well as the air.

It is impossible to discuss the history of the Banks without coming back again and again to the shipwrecks and the factors that caused them, because they, more than any other single factor, shaped the area's history. Some of the wrecks still can be seen—a few visible only as weather-beaten skeletal structures, peeping a few feet above the sands, and others, as in the case of one World War II LST, retaining most of their original shape.

These wrecks are there because it is just off the point of Cape Hatteras that the northward-surging Gulf Stream runs head-on into the cold Labrador Current running down from the Arctic. The point of their meeting is marked vividly by massive confrontation of wave against wave that tosses water and spume as high as a hundred feet into the air. And from this is formed Diamond Shoals, its constantly shifting sand bars pushing more than a dozen miles

Wreck of World War II landing craft on Cape Hatteras beach.

Bruce Roberts

A good day's catch, the whine of envious gulls, and a Carolina moon.

into the ocean.

The same oceanic factors that created the shoals and caused the wrecks, however, have brought eminence of another sort to the Outer Banks. It seems that fish thrive under the same conditions that sink ships. As a result the Banks are known, and deservedly, as "Game-fish Junction," and more recently the "Blue Marlin Capital of the World." More than 50 types of gamefish, ranging from the prized marlin to channel bass, trout, and blues, have been caught along the shoreline or from boats in the sound or ocean; several of these catches have established world records. The best fishing is from April to November. Numerous guides, boats, and beach-buggies for the surfcaster are available. The larger charter boats for Gulf Stream fishing are based at Oregon Inlet and Hatteras. Two ocean fishing piers are located at

Kitty Hawk, two at Nags Head, and one at Rodanthe on Hatteras Island. All are open from spring through fall.

Surfcasting tournaments are held each October at Nags Head and Hatteras, and a unique Short Course in Sports Fishing, sponsored by North Carolina State College, is held each June in Nags Head. An international blue marlin tournament is staged each year off Hatteras.

Mid-November finds the opening of waterfowl hunting season in the area, and shooting is good until early January for ducks and geese on the sounds and marshes separating the Banks from the mainland. Hunting guides may be obtained in the communities along Currituck, Albemarle and Pamlico sounds, and on Bodie, Roanoke, Hatteras, and Ocracoke Islands.

Those who had rather sight than shoot will find their fun at the Pea Island National

Walter A. Damtoft

Children understand beaches and their possibilities.

Wildlife Refuge, extending for 13 miles south of Oregon Inlet. The refuge lies along several heavily traveled lanes of the Atlantic Flyway, and both migratory and nonmigratory birds use the refuge for wintering and nesting. The most spectacular visitors are Greater Snow Geese, which pour in by the thousands each November and remain until early January. Walkways and observation platforms are provided for photography and bird watching.

This refuge is part of the earlier-mentioned, 45-square-mile Cape Hatteras National Seashore Area, which includes 70 miles of ocean front between Whalebone Junction and the southern tip of Ocracoke Island. Park facilities include four seaside campgrounds (at the north and south shores of Oregon Inlet; at Cape Hatteras and at Ocracoke); Coquina Beach on Bodie Island, sporting bathhouses, lifeguards, and a visitor center; a fishing center at the north shore of Oregon Inlet; and a supervised bathing beach on Bodie Island.

The four campgrounds include comfort stations but no utility outlets for trailers. You can stay for 12 days before you'll be asked to move on—but be sure to bring mosquito nettings and extra-long tent stakes for use in the sand. Further information on park facilities and services can be obtained by writing to the Superintendent, Cape Hatteras National Seashore Recreational Area, Manteo, North Carolina.

State-operated liquor stores are open from 9 a.m. until 9 p.m. at Nags Head and Manteo. Light wines and beer are available at a number of restaurants. Bars and mixed drinks do not exist. It is possible, under North Carolina's unique liquor laws, to carry your bottle into some restaurants and mix your own—but be sure to ask before you carry.

The largest concentration of hotels, motels, and lodges is in the vicinity of Nags Head, Kitty Hawk, and Kill Devil Hills at the northern end of the islands. The new bridge, however, has spurred construction of facilities all along the Outer Banks, and all villages have accommodations of some sort. An airport at Manteo provides charter service, and a new airfield also exists at Buxton on Hatteras Island.

One point should be remembered and looked for by all who visit the Outer Banks: The Atlantic Ocean still is mistress of these islands, and she is a jealous mistress.

At one spot along the highway, you can look to the landward side of the island and see the rotting remains of a bridge among the marsh grasses. This bridge once spanned an inlet that no longer exists.

Drive farther south and you'll see where dredges rejoined an island that was split by the driving force of a hurricane a few years back. Drive north, and you'll find the famous "walking dunes" that move constantly as the wind shifts their contours.

Read your history books and you'll find that Oregon Inlet, across which the new $4,000,000 bridge now stands, was solid land prior to two severe storms in 1846 that cut Hatteras Island in two—and since its creation, the inlet has moved southward at least a mile.

In other words, the bridge does not mean the ocean has allowed the Banks to become a permanent part of the mainland. The Atlantic has declared a temporary truce. Nothing more. ◆

Bruce Roberts

Old ship timbers entombed.

ALASKA

By Ed Fortier

ALASKA's wilderness can be a merciless teacher. Break her unwritten laws and rules, and you may pay with your life.

As my dory eased onto the beach of Knik Arm's northwest shore on that memorable day, I had no idea that within minutes I would be relearning a basic lesson.

Five of us were embarked on a moose hunt, using my Point McKenzie cabin as headquarters. We were arriving the day before the season opened in mid-August to do a little scouting for signs and be all set to hunt at daybreak.

The day was clear and calm. The first leaves were turning red and gold at the landing point six miles north of my cabin. My companions would take the boat down to the landing while Chris, 12-year-old son of a fellow hunter, and I hiked back to the cabin on an old moose trail that skirted the coastline.

Chris carried his single shot, .410 gauge shotgun, just in case we kicked up a grouse. I wasn't going to be hunting moose, and my .300 magnum rifle was too heavy to carry on a six-mile hike, sole purpose of which was to prospect for moose tracks and rub shoulders with the outdoors.

But the country was wild, and I didn't want to travel unarmed. I satisfied my requirement for protection by taking a light, semi-automatic .30 caliber carbine of World War II vintage, belonging to Chris' father. I had never shot the gun, but knew how it was supposed to operate.

Long before we reached the top of the 100-foot cliff, we heard the hum of the big outboard taking our friends south to the cabin. As we paused to rest, I asked Chris if the carbine was accurate.

"It shoots pretty straight, but sometimes it misfires, and sometimes, when it does fire, the next shell won't move into the chamber," explained my young friend.

I had no premonition of danger as we reached the heavy timber atop the cliff. We moved deeper into the forest of spruce and birch. This was the real wilderness. We hit the game trail and turned south.

Suddenly, as we entered a clearing about 20 feet in diameter, some animal raced ahead of us through the trail's shoulder-high grass. Before I could speculate on its identity, the waving grass reversed itself and whatever had run away was now heading straight for us and fast.

We stood our ground as a big black bear exploded out of the grass, missing my legs by inches. Whether he missed by design or because the normally bad eyesight of bears put him off target, I'll never know.

He was big and mad and my young friend and I were badly shaken. His first rush had

On the Shoulder
Of the Continent,
A Wilderness
That Can Take Care of Itself

taken us by surprise. Now we were ready for him—or should have been. But a black bear weighing 400 to 500 pounds is no quarry for a misfire-prone .30 caliber rifle and a single shot .410.

"My knees are knocking," said Chris as we heard the bear grunting and snorting in the heavy cover ahead of us. The bright sun couldn't dispel the deep chill inside us.

"So are mine," I assured him. "Keep your hammer cocked, but don't fire unless I do, and then reload and keep shooting at his eyes."

"Why did it charge?" asked Chris.

"Either a big male with a kill up ahead that it wants to protect or a sow with cubs. Our only chance is to let it cool down and then beat it back to the beach."

I knew it would take a one in a million shot with the carbine to kill the bear at 20 feet, and at that distance I'd get only one shot.

"Unless we can kill it, we can't risk just wounding it and being mauled. We can't run and we won't have time to climb a tree. Have to tough it out," I told Chris.

There was no help to be had for the hollering. I couldn't have had a better partner for the showdown. Chris' knees might have knocked, but he didn't panic and he didn't retreat.

Just then the bear stood up on his hind legs 50 yards up the trail and watched us for maybe a full minute. Ears erect, huge paws on his chest, he (or she) was measuring us even as we were measuring him. I had to know if the carbine would fire so I aimed a shot 20 feet over his head. The bang didn't scare the bear but it brought new terror to me. The firing

mechanism had failed to move a new shell from the clip to the breach. I was carrying a one-shot rifle.

I silently cursed my stupidity and laziness for not bringing the .300 magnum. A well-placed 180-grain slug from my heavy magnum would drop our angry enemy in his tracks.

There were more rushes, but none in which the bear broke into our little clearing. He circled us, grunting and growling in the heavy undergrowth, stood up several times and watched us frozen in our tracks.

The big black kept us pinned down for 45 minutes. Slowly, carefully we backtracked to the edge of the cliff and finally reached the comparative safety of the open beach.

The reason the bear rushed us remains unknown and academic. The sad fact is that I wasn't properly equipped for the surprise encounter. Laziness is my only excuse for not taking my own rifle. And if that first mad rush had come six inches closer, I might have paid for it with my life. Worse, a young boy might have died or been crippled because I wanted a nice, easy walk in the woods.

Chris and I were lucky to complete our refresher course on wilderness rules with only a scare for our penalty. Better hunters and outdoorsmen than I have been denied a second chance.

☆　☆　☆

Standing alone on the clean, rocky shore of a nameless lake, you watch the floatplane which brought you take off and become insect-size as it disappears through a pass in the high peaks.

The strange sound of silence fills your ears as you study the white-capped mountains and

Mount McKinley—the view from Bunco Lake.

Mac's Foto

clear, still water. The nearby pile of camping equipment and fishing gear identifies you as a civilized intruder. It suddenly seems small and inadequate. Realization that there is probably not another human being within 100 miles in any direction produces a sense of exhilaration, perhaps a trace of fear.

You are alone in Alaska's wilderness, just about as solitary as a human being can be this side of mid-ocean or outer space. For many Alaskans the fact their state is a vast wilderness area is a badge of distinction. The modern Thoreaus, and there are many, view the other 49 States as a sea of civilization with a few islands of wilderness.

The way in which Alaska's outdoors dominates its people is best understood by a few statistics. The present population is about equal to the 254,698 residents counted in Wichita, Kansas, in 1960. With 200,000 Alaskans living in cities, towns and on military bases occupying not more than 400 square miles, it is evident that there are only about 50,000 persons in the remaining 586,000 square miles—

a bountiful 11.7 square miles of breathing space for each outdoor-lover in residence.

That this rugged frontier is not easily bent to man's will is demonstrated by the fact that after the white man's presence on the premises for more than 200 years, the state has less than 4,500 miles of roads outside cities and towns.

As compensation for its lack of roads, Alaska offers the outdoor-lover such attractions as 175 named glaciers in southern Alaska alone, a sky full of mountain peaks that top the tallest in the South 48, the nation's entire supply of 20 active volcanoes, a mainland coastline of 4,750 miles which stretches to 33,904 when the hundreds of islands—most of them uninhabited—are counted. Added largesse for naturalists and sportsmen is a bountiful supply of the continent's biggest big game, millions of birds and waterfowl, plus lakes and streams in which more fish die of old age than are caught.

There are no hydroelectric dams on any major river in Alaska, and no bridge crosses the Yukon or Kuskokwim, largest rivers in the state. Except near cities, "Keep Out" and "No Trespassing" signs are absent.

The importance of Alaska to an outdoor-turning nation was pinpointed recently by the Outdoor Recreation Resources Review Commission in its report to Congress. The ORRRC concluded:

"Alaska is a storehouse of recreational opportunities. In this new State, with far less than 1 per cent of the total national population, are 31 per cent of the lands in the National Park System, 64 per cent of the public domain, 65 per cent of wildlife refuge lands, and 11 per cent of the national forest acreage."

Alaska's outdoors is so vast and varied a force, and of such spectacular dimensions, that its full effect on first encounter is overpowering —whether you arrive by car, boat or plane. Such words as isolation, majestic, solitude, desolate, wild and grandeur take on new meaning.

The discovery that nature and her array of powerful props and elements are in command and really only tolerate man in the Far North can be ego-deflating and spirit-rejuvenating. At its best, your confrontation with Alaska's outdoors will make you feel small in a good way.

After more than 20 years of hiking, hunting and fishing over Alaska, I am convinced that the key to an individual getting the most out of our special outdoor kingdom is wise management of both time and money. For anyone to attempt to experience all the moods, to know intimately all the flora and fauna of every corner of Alaska in a month, summer, year or lifetime is folly. Her outdoor treasures are dispensed on nature's terms or not at all. The rare tonic to be sipped from witnessing the Aurora Borealis, a caribou migration, erupting volcano or red salmon run is beyond the power of man to arrange at will.

If your adventure into Alaska's outdoors is to be satisfying, careful planning is necessary. First, decide what you want to see and do, and how much money you can spend in the process. This decision will determine your destination.

So large that some of its old-timers are complete strangers to other areas, Alaska is best evaluated by California-size regions. The island-laden panhandle or Southeast is actually a northern extension of the British Columbia coast.

The mountainous southern and western section ranges from Cordova to Attu Island, a distance of nearly 2,000 miles. The more flat interior is drained by the Yukon River from the Canadian border to the Bering Sea. The true Arctic extends from the Brooks Range north to the Arctic Ocean. Each area has special attractions for outdoor-lovers; each has its "ours is best" boosters.

Now accessible as never before, Southeast Alaska presents the first act of Nature's Alaska show. The new state-owned ferry system provides six-day-a-week service from Prince Rupert, British Columbia, to Haines and a link with the highway system to interior and western Alaska. (Alaska's marine highway will soon connect with Canadian ferries sailing from Vancouver.) Cost for the ferry ride is $28.50 per person and $96 for the average car. Stops are made at Ketchikan, Wrangell, Petersburg, Juneau, Skagway and Haines. Add 12 hours to the regular 30-hour trip if Sitka is a port of call.

You are cruising through the 18-million-acre Tongass National Forest, largest in the nation. It is a rain forest world ruled by giant Sitka spruce and western hemlock, populated by more whales, porpoises, deer and bear than people.

This lush realm is ruled by the U.S. Forest Service, but it is far from untouchable. More than 100 Forest Service cabins and shelters are

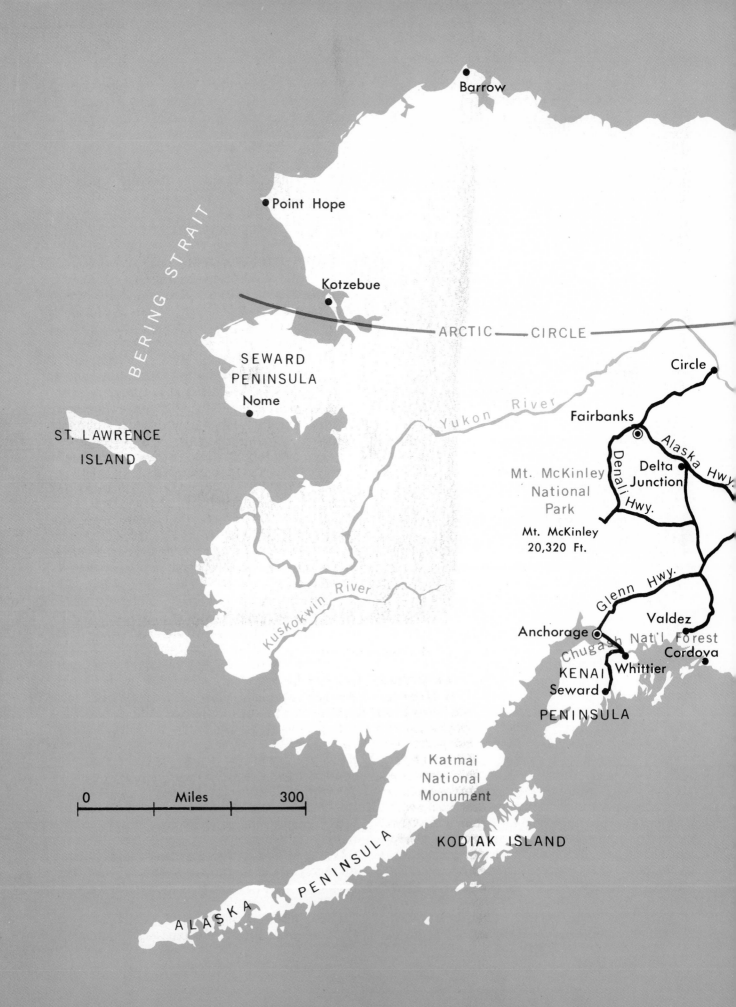

Barrow

Point Hope

Kotzebue

BERING STRAIT

ARCTIC — CIRCLE

Circle

SEWARD
PENINSULA

Yukon River

Nome

Fairbanks

ST. LAWRENCE
ISLAND

Mt. McKinley
National
Park

Delta
Junction

Alaska Hwy.

Denali Hwy.

Mt. McKinley
20,320 Ft.

Kuskokwin River

Glenn Hwy.

Valdez

Anchorage

Chugach Nat'l Forest

Cordova

KENAI

Whittier

Seward

PENINSULA

Katmai
National
Monument

0   Miles   300

KODIAK ISLAND

ALASKA PENINSULA

ALASKA

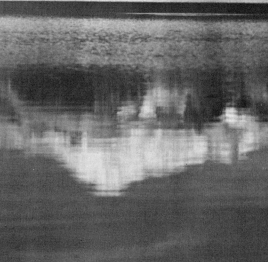

Skagway ●
Haines ●
Glacier Bay ● Juneau
Nat'l Mon. ☆
ADMIRALTY
Tongass
Sitka ●
● Petersburg
National ● Wrangell
Forest ● Ketchikan

◉ Prince Rupert
(British Columbia)

located at strategic locations for hunting, fishing and scenic panoramas. All that is required of the user is a sleeping bag and food. Most are accessible by boat or plane from the nearest ferry stop.

Practically the entire area is open to hunting and fishing in accordance with state fish and game laws. King and silver salmon and halibut abound in bays and inlets, with freshwater streams and lakes yielding Dolly Varden, rainbow, cutthroat, eastern brook trout and steelhead.

Brown bear are common on Admiralty and nearby islands, mountain goat roam the rocky crags, and there are a few moose. Top targets for hunters are Sitka black-tailed deer, so numerous there is a five-month season and bag limit of four. State biologists estimate the deer density may exceed 20 animals per square mile. But there is more to Southeast than fish and game.

Glacier Bay National Monument, one of nature's most massive wonders, is located 100 miles northwest of Juneau—a half hour flight by plane or a day's cruise by boat from the state capital. Fed by the world's largest icefield in the St. Elias Range, 20 glaciers meet the devouring sea in this 70 by 90-mile monument which is practically as unspoiled as when it fascinated John Muir 85 years ago. Construction started in 1965 on a guest lodge for the National Park Service which administers the area.

More civilized and better known among those who seek to dissect the mysterious blue-green spectrum of a glacier's face is Mendenhall Glacier, a 12-mile ride from Juneau. The U.S. Forest Service operates a Glacier Visitor Center at Mendenhall, only installation of its kind in the world.

End of the Panhandle's world of blue sea, green forests and white-crowned mountains comes at Haines, salt water terminus of the Haines Highway. This 159-mile road links the marine highway ferry route with the Alaska Highway. Bird lovers who reach the Chilkat River flats near Haines at the right time in autumn may see as many as 3,000 American bald eagles feeding on salmon.

Southeast Alaska's outdoors can also be entered from the south by Pacific Northern Airlines with daily jet service to Ketchikan and Juneau from Seattle. Alaska Coastal-Ellis Airlines makes scheduled flights to smaller towns.

Summer cruise ships serve the area and plane charters can be arranged.

Mecca for Alaskans and visitors devoted to pursuit of the outdoor life is Anchorage, home for almost half of the state's residents. Evidence that many of Anchorage's 100,000 citizens are outdoor addicts is everywhere. The per capita ownership of boats, planes (one-fifth of the world total of float planes), guns, cameras, sleeping bags, fishing equipment and skis is among the highest in the nation.

This staging area for the "bush" or roadless back country is reached via three airlines arriving daily from Seattle (one-way fare from Seattle is $99.56), and from Europe and Asia by five international carriers. Other visitors drive or come by bus over the Alaska Highway, a distance of 1,642 miles from Dawson Creek, British Columbia, or take the ferry-engineered shortcut from Haines, a ride of 742 miles.

Follow any compass heading from Anchorage and you can find what outdoor purists are now emphasizing as a "quality experience."

Accessible by road to the east is the Chugach National Forest, second largest in the nation, and its Mt. Alyeska, boasting the state's finest ski slopes. Pride of the Chugach is Portage Glacier, where an ice river can be seen at work reshaping the earth. A short train ride through a mountain tunnel puts you in Whittier on Prince William Sound, where charter and excursion boats make tours of the primitive, island-rich fjords and bays. A sharp blast of a boat whistle two miles from Columbia Glacier sends tons of ice cascading into the sea.

South of Portage Glacier on the Kenai Peninsula lies Seward, hotspot for silver salmon fishermen during late summer and fall. Dominating the west side of the Peninsula is the Kenai National Moose Range, a major outdoor magnet for Alaskans. Famed as the home of the giant Kenai moose, the Moose Range abounds in wildlife and birds — 146 species.. Hunting is permitted in accordance with state game laws and three species of trout and five of salmon are caught in the 125 lakes on the Range.

It is here on the 1,765,400-acre Moose Range administered by the U.S. Fish and Wildlife Service that the compatibility of industry and nature is getting an acid test. The Swanson River oilfield's 53 producing wells lie within the Range. Present consensus is that oil and moose can be successfully mixed. An oil exploration bonus for

Mac's Foto

Hunter Mort Proctor of Vermont checks his gear.

outdoor-seekers has been use of development roads which penetrate a once-forbidding wilderness.

If your trail to the outdoors leads southwest of Anchorage, you will have finished with roads. Kodiak Island, home of the largest carnivore on earth, can be reached once a week by state ferry from Seward (round trip, $27; car under 20 feet, $110) or Homer (round trip, $20; car, $84) or by plane from Anchorage (round trip, $73.50).

Three fourths of the historic 3,500-square-mile island is included in the Kodiak National Wildlife Refuge administered by the Fish and Wildlife Service. Purpose of the roadless refuge is to preserve a natural habitat for the estimated 1,500 Kodiak bear on the island. Hunter harvest of the giants who weigh up to 1,400 pounds ranges between 150 to 200 yearly.

A guide who knows Kodiak well has said:

"I wish Ernest Hemingway could have made it up here just once. He would have been hooked, and we'd now have Alaskan songs to equal those Robert Service wrote for the Yukon."

Northwest of Kodiak on the Alaska Peninsula is the 697,590-acre Katmai National Monument, largest area administered by the National Park Service. Once visited only by the most intrepid traveler, the Valley of 10,000 Smokes is in the process of being opened to the world. Stark evidence of the 1912 eruption of Mt. Katmai is still visible in the ash and lava-filled valley.

Northern Consolidated Airlines, concessionaire for the monument, demonstrates the way in which wings are reaching into remote corners. An F-27 propjet carries valley seekers from Anchorage to King Salmon, where they transfer to a twin-engined amphibian for the flight to NCA's Brooks River Camp. The journey

Mac's Foto

On Mount Alyeska, south of Anchorage.

ends with a 21-mile ride to the volcanic valley.

Jim Dodson, NCA vice president, says it is possible for a New York fly fisherman to board a jet at 7 a.m., and the same day catch a Brooks River rainbow for his lunch. Total cost for the continent-spanning trip, including four days at Brooks River Lodge, is $671.15.

The great brown bear country stretches south of Katmai to the end of the Alaska Peninsula. As many as 100 of the mammoth bear have been counted on an August day fishing salmon on Meshik and Aniakchak Rivers.

A major, little-known outdoor resource, the treeless, rainy Aleutians are the stage where the sea otter is fighting and winning its battle for survival. Almost extinct 50 years ago, this most-prized of fur bearers has come back until more than 20,000 inhabit the stormy island chain, adding up to most of the world's sea otter population.

Extending 1,100 miles from Umnak on the east to Attu in Asiatic waters, the Aleutian Island National Wildlife Refuge is the nation's second largest (2,720,350 acres).

The bleak islands are home at some time of every year for millions of shore birds (more than 142 species). The nation's entire black brant population and other species of geese feed on the eelgrass beds of Izembek Bay on the west end of the Alaska Peninsula for two or three months every year. To protect the waterfowl that rely on the eelgrass, the Fish and Wildlife Service acted in 1960 to maintain the vital food supply by establishing the 415,000 acre Izembek National Wildlife Refuge.

The hunter or bird watcher in the South 48 who cares about wild geese may not be aware of it, but he has a vested interest in this distant refuge. David Spencer, supervisor of Alaska Wildlife Refuges, explains his agency's timely concern with Izembek's rare store of food:

"The eelgrass beds of Izembek Bay are among the most extensive in the world. This food resource is the basis for a vast food chain, supporting hundreds of thousands of waterfowl in the fall. Eelgrass is a fragile, transitory growth, easily destroyed by man-made disturbances and pollutions. It is necessary that we know the conditions for its continued existence so that we can evaluate changes and apply any necessary measures to insure its survival."

Raucous proof that man can save wildlife from extinction can be heard on the tiny Pribilof Islands north of the Aleutians in the Bering Sea.

Bob & Wilma Knox

Ward W. Wells

Eskimos hunt walrus and seal in the Bering Sea.

Summer home of several million barking, bawling fur seals, the Pribilofs are believed by some naturalists to hold the greatest concentration of mammal life on earth. Reeve Aleutian Airways makes the four-hour flight from Anchorage to St. Paul Island once a week during summer months. Round-trip fare for the two-day trip, including meals and lodging, is $160.

Other Bering Sea attractions for the wildlife watcher who dares to be different, can afford to charter an airplane and is not fussy about where he sleeps, are Nunivak Island, home of the only sizable musk-ox herd in the U.S., and Hagemeister and Walrus Islands, major gathering grounds for walrus.

Alaska's finest attraction for those who want to shoot wild game with a camera or study it for their memory file is Mount McKinley National Park, 2,030-square mile preserve dominated by the continent's highest mountain, 20,320-foot Mount McKinley.

The Indians call the massive peak, "Denali," which means "The Great One." And when seen in its perpetual snow cloak, rising straight up 18,000 feet from its base, Denali seems a far more appropriate name for this ruler of the wilderness.

McKinley Park can be reached by the Alaska Railroad from either Anchorage (round trip, $18.70) or Fairbanks (round trip, $28.50), as well as by roads from both cities. Admission is free and there are facilities for campers. Park officials recommend three to five days for a good look at the Park. Camper and trailer dwellers can manage on $4 a day. A road extends 60 miles from Park headquarters to Camp Eielson (bus fare, $15), and 83 miles to Wonder Lake (bus fare, $20) for spectacular views of "The Great One."

Unmolested by hunters, wild game is plentiful, ranging from solitary Toklat grizzlies, moose and wolves to herds of caribou and bands of Dall sheep. More than 120 species of birds nest in the park. Sport fishing for grayling and trout is permitted.

Rates at the McKinley Park Hotel are $13 a day for two without bath and $18 with bath. So popular is McKinley Park with outdoor-lovers that serious consideration is being given to enlarging it. The visitor total has climbed from 10,662 in 1957 to 19,175 in 1964.

Mountain climbers aiming to assault Mount McKinley must receive permission from the National Park Service. No party of less than four is permitted to attempt the high climb, and it must meet rigid standards to challenge one of the world's coldest and toughest climbs.

The door through which visitors enter Alaska's vast interior and roadless Arctic is Fairbanks, the state's second largest city, and northern end of the Alaska Highway, 1,525 miles from Dawson Creek, British Columbia.

Alaska's farthest-north road point is Circle City on the Yukon River, terminus of the Steese Highway. Here, on the banks of the great river is the southern edge of the Arctic. You can invade this starkly beautiful land of tundra and the midnight sun by taking tours offered by Alaska Airlines from Anchorage and Wien Alaska Airlines from Fairbanks.

Conducted from June through September, the Wien tours range from $137.50 for a two-day trip to Kotzebue to $243.35 for a four-day visit to Nome, Kotzebue and Barrow. The same airline makes regular flights from Nome to Gambell on St. Lawrence Island in sight of Siberia, and from Kotzebue to Point Hope, one of Alaska's most primitive Eskimo villages. Alaska Airlines offers a two-day tour to Nome and Kotzebue for $136.25.

Special preserve for naturalists and biologists is the Arctic National Wildlife Refuge, largest in the U.S. Occupying 8,900,000 acres in the northeast corner of Alaska, this pure wilderness can be reached only by air. Large enough to be biologically self-sufficient, it is the home of polar, grizzly and black bear, moose, caribou, Dall sheep and smaller animals. David Spencer, Alaska Wildlife Refuge supervisor, estimates not more than 200 humans visit the Arctic refuge in a year, although hunting and fishing are permitted.

If the population levels of the big game herds which it shelters and feeds are an indica-

Dozing walrus on the islands in Bristol Bay.

Ward W. Wells

tion, the managment of Alaska's outdoor is succeeding. Here are current estimates on populations of major species, and all, except brown and grizzly bear, are thriving: Deer — 200,000 to 250,000; moose—75,000 to 100,000; Dall sheep—30,000; caribou—400,000 to 500,000; black bear —6,000 to 7,000. The state's main herd of 400 to 600 bison is pastured in the Delta Junction area.

The 41,184 resident and 5,008 nonresident hunters who took to the field in 1964 harvested 12,000 deer, 8,743 moose, 25,000 caribou, 1,500 black bear, 627 brown and grizzly bear, 918 sheep and 600 goats.

Both the abundance of the game and the vastness of its habitat are reflected in the bag limits and seasons—most liberal and longest of any state. It is legally possible to hunt some species of big game throughout the year. South of the Arctic (where there is a year-round season and no limit on caribou) a hunter can take one moose, three caribou, four deer, two elk, two goats, one sheep, one brown or grizzly bear, one polar bear, three black bear and one walrus.

Basic requirement for a nonresident nimrod is the purchase of a hunting license for $10, and a big game tag for each animal killed. Tags range from $150 for a polar bear and $75 for a brown or grizzly to $10 for a black bear or deer.

Alaska's big game laws cover 50 pages of fine print, and thorough knowledge of them is a must. For hunting purposes, the state is divided into 26 game management units, each with its own limits and seasons.

Nonresidents are no longer required to hire a registered big-game guide. As a consequence, the number of hunters arriving from the lower states via the Alaska Highway in campers is increasing. The visiting sportsman who can't afford a guide will have his best chance to bag an Alaskan big game trophy in the Gulkana River Basin northeast of Anchorage.

Roaming the 18,000-square-mile area is the Nelchina herd of 70,000 caribou. State game biologists seek a higher kill to prevent overcrowding. This prime hunting ground is bisected by the Glenn Highway, bordered on the north by the Denali Highway and penetrated by half a dozen short roads. Season on caribou extends from August 10 to March 31.

Roadside hunting is best during late fall and winter caribou migrations. This country can

be brutal and unforgiving. The hunter new to Alaska who charges off alone into the wilderness in pursuit of game is inviting trouble. At best, he may trigger a costly search; at worst, he may never be found alive.

Big game hunters with a burning ambition to take a handsome trophy and the money to satisfy it are the mainstay of Alaska's more than 200 licensed guides. In hiring a guide, the hunter enters into a contractual agreement, and it is wise to ask for references. Guide requirements are strict and there is a professional code. The man who specializes in dissatisfied customers is soon without a license.

The state's top guides are sportsmen and conservationists. They have a vital interest in making certain that the merchandise on which they depend for a living is not seriously depleted or senselessly destroyed.

Attesting to the quality of their service is the fact that some hunters return year after year to hunt with the same guide. Most use planes to get hunters into game-rich country, and the client from Chicago may arrive in Anchorage by jet, transfer to a smaller commercial plane for a flight to a remote settlement, where he will be met by his guide and flown to his destination in a small plane. Others use pack horses, boats or tracked vehicles to put their hunter on target.

Costs vary, depending on the skill and reputation of the guide, but the standard price of established producers ranges from $100 to $150 a day, and includes everything the hunter needs except his rifle, camera, clothing and ammunition.

If you are a stranger to Alaska, a guided hunt will improve your chances of success. In 1963, for example, guided hunters from 41 states and 12 foreign countries took 1,110 head of big game in Alaska. The average number of big game animals taken for each guided party was 2.9.

The bleakest outdoor stage on earth is the backdrop for polar bear hunters who search the Arctic ice pack each spring for the huge white beasts. Kotzebue, Barrow and Point Hope are points from which planes take off during late February through April in quest of the white bear. Nonresident hunters took more than half of the 251 polar bear shot in 1964.

Now being discovered as exotic quarry are walrus, which a few bold sportsmen hunt from Eskimo-manned skin boats, and Beluga whale,

A moose taken on Kenai Peninsula.

Ward W. Wells

both shot and harpooned from fast, open boats. For the really jaded hunter who seeks excitement, wolf hunting from the air is recommended. Armed with a permit and flying guide, the hunter zeroes in on the 150-pound black or gray timber wolf with a shotgun during a firing pass.

"Gunning wolves from the air is real sport, sometimes very tricky," says Ward Gay who takes hunters out in his Super Cub for $35 an hour in March and April.

Commercial fishing is Alaska's principal industry and sport fishing its major avocation. Nonresident anglers can join the piscatorial pursuit with purchase of a 10-day license for $5 or a season's license for $10. Pressure on lakes and streams near roads adjacent to population centers is extremely heavy, but the serious fisherman can find action if he's willing to drive half a day.

The Clearwater River near Delta Junction on the Alaska Highway is one of the North's most beautiful and productive grayling streams. Lake Louise, Tangle, Summit and Paxson Lakes and the Gulkana River, all south of Fairbanks, can be reached by road. The Chitina and Nabesna roads northeast of Anchorage pass excellent trout and grayling waters. The Kenai, Moose, Russian, and Swanson Rivers on the Kanai Peninsula are consistent producers, as are lakes and streams in the Matanuska Valley.

Guides and pilots in every major town sell fly-in trips that are equivalent to leasing a lake or a mile of virgin stream for your private use. Costs range from $25 to $250, depending on the distance and length of stay. Float trips, in which anglers are landed at the headwaters of a

Ward W. Wells

Brook Falls, Katmai National Monument.

wilderness river and float down to a predetermined pickup point are becoming popular.

If you insist on the din and noises of civilization with your fishing, avoid the distant lakes.

Ted Almasy, McGrath guide who specializes in fishing the little-known Tikchik Lakes, saw only two humans in three seasons. I have fished for five days at Iniakuk Lake in the Arctic without seeing another soul except my two companions.

Stores in Anchorage, Fairbanks, Juneau and Ketchikan stock every type of clothing, cameras, film, camping gear and sporting goods needed for an excursion into the outdoors. Prices are generally higher in Alaska, and vary considerably within the state. Restaurants get from $2 to $10 for dinner; hotel and motel rates start at about $5 a day and go up to $20 in larger hotels. Gasoline prices for regular spread from 40 to 60 cents a gallon, and a quart of milk or loaf of bread costs 35 to 60 cents, depending on location. As a general rule, the farther you are from Seattle, the higher the prices.

Three essentials to outdoor recreation in Alaska are protection from rain, insects, and sore feet. A raincoat or jacket is standard garb in southeast and southern Alaska, and recommended for the interior and Arctic. Mosquitoes grow big and bite hard over most of the state from May to midsummer. Gnats are bothersome from late July until mid-September. But the absence of snakes takes much of the sting from the bug bites.

Hip boots or waders are used by most fishermen. Sturdy leather boots are favored by Alaskans for hiking and high country hunting. Informal, warm clothing is always in style in Alaska.

Experience in camping without luxury conveniences will serve you well in the North. By standards of more settled states, Alaska campgrounds are quite primitive.

The most important item you can bring north is an ample supply of time. The family taking two weeks to drive over the Alaska highway to "see Alaska" and then return is inviting a severe case of highway nerves. A minimum of three weeks is needed for the trip up and back and a month is more satisfactory.

A dangerous end result of budgeting too little Alaska time is a natural reaction to speed up your experience in the face of bad weather or poor road conditions. Alaska's wilderness can destroy your hasty challenge without any trace of it having been made. There are old travelers and bold travelers in this outdoor stronghold, but there are few old, bold travelers.

Strangely, it is the older Americans, many of them retired, who appear to be breaking the

Mac's Foto

The Lowe River in Keystone Canyon near Valdez.

discovery trail to recreation in Alaska. Many tour operators report most of their clients are over 50.

Evidence that Alaska's outdoor rewards are within reach of the average citizen can be found throughout the summer at the general delivery windows in the Anchorage and Fairbanks Post Offices. It is here that the senior citizens, after an unhurried trip, report in growing numbers to collect Social Security checks which have been forwarded.

Winter brings a special beauty to Alaska, and the number of visitors who want a December or February outing in the "Frozen North" is slowly increasing. A tolerance for cold, snow and short days plus a rugged physique are requisites.

That Alaska's outdoors is available in

203

abundance for enjoyment now is beyond dispute. But what of tomorrow? What chances do future generations have of enjoying this untamed national resource?

In the opinion of this observer, the outlook is good and getting better.

I believe we are seeing our wilderness through more appreciative eyes. We are learning that experiences we consider run-of-the-mill may be the highlight of a lifetime for the sportsman from Kansas City. There is growing belief that in the final analysis our massive outdoors is not an enemy of progress and may, in fact, be a key to our future rather than a barrier.

"There has certainly been a growing awareness of the obligation to preserve our outdoor heritage for future generations," comments David Spencer, Wildlife Refuge supervisor for Alaska.

In overseeing 65 per cent of the nation's wildlife refuges, Mr. Spencer watches for "slightly eroding events—a road here, a powerline there, streamside settlement, a fuel dump— minor things that gradually change a wild country to a developed country."

Equally encouraging for outdoor-minded Americans is the quiet revolution that has occurred in the management of Alaska's game and fish resources by both federal and state agencies.

Fifteen years ago this priceless treasure was controlled largely by overworked game wardens. Today, with the exception of a few enforcement officers, members of Alaska's Department of Fish and Game are college-trained scientists. Supported by a multimillion-dollar budget, which in itself shows taxpayer recognition of the worth of our outdoor resource, these men are developing systems and principles of wildlife management that are being studied by other states and nations. Working conservationists with a clear concern for future seed, the scientific managers are not opposed to harvesting a renewable game and fish crop. But they are determined and empowered to keep it renewable.

Major enemy faced by the U.S. Bureau of Land Management, landlord for most of Alaska's western and interior wilderness, is forest fires. This Federal agency is now in the process of transferring to state ownership 102,000,000 acres of land which the state must select by 1984. The future of a big chunk of Alaska's outdoors will thus rest with the state Division of Lands. Although the selection process has just started, the state is showing some awareness of the need to reserve lands for public recreation. For example, all disposal of land along fishing streams includes a 15-foot pedestrian easement for fishermen.

Steve McCutcheon, Anchorage photographer and guide, has visited every corner of Alaska in his 50-year romance with the outdoors. "Opportunities for enjoying Alaska's outdoors are greater now than every before," he comments. "The fish and game continue in plentiful supply, and are much more accessible, thanks to the airplane.

"We can now reach wilderness destinations in a few hours that were once a week's or month's hard travel, if reachable at all."

In the final analysis, whether one finds a "quality experience" in Alaska's outdoors will depend on the individual. It is not necessary to climb a mountain, shoot a moose, or race down a wild river to find memory-making adventure in our outdoors. Some of nature's most beautiful spectacles are free for the seeing.

When he saw the northern lights on a July night in Alaska 85 years ago, famed naturalist John Muir wrote:

"In form and proportion it was like a rainbow, a bridge of one span five miles wide; and so brilliant, so fine and solid and homogeneous in every part, I fancy that if all the stars were raked together into one windrow, fused and welded and run through some celestial rolling mill, all would be required to make this one glowing, colossal bridge."

Thus did one observer describe a quality experience in America's Far North. ◆

There's more in Alaska than ice and snow.